Malcolm Knox is the autls
Summerland and *A Priv*d
Victorian Premiers' Awae
and the Commonwealth .... Prize (SE Asia and Oceania region). He was literary editor of *The Sydney Morning Herald* and won a Walkley Award for investigative journalism in 2004. He lives in Sydney with his wife and two children.

SECRETS OF THE JURY ROOM

MALCOLM KNOX

RANDOM HOUSE AUSTRALIA

Random House Australia Pty Ltd
Level 3, 100 Pacific Highway, North Sydney, NSW 2060
http://www.randomhouse.com.au

Sydney   New York   Toronto
London   Auckland   Johannesburg

First published by Random House Australia 2005

Copyright © Malcolm Knox 2005

All rights reserved. No part of this publication may be
reproduced, stored in a retrieval system, or transmitted
in any form or by any means, electronic, mechanical,
photocopying, recording or otherwise, without the prior
written permission of the publisher.

National Library of Australia
Cataloguing-in-Publication Entry

Knox, Malcolm, 1966–.
Secrets of the jury room.

Includes index.
ISBN 978 1 74051 224 4.
ISBN 1 74051 224 3.

1. Jury – Australia. 2. Jury duty – Australia. I. Title.

347.94052

Typeset in Sabon by Midland Typesetters, Maryborough, Victoria
Printed and bound by Griffin Press

*For my parents,
who supported me when I went to law school
and when I dropped out.*

Contents

AUTHOR'S NOTE xi

INTRODUCTION
A Ticking in the Box 1

CHAPTER ONE
The Fall of the House of Rusher 17

CHAPTER TWO
Panel Beating or How Jurors and Lawyers Cull the Pool 35

CHAPTER THREE
Challenging the Challenge 55

CHAPTER FOUR
The Foreman was a Storeman 68

CHAPTER FIVE
The Defence Opens 83

CHAPTER SIX
Meet Your New Family 94

CHAPTER SEVEN
Let Them Eat Fruit: How Juries Subsist 114

CHAPTER EIGHT
Undercover: 'Spike' in Silverwater   130

CHAPTER NINE
Children Overboard on the Lower Ground Floor
or The World as Seen from a Room Without Windows   152

CHAPTER TEN
The Star Witness: Les is More   164

CHAPTER ELEVEN
Survivor XII: The Jury Room   195

CHAPTER TWELVE
'Ladies and Gentlemen . . . I Call Steven Rusher'   215

CHAPTER THIRTEEN
Summing Up or How Jurors are Sold a Bill of Goods by Men in Gowns   235

CHAPTER FOURTEEN
One Angry Man: How Juries Deliberate   253

CHAPTER FIFTEEN
Twelve Angry Suggestions   294

CHAPTER SIXTEEN
Going Home   301

NOTES   318

BIBLIOGRAPHY   337

TEXT ACKNOWLEDGMENTS   341

INDEX   342

Secret? What do you mean, secret?
There are no secrets in a jury room!
– Juror played by Lee J. Cobb in *12 Angry Men*

Author's Note

Australians haven't read a book like this before. Our law has done everything possible to stop this book being written. Let me explain why.

The original version of this book was printed, bound and shipped to book stores in 2002. On the eve of publication, I was in Mildura with my wife and son, on our way back to Sydney after visiting relatives in Broken Hill. I got a phone call from my publisher, who said: 'Our lawyers are saying we have a problem.'

The problem was, a man who was in the book was hell-bent on stopping it coming out. This man, 'J', had been the accused in the criminal trial on which I'd sat as a juror. J had heard about the book, and although everything I'd written about him was available to anybody from court records, he wanted to stop publication. If details of his case got out, J said, he would suffer possible prejudice in any upcoming trials he might be involved in. The book would be in contempt of court. It could, theoretically, land me and my publisher in jail.

When I took the phone call, I laughed off the threat. Firstly, the chance of him sitting in front of a jury on this same matter was, in my opinion, zero. Secondly, the chance of my book falling into one of those 12 jurors' hands was a fraction of zero. Thirdly, it would require that juror to disobey his or her duty, laid out with great seriousness by the judge in that hypothetical trial, and be influenced by the book. Fourthly... but why go on? The sequence of probabilities was like getting hit by lightning and attacked by a shark at the same time. It just wouldn't happen.

Unfortunately, courts don't think this way. They don't calculate odds or speculate on likely results. Courts deal more happily in iron rules. In this case, J held a trump card, which was that he was trying to protect his rights under criminal law. He was fighting for his freedom. We, on the other hand, were only arguing for a 'commercial' end: to publish a book. The weakest argument from criminal rights will beat the strongest commercial imperative. Never mind that his chance of suffering from this book's publication was a million to one. That million-to-one chance was enough.

I don't disagree with this principle. J's rights under criminal law are more important than my wish to get a matter out for public discussion. The right to defend yourself, under criminal law, *should* override a writer's imperatives.

So, in good faith, we backed off. J's lawyer told us the matter would be settled within a couple of months. We waited. But then J had a problem with resolving his appeal ... then another ... and as the months dragged on, anyone but the courts could see that a pattern was emerging. J had located the better nature of our justice system – its integrity in protecting accused criminals – and turned it back on itself. He manipulated his rights to delay the process. He contrived adjournments, then got the adjournments adjourned. A dog ate his homework. His lawyer let him down. He had a headache. He was washing his hair that day. And so on. He was making a monkey of the courts, standing on his rights only to use them to create more delays. If you want to make your life a court case, and prolong it forever, you can. Your court case can be like your gold teeth, living on when you are nothing more than dust and ashes and a bad memory. It seemed to suit him to prolong and postpone, to be able to say, for as long as he was behind bars, that his conviction was 'under appeal'. When you're in jail, I suppose, you do whatever keeps you going.

Author's Note

If J's connivance were the only barrier between this book and you, the reader, that would be frustration enough. But consider how hard it is for a juror to tell his or her story in the first place. The Jury Act forbids anyone from asking a juror a question about a trial. Anyone. Not even a judge can compel a juror to discuss a trial. And if a journalist, or an editor, or, as has happened, a radio announcer, tries to tease out a juror's story, then that interrogator can go to jail. It's called 'soliciting' a juror, and it carries a criminal penalty that reflects how seriously our law treats the privacy of the jury room.

In this case, I happen to be a writer who was on a jury. I've volunteered my story. Nobody, not even in the editing of this book, is allowed to ask me to clarify or elaborate on anything that happened in the jury room.

The next obstacle is the section of the Jury Act that says a juror cannot identify other jurors. That's fair enough. In this book, I disguise and amalgamate each of the jurors until they won't even recognise themselves.

The next roadblock is tougher. You cannot, by law, discuss the deliberations that happened inside the jury room for gain. What are 'deliberations'? Do they include everything the jurors say from the beginning of the trial, or just what they say after the sign goes up on the jury room door, 'Jury in Deliberation', at the end of the trial? There is no case law telling us exactly what this means in practice. I asked the NSW Director of Public Prosecutions, Nicholas Cowdery QC, how far I could go. He said: 'Avoid any discussions where jurors were discussing the accused's guilt or innocence; where you were deliberating on the verdict.'

That would be fair enough, but if you took the deliberations out of *12 Angry Men*, you'd have a one-minute movie. The deliberations are what make a jury, what reveal all the hidden tensions. Deliberations are like a neon strip light over your bathroom mirror: they bring all the spots and blemishes to the surface.

Censorship in courts runs against the grain of history. From the 1500s, English common law has been illuminated by publicity. When law courts on the Continent degenerated into secret clerical inquisitions, the English saw the open trial as a protection against tyranny. Yet the jury room has become what one judge called 'the blackbox of the judicial system' in order to protect the 'safety' of the verdict, which might be compromised if jurors revealed how they came about it. The Australian Law Reform Commission reported in 1987:

> *The quality of finality is lost if jurors, immediately after the verdict, have carte blanche to describe to anyone such things as their own doubts or second thoughts on the matter, the alleged doubts or second thoughts of any other juror, the compromises or shifts of opinion that took place in the jury room, the different grounds that led to a seemingly unanimous decision, or the conflicting or inaccurate impressions of the law or the evidence which were formed within the jury room.*

That report came after a crisis in the mid-1980s, when some jurors spoke out publicly against decisions they'd been involved in. Jurors from the Ananda Marga, Norm Gallagher, Lionel Murphy and Maher–Donnelly ('bottom of the harbour' tax scheme) trials aired their views on deliberations. In the aftermath, applications by prospective jurors to be excused trebled and the NSW Jury Act was tightened to stop jurors blabbing.

Justice Carter told the jurors in the complex Maher–Donnelly case:

> *What happened in there is your business and nobody else's. I urge you to maintain the confidentiality of what occurred. Any attempt to ascertain your views about the trial or anything connected with it would be thoroughly*

> *mischievous. So, too, would any attempt by a juror to*
> *volunteer views for publication.*

Nonetheless, one juror from that case, 'Tom', spoke to the *National Times* in 1985:

> *The others started moving down to the other end of the*
> *room, away from me. One man was really worried*
> *about how stupid we would look if we couldn't reach a*
> *unanimous decision. I felt alienated and the prospect of*
> *spending a weekend with these people did not look*
> *good. I made up my mind to abstain from voting on*
> *count one if I could secure a not-guilty on the other*
> *three charges.*

After 1987, the Jury Act was tightened to place a hermetic seal over the jury room. One of the more celebrated violations of the Act was in 1999, when radio announcer John Laws (who had interviewed jurors from the Lionel Murphy trial) broadcast an interview with a woman juror who disagreed with her jury's acquittal of a murder suspect. Laws was convicted under the Jury Act for 'soliciting' information from a juror. Supporting the decision, the president of the NSW Bar Association, Bret Walker SC, told the ABC:

> *We're not allowed to know what goes on inside a jury*
> *room because we can never be satisfied we'll know either*
> *accurately or in a climate of sufficient calm to protect the*
> *security of the verdict.*

To carry out candid jury-room discussions, and to live without fear of reprisals from a participant in the case, jurors do need a measure of secrecy. Nobody can dispute that. Courts also want to stop a juror racing out to publish a sensational story about a big trial, as often happens in America. But while the intent of the ban is to insulate juries from criticism, corruption or embarrassment, it also insulates them from any balanced appraisal. A juror who contacted me said she was traumatised by her case and had nowhere to turn:

> *There are so few people one knows who have served on a jury that it is difficult to vent your feelings about the experience to a sympathetic ear. Unless you have served as a juror it is impossible to fully understand the depth of emotion that is felt and the immense difficulty of the task forced on you. Not being able to talk about the case is tantamount to torture.*

There's a wider point to be made here. Why involve the public in the legal system if you don't allow them to talk about it? Surely the value of lay participation is, as Australian academic and leading jury researcher Mark Findlay says, that jurors can 'broadcast more widely among associates the positive and negative aspects of the experience'.

What actually happens, Findlay writes, is the opposite: the secrecy laws discourage 'an informed assessment of the jury':

> *What juries actually understand of their role and responsibilities is not widely appreciated. The elements of the criminal trial which influence a jury's decision are far from clear, as are the issues of evidence and procedure which impede a juror's comprehension. Even issues such as when and how jurors determine guilt or innocence have been kept almost religiously from public view . . . Yet while the anonymity of jury decision-making is said to allow for the community conscience to prevail, the secrecy of the jury room locks this expectation away from public verification.*

Author's Note

Trial lawyers, of course, would love to know more about what goes on in the jury room. They spend much time guessing in the dark about what tactics work and what backfire. If there were an avenue for dialogue between juries and the outside world, trial lawyers could test their theories against reality. As one Sydney barrister, Murugan Thangaraj, puts it:

> *Lawyers do run into jurors after a trial. You can't buy them a beer, but you can listen to them, and they often want to talk. It pisses me off about the Jury Act that there isn't more jury feedback. It would help lawyers become better at our work.*

But instead, as Nicholas Cowdery says: 'It's blind man's buff. We don't know what goes on in the jury room.'

Do we really want to know too much about juries? It's a question of faith. Critics of the jury system, such as British QC Sir Louis Blom-Cooper, say if we knew what went on in the jury room then 'the whole thing would collapse'.

But if more information would allow us to criticise juries more openly, it would also allow us to defend them more openly. What research has been done only restores faith in juries' ability, against the odds, to get it right. The jury system isn't a hothouse flower that needs to be sequestered. It's not a mysterious wife kept in purdah. It's robust and big enough to take the heat. It doesn't need repressive 'protection'.

As justification for his jury exposé, a book called *Trial by Jury*, American juror Graham Burnett stresses the enduring importance of publicity:

> *. . . there are things to be learned from the way events unfolded (about the law, about justice, about truth and how we know it), and. . . the jury room is a most remarkable – and largely inaccessible – space in our society, a space where ideas, memories, virtues and*

prejudices clash with the messy stuff of the big bad world. We expect much of this room, and we think about it less often than we probably should.

It's time to let the world in on the secret.

For three years I tried to work out how to publish this book without going to jail. I'm okay on the soliciting part: I haven't been solicited, nor have I solicited anyone else, to tell their story. The other former jurors who appear in this book have come forward under their own steam.

I'm in the clear on the identification of jurors in my trial. They are not identified. There remains our friend Mr J. Even if blind Freddy knows J will never stand trial on this matter again, I still have to disregard Freddy and pretend there may be some future juror, some disobedient or renegade soul, who reads this book during a trial of J. I have to ensure that that juror will not recognise J.

I must, therefore, disguise him. I must work on him with a novelist's skills: cobble him together out of ghosts, memories, fantasies, and little bits of real people. Consequently, he's become someone completely different. His life story is different. His motivations, his appearance, and of course his name are different. The context of the accusations against him is different, his lawyer is different, the witnesses for and against him are different. No future juror can recognise him or prejudge him because – dear hypothetical rogue juror – the man you will read about in these pages is not J at all. You don't know what is real and what I'm making up. He's become a character from a writer's imagination. And the discussions in the jury room that I'll talk about are also the magic lantern show of imagination. While the details are embroidered, however, what follows is an honest account of my own experience as a juror.

Most of the material in this book is factual – everything that doesn't involve J directly is dead straight nonfiction. But the events that halted publication of the 2002 version of this book have forced me to drape J, and others, in costume and disguise. In doing so, I hope to have penetrated beyond the literal recording of facts, and reached the kind of truth that novelists, rather than historians, attempt to find. That is, a truth that lies deeper than the particular. With three years of reflection behind me since this book was first about to be published, I think I understand much better what it means to be on a jury. I understand with more clarity the centrality of our jury system to what we like to call 'democratic' society yet so often fail to follow up with more than lip service. And that's what this book is about. It's not about J, it's not about me, it's not about any individuals in that trial. It's about the jury.

Introduction

A Ticking in the Box

Jury service is viewed by some as an onerous and unwelcome duty, and by others as a precious and inalienable right, but we have been told that those who start their service holding the former opinion often end up by holding the latter.
                    – British Home Office report into juries, 1965

In the silence of night I can hear it. Like an internal wristwatch, the graphite valve implanted in my heart opens and shuts with a sharp snip, rationing out my remaining time at around 80 beats per minute. Normally, lying in bed is the only time I hear it. Daytime ambient noise and talk, and concentration on outward things, muffle the ticking. But this wasn't a normal situation.

Mid-morning, the trial's last day: I entered a lower-ground-floor courtroom of the NSW District Court, feeling that my heart was ticking so loudly it might set off a bomb scare. It raced at twice its normal rate; sweat condensed on my hands and forehead; a morbid weight dragged on my shoulders.

Five weeks since meeting in this place, 11 strangers and I were ready to deliver our verdict. We'd come from the broad torso of society, from everywhere except the extreme top (who manage to get out of jury duty) and the bottom (who slip out of the eligibility lists). We'd come with varying degrees of willingness, knowledge, commitment and sympathy; we'd listened to a story of tragic drama that would have inspired Shakespeare; and we'd somehow formed ourselves into an entity that could come to a decision and speak with one voice. We'd gone up blind alleys and negotiated our escape. We'd bent to the State, and sometimes tested its authority. We'd argued over the riptides of world and national affairs. We had disputed the issues facing us as we exercised our other democratic freedom, as voters in elections. But whereas, as voters, we were drops in an ocean, as jurors each of us bore an awesome responsibility, direct and immensely potent, over the future of the man facing us. We had approached those two democratic roles – as voters and as jurors – with vastly different degrees of seriousness. As voters we were lazy, prejudiced and gullible. As jurors we tried our best, under each other's daily scrutiny, to be diligent, fair and forensically sceptical.

We'd grown familiar with the accused, acknowledging him each day like a nodding acquaintance on the bus. Sometimes the whole apparatus of the court had seemed to dissolve away, leaving two poles of energy: him and us, accused and jury, the only people who mattered. We were familiar with the facets of his great sheeny forehead, angling the courtroom light; with his mannerisms and his emotions. We knew more about his life than we knew about our closest friends'. And today, we'd come to decide whether this man had been wronged or had done wrong. The consequences of an error presented themselves with a stark clarity that most of us try to avoid in our everyday lives. By convicting, we might be putting an innocent man in jail for years. By acquitting, we might be enabling him, actively abetting him, to commit murder.

The violent ticking of my heart was only the most immediate physical sign. Since early in the trial, the skin on my hands had been peeling away from the fingertips: a common reaction, I was told, to uncommon stress. I was sleeping fitfully and amped myself up each day with tea and coffee, which normally I didn't drink. I harboured feelings of unnatural intensity towards the other people in this courtroom. I was desperate to get away, yet fanatically committed to seeing this through and doing the right thing.

That last day, literally judgment day, was our shortest in court. We convened, resuming our discussion of the previous afternoon. We played devil's advocate for each other. The foreman travelled the room and asked us for our verdicts individually. He asked again, inviting any doubters to come forward. And then, surprisingly quickly, it was over. We returned to the court and watched the accused as the foreman delivered the verdict. The judge thanked us and wrapped up as perfunctorily as if finishing a meeting that had lasted one hour, not one month.

Relieved as I was when I walked free of the courthouse, the trial would not leave me. A month-long plug had been pulled out of me, and afterwards I couldn't stop talking about this thing I had been through. Like a wound that only hurts when it begins to heal, the trial nagged and chafed at me from the moment it was over.

I know this sounds weighty, but there's no other way I can put it. I felt that I had peered into the soul of our democracy, and had come out both enlightened and disenchanted: enlightened by the discovery that I and my fellow citizens could be trusted to think clearly, a trust I'd doubted I possessed until now; and disenchanted by how many obstacles the trial process had laid in our path. I was relieved, yes, but angry too.

I'd travelled a long way in that month. Having tried to get out of jury service, having believed jurors must be blithering idiots too dull or too dispensable to get out of it, having thought that to trust 12 people dragged in off the street was a system 200 years out of date, I'd arrived at a position where I now believed jurors were not only an essential safeguard to liberty but that being on a jury should be a duty that is almost impossible to evade. I walked out of the court a convert.

Yet I was angry that we had been denied basic help and respect, made to feel like prisoners, enclosed in a cocoon of ignorance. Our native intelligence had been insulted, yet, paradoxically, our knowledge of the criminal trial process had been ridiculously over-estimated. I felt that we reached a satisfactory verdict despite, rather than thanks to, the court.

It sometimes felt as if the court saw us, the jury, as a necessary evil.

After the trial, I started reading about juries, and found a miraculous thing: the hurdles we had overcome have been placed in front of juries for centuries. Our experiences, as jurors, were remarkably similar to what had gone before. We were not alone. We were the latest participants in a long, long conversation.

'Jury service,' said Thomas Jefferson in the 1770s, 'is the school by which the people learn the exercise of civic duties as well as rights.'

But was it really? Mark Twain thought Jefferson's pronouncement was just the type of high-minded guff you'd expect from a nation-building, constitution-writing statesman. Twain wrote:

> *The jury system puts a ban upon intelligence and honesty, and a premium upon ignorance, stupidity and treachery. It is a shame that we must continue to use a worthless system because it was good a thousand years ago.*

Worthless? The French observer of American democracy Alexis de Tocqueville came away with a different view: 'By making men pay attention to things other than their own affairs, jury service combats individual selfishness, which is like rust in society.'

Fine words, but as a Frenchman de Tocqueville was bound to be impressed by the novelty of juries. Charles Dickens, through Mr Bumble in *Oliver Twist*, was more hardened to the daily reality: 'Juries is ineddicated, vulgar, grovelling wretches.'

The English historian Thomas Plucknett thought the problem lay not just in the type of people who got on juries, but in their unaccountability: 'The jury states a simple verdict of guilty or not guilty and the court accepts it, as unquestionably as it used to accept the pronouncements of the hot iron or the cold water' of the religious 'trial by ordeal' that juries had replaced in the 13th century.

The constancy of the arguments, from the 1200s to the 2000s, is both a reassurance of the continuity of human consciousness and a depressing reminder that the argument over juries is no nearer resolution now than it was 800-odd years ago, when juries first appeared in English law.

If it's been said about humanity, chances are it's been said about the jury. Novelists, screenwriters, playwrights and poets have all had a go, and among the generations of judges, lawyers, politicians and academics siding for or against juries, Victorian law professor Tony Blackshield has linked it with our deepest myths and fables: 'In "The Emperor's New Clothes" it takes an innocent little child to stand up and say, "There's nothing there." We have been relying on the jury to stand up and do that.'

Yet the role of the jury, while seemingly fixed in aspic, has also spoken directly to changing times. In the days when juries were literally a check on the tyranny of kings, the most important quality of the juror was that he knew the accused and the accuser, or if he didn't he could find out about them. His knowledge of the intimate details of a dispute prevented the imposition of random justice from afar. Nowadays, by contrast, the essence of the juror is that we come to court as a blank slate. If a juror knows too much about the case, he or she will be disqualified. In NSW in 2004, a guilty verdict was overturned on appeal because some jurors had illicitly conducted their own investigation, visiting the scene of the alleged crime, a gang rape. This more recent ideal, of juror-as-ignoramus, has always lent itself to lampoonery, such as when Twain observed: 'We have a criminal system which is superior to any in the world and its efficiency is only marred by the difficulty of finding twelve men every day who don't know anything and can't read.'

The apparent dullness of jurors has been counterbalanced by their deeper sense of 'real', rather than legal, justice. Commonsense has won its most notable victories when juries have taken the law into their own hands. In 19th-century America, while a brilliant man like Twain was poking fun at juries and equally brilliant and expert Harvard professors were asserting the affinity of black people to chimpanzees, juries led a rebellion against a law punishing people who harboured escaped slaves. In 17th-century England, jurors drew their line in the sand by refusing to convict Quakers for preaching in the street, even though it was against the law. In NSW, the struggle for the jury system was part of the wider struggle for democracy, for emancipated convicts to have the same rights as free settlers. The advent of juries was an important step in our transition from penal colony to self-governing State, and when Australia was federated, the right to jury trial for federal crimes was the only right laid out in our Constitution. Defending this right as a High Court judge, Sir William Deane said the jury 'reflected a deep-seated conviction of free men and women about the way in which justice should be administered in criminal cases' and any winnowing down of jury trials was 'a potentially mischievous mockery' of the Constitution.

In America, juries became the de facto shadow government in the lead-up to the revolution, ruling for home-grown institutions and values against English tyranny, and the jury system was enshrined in Article III of the US Constitution. Juries asserted commonsense over bureaucratic imposition, expressing the people's will more candidly than written laws.

Yet in our time, the arguments for and against juries are still fighting like a pair of caged cats. For every pro-jury commentator, like Australian academic and leading jury researcher Mark Findlay, who says juries are 'ahead of formal law reform, and perhaps more in touch with contemporary attitudes' than parliaments or judges, there's another, like American academic B.S. Oppenheimer, who'll argue:

> *We commonly strive to assemble twelve persons colossally ignorant of all practical matters, fill their vacuous heads with law which they cannot comprehend, obfuscate their . . . intellects with testimony which they are incompetent to analyse or unable to remember, permit partisan lawyers to bewilder them with their meaningless sophistry, then lock them up until the most obstinate of their number coerce the others into submission or drive them into open revolt.*

Juries have acquitted Ku Klux Klansmen, anti-abortion arsonists, O.J. Simpson, and the police who bashed Rodney King. They convicted Lindy Chamberlain and Lionel Murphy. Every day, jurors acquit (or convict) someone because he looks like their nice (or nasty) Uncle Phil, because they believe the accused has suffered enough already (or not enough), or, worse, because they would rather go shopping than thrash out their decision properly. These were the kinds of juries Auberon Waugh had in mind when he said: 'We know, as a nation, that we are no longer fit for jury service.'

Any discussion of juries must weigh them against the alternative. Originally, the alternative to juries was clerical or royal fiat. Now, it's a question of juries or judges – ignorance versus professionalism, lay wisdom versus judicialism, commonsense versus legal sense.

Here too, nothing is settled. On the one hand, Mark Findlay writes that 'a group of 12 diverse people will, between them, arrive at a less subjective or individually partial decision than would a single judge who typically is middle-aged, middle-class, Anglo-Saxon and male.' The very strength of the jury, he argues, lies in each juror's accountability to commonsense, conscience and the opinion of the 11 others in the room – rather than the accountability to legal precedent and the threat of public condemnation that hangs over judges.

But aren't judges the experts? Isn't leaving the facts in lay hands a great error? American judge Hiller Zobel, who presided over the case of Louise Woodward, the English nanny accused of murder, thought giving juries control over verdicts was akin to 'asking the ignorant to use the incomprehensible to decide the unknowable'. Even pro-jury observers, like New Zealand professor Warren Young, question leaving the 'fate of the accused ... in the hands of 12 members of the community who (probably) have only just met each other, are (probably) unfamiliar with the court process, and who (probably) are feeling almost as stressed by the situation as the accused'.

Stressed – yes, I knew what that meant after the trial on which I sat. But the question I was left with was this: Given the obvious shortcomings of the jury system, should we try to improve it, or just ditch it?

I went in search of experts. But, even though nearly everyone holds a categorical opinion about juries, there is no such thing as a jury expert. (Perhaps one follows the other.) This was what I discovered as I inquired deeper into our jury system. It arouses great passions, yet is one of the few areas of our society that remains a genuine mystery.

Judges and trial lawyers have wide-ranging, heartfelt and interesting opinions about juries, but they are excluded from being on one. All their accumulated knowledge of juries is, by their own account, guesswork. I spoke with serving and retired judges whose attitudes ranged from exasperation to admiration. They estimated the proportion of 'unsafe' jury verdicts as anything from one in four to one in 40. But ultimately, judges, like the lawyers who try to divine throughout a trial which way the jury is leaning, know nothing first-hand.

I sought out criminal trial lawyers to uncover their ideas about juries and the tricks of their trade. I make no claim to have found a large or representative group of lawyers. It seemed to me that prosecutors were less colourful than defence counsel, for, as the NSW Director of Public Prosecutions, Nicholas Cowdery QC, told me, 'The prosecutor represents the entire community, while the defence counsel only represents one person.' Rule 20 of the NSW Bar Association says: 'A barrister appearing for the Crown in a criminal case is a representative of the State and his function is to assist the court in arriving at the truth.' The prosecutor's role is, theoretically at least, strictly circumscribed. On the other hand the defender can be, in barrister-novelist Nicholas Hasluck's words, 'something of an anarchist'. Among criminal defence lawyers, I went to Forbes Chambers, the first port of call for most criminal defendants in Sydney, and received candid and in-depth help. I spoke with barristers Tom Molomby SC, Ian Barker QC, Henry di Suvero, Nicholas Cowdery QC, the prosecutor and solicitors in what I came to know as 'my' trial, and several other barristers and serving judges who assisted me on condition of anonymity. Lorana Bartels, then a research solicitor with the DPP's office, gave me access to Crown prosecutors' views on the issue of majority verdicts, from a survey she conducted for her master's thesis in 2001.

Were this a book about lawyers, I'd have taken a larger and more representative sample. But it's about jurors, that huge elusive mass of citizens who enter Australian courtrooms at the rate of about 40,000 per year and are, according to Findlay:

> *... expressly and implicitly silenced as a result of intimidating courtroom "drama" and environments, coercion in the deliberation room, and instructions from judges, lawyers and court officials; and are kept silent as well by a general lack of knowledge about their rights and privileges.*

Is it necessary to know something from personal experience in order to call oneself an expert? Socrates said all doctors should have suffered from the diseases they have to treat, though he pulled back from recommending that all judges should have committed the crimes they judge. But it seems to me – and to the many lawyers who have told me they would dearly love the forbidden experience – that you cannot truly know what the idea of the jury means unless you have served on one.

Nonetheless, a juror's expertise is intense but limited. Since I wrote an article about juries in *The Sydney Morning Herald* in 2002, I have been approached by dozens of jurors telling their stories. These fascinating insights form part of the body of knowledge from which I have drawn this book.

The mystery of the jury room is reinforced by laws 'protecting' its secrecy. The Anglo-Australian ban on revealing jury-room deliberations does not extend to the United States. American juror accounts on television, in newspapers and magazines and in books is one reason why the bedrock of our knowledge about juries comes from America. My knowledge of juries has been deepened by American jurors Graham Burnett, Johnathan Carter, Mara Taub and Mary Timothy, among others who have written books about their jury duty.

The American experience has also fused with popular culture to create a sometimes confused portrait of juries. The NSW jury summons contains a brochure that warns against expecting 'what you may have seen in television shows'. A NSW Supreme Court judge and former Attorney-General, John Dowd, customarily opens trials by warning jurors not to expect the same process they see in American movies and courtroom television shows. Well may he worry. Part of the difficulty all jurors have adjusting to a criminal trial is that it is neither as action-packed nor as neatly resolved as the TV courtroom drama. There's rarely a Perry Mason to produce the smoking gun at the last minute. Liars don't always blink. In my researches, I've watched about a dozen films with a significant jury-room element. The best, I think, remains Reginald Rose's 1957 adaptation of his play *12 Angry Men*, founded on his experience as a juror. I came to understand very well the words of Alex Kozinski, a US Circuit Court judge who decided to be a lawyer after watching *12 Angry Men*:

> *As I sat there watching, struggling with the language, trying to figure out the jury's function in American law (Why, I wondered, didn't they just convict by a vote of eleven to one and go home?), my whole adolescent conception of certainty, of knowledge itself, was shaken. The case against the defendant seemed so airtight; the reasons offered by the eleven sounded so irrefutable. I couldn't imagine how (or why) anyone could reach a different conclusion. Then, as one reason after another started to come apart, as inconsistencies crept into the picture, as jurors began changing their votes, I came to understand that truth does not spring into the courtroom full-blown, like Athena from the head of Zeus. Rather, facts have to be examined carefully and skeptically, moved around and twisted like pieces of a puzzle before they will yield a complete picture.*

Riveting as it is, *12 Angry Men* does stretch credulity. There are few known cases of a Henry Fonda swinging all 11 votes his way. Two-thirds of juries end up with the same verdict they carry into deliberations. Fonda breaks just about every law in our Jury Act during the film. But at the same time, the *idea* of the jury room is portrayed in *12 Angry Men* with compelling clarity. Something in the claustrophobia-induced chemistry between 12 strangers under immense pressure is common to all juries, even those most harmonious and judging the easiest cases.

What film, television and other fictional jury rooms do, though, is create a deceptive idea of the exceptional juror. Henry Fonda stands against the tide. In the 1987 film *Suspect*, Dennis Quaid plays a juror who goes out, investigates the crime himself – finding the real murderer – and lives happily ever after with the defence attorney (played by Cher). At one stage, Quaid helps Cher by dropping a hint to test out whether the accused is right- or left-handed (having discovered independently that the murder was committed by a left-hander). Outside the court, he approaches her but is rebuffed:

> Cher: *I'm not allowed to talk to you, Mr Singer.*
> Quaid: *The least you could do is thank me, counsellor.*
> Cher: *Thank you? What I should do is go to the judge and have you thrown off this panel.*
> Quaid: *Nobody twisted your arm to use that information. I was just offering to help . . .*
> Cher: *If you really want to help me, leave me alone. Jury tampering is a felony.*
> Quaid: *You haven't tampered with me. Yet.*

In a number of other popular-culture representations – the films *The Juror* and *Trial By Jury*, the John Grisham novel *The Runaway Jury* – juries are tampered with by participants in the trial. Sometimes they bend to the threats, sometimes they stand up against them. Always, the hero-juror is the one who breaks the rules.

While unrealistic, these portrayals do inform our underlying cultural knowledge of juries. In the jury on which I served, one juror expressed a fear of reprisals from the accused, which she acknowledged was unfounded, but 'I've watched too much TV.' At times during the trial, I wondered if come deliberation time I was going to have to do a Henry Fonda and stand up against the majority. But in real life, the task is far more subtle – a juror must not seek to provide the telling piece of evidence, but rather to help in the uniquely consensual concert of achieving unanimity.

Filmed jury stories do cross over with real life. In 1993, the ABC broadcast a teledrama, *Joh's Jury*, which was based on juror accounts of the perjury trial of the former Queensland

Premier Sir Joh Bjelke-Petersen. (I found this, alongside *12 Angry Men*, the superior 'jury movie', so much so that the day after I saw it, when by chance I ran into the actor who played the infuriating jury foreman Luke Shaw, I told him that my first impulse was to take a swing at him.) *Joh's Jury* is about another exceptional juror, Shaw, who blocked a verdict and misrepresented the jury to the court.

After the screening of *Joh's Jury*, Michael Quinn, the president of the Queensland Criminal Law Association, said it was 'irresponsible in the extreme . . . a fundamental attack on the jury system . . . it seems to suggest that the jurors' deliberations in the jury room should be made public.'

I disagree. I found *Joh's Jury* wonderfully educational, if exasperating, and it seems I'm not alone. In a NSW study of juries, one juror confessed to watching *Joh's Jury* 'not just once but four times, in order to obtain guidance on how a jury should deal with disagreement among its members.'

The more we know about juries, the better. And there's no doubt that popular culture and media stories help us understand how people act on juries, as Findlay has pointed out:

> *Accepting that community confidence in the jury is high, and disproportionately so when considered against detailed public knowledge of what juries do, it is stories of the jury rather than real experience which tend to feed public opinion. These stories come through radio, television, theatre, press and film. Therefore the way juries are reported on or represented through the media becomes a legitimate source of information for research.*

That quote comes from one of the few serious attempts to understand juries in Australia. In the early 1990s, Findlay and a team from the University of Sydney polled 637 jurors and 881 non-jurors for a 1994-published study that remains the most comprehensive done here. In 2001, Professor Michael Chesterman and a team from the University of NSW interviewed 175 jurors from 41 criminal trials, mainly on how they had been affected by publicity surrounding their trial, but also on other aspects of the jury experience. Overseas, a hugely informative survey was conducted in 2000 by a New Zealand team led by Professor Warren Young, interviewing 312 jurors with a wide brief. Before that, the NSW Law Reform Commission had done a survey here in 1985, a British Royal Commission was conducted into juries in 1993, and there have been several American jury surveys, with academics there not bound by our jury-secrecy laws.

At the end of each of the academic jury surveys there is usually a list of recommendations to law-makers. What strikes me is how the same recommendations recur. There are five or six ways in which jurors can be helped, very easily, to reach a 'safe' or evidence-supported verdict. These involve the conditions under which jurors work, the process of 'getting off' jury duty, the way judges and lawyers present information, and juror input into a trial. When asked, jurors come up with the same requests time and again.

During the time I researched and wrote this book, the NSW Government enacted four changes to the jury system. One was to allow crime investigators to interview jurors about offences committed by jurors. One was, contrarily, to destroy all juror records so that a convicted criminal won't be able to track ex-jurors down. (Jurors' right to privacy is all very well, until the State wants to breach it, and then it's okay.) Trial by jury in civil matters has been all but abolished. Politicians and their shills attack the jury system every time an unpopular verdict comes out. And finally, parliament threatened jurors with jail if they conducted their own inquiries into the accused person. Meanwhile, nothing is done in response to the carefully researched, properly founded recommendations to help juries do their jobs better. In 2005, the influential Sydney barrister Bret Walker SC suggested that jurors should be interviewed after a trial. His aim seemed less to aid jurors than to discover where they'd gone wrong. 'Don't think juries can't be negligent,' Walker told *The Sydney Morning Herald*'s Michael Pelly.

In politics, it's a lot easier to seem tough by threatening sweeping steps against juries than to assist them, because juries represent no vested interest, no public partisan body. Working in the shadows, juries enjoy a necessary privacy. But that very privacy makes them vulnerable to attack. The result is that juries are, collectively, powerless to speak for themselves, and open to uninformed speculations. Juries can be negligent? How would a barrister, or for that matter a politician, know? When I spoke to trial lawyers, the common thread was their confession that they are stumped, constantly, by the mystery of what goes on behind the closed door of the jury room.

When we 12 walked out of the Downing Centre for the last time, we melted back into our communities. It was too early in the day for a farewell drink, and no big get-togethers were planned. A week later, I bumped into our foreman. Two newspaper reports about the trial had appeared after our verdict, and I asked if he'd seen them. 'Nah,' he said. 'I don't care. As far as I'm concerned, the minute it was over I'd forgotten about it.'

Most jurors are happy to be anonymous. But meanwhile, our democratic rights are seized and impounded by the jury's more vocal and organised enemies.

By the end of the 20th century a growing number of observers were coming to see the retreat from jury justice as part of a general retreat from democracy. The Canadian philosopher John Ralston Saul thinks attacks on the jury system 'are not about justice, they're about power. They're about this idea that the expert has the truth, and ordinary people aren't up to the task of making important decisions.' Saul sees the reduction of juries, 'for which I have no sympathy', as a reflection of the wider theft of power from citizens.

It is ourselves who remain the most vulnerable to this theft, as American commentator Alexander Cockburn has pointed out succinctly:

> *When a US president blunders or commits an illegal act, no one suggests that the presidency be abolished. When a professor is caught in acts of plagiarism, no one calls for repeal of the tenure system. But when democratic power blunders or is abused there are prompt calls for the institution to be abolished.*

Like participatory democracy itself, the jury system has all the best enemies: business and political elites; those who are intolerant of and impatient with Joe and Joanna Public; those who think experts can solve every problem. Those who get out of jury duty and those who are never required to serve on juries are usually its strongest opponents. Those who have been jurors are its strongest, yet most anonymous, supporters. When I stepped out of the District Court after a month as a juror, I was bursting, like a diver who has been too long in the deep, with a story to tell.

Chapter One

THE FALL OF THE HOUSE OF RUSHER

Only Steve Rusher will ever know what he had in mind when, on the Easter weekend of 2001, he packed two false passports and his son Steven Jr onto an Amtrak train from Los Angeles to Vancouver.

Only Rusher will know if he was simply embarking on a desperate quest to protect his five-year-old boy, or if he had something more sinister in mind. He might have been acting under the influence of paranoid fantasy; or he might have been weaving new fantasies with manipulative intent, to conscript others to his quest. He might have been constructing lies as a fall-back, in case he got caught. He might have been trying to convince himself that he was acting nobly. Whichever it was, we don't know, because Steve Rusher has always maintained his innocence.

Tall and forceful, with a thick wave of dark blond hair, Rusher was already breaking the law when he took Steven Jr onto the train at Union Station. SJ, as his father called him, had been staying with Rusher for the routine visit that the courts had ordered while Rusher and SJ's mother sorted out their ongoing custody dispute. Just that week an LA County Court decision went against Rusher, reducing the number of days a month he could spend with SJ from eight to four. After the loss, he was boiling. He used a business connection in Los

Angeles to obtain false passports for himself and his little boy, under the names Warren and David Huck. When SJ came to visit at Easter, Rusher took him on an adventure to the far end of the earth.

Whatever Rusher had in mind then, he could never have guessed how long he would be staying in Australia. He and SJ flew from Vancouver to Sydney on an Air Canada service, and stayed in a flat at Coogee beach. Rusher, who had brought around US$60,000 in cash, purchased an old-model Nissan Pintara for $4,200 and set off with SJ towards Melbourne. His ultimate destination was Hobart.

But for some reason Rusher abruptly turned around in late May 2001 and drove north, through Sydney, to the Gold Coast. He rented a flat and dropped into a local libary to send and check emails. He asked for help from one of the library staff, a man named Les McAtee.

In the past few years, Steve Rusher had suffered the loss of fortune, reputation, friendships and family. He had been ruined in business, his third marriage had disintegrated in the most humiliating way, his qualities as a father had been vilified in court, and he was being denied contact with the one person he unambiguously cared for: his son. And now his real problems started.

This was Rusher's second visit to Australia. In December 2000, Rusher and his wife of ten years, Lorna Fiona Emery, had formally separated. Fiona, as she was known, wasn't just leaving Rusher. A week after the separation, she took SJ to Australia – to Tasmania, no less, as far from her husband as possible – to reunite with a close friend from her pre-Rusher life.

Furious, Rusher followed Fiona and SJ to Hobart and started proceedings in the Family Court of Australia to have SJ returned to the United States. Fiona said she was seeking Australian residency with her Tasmanian lover, but the judge said she would have to take SJ back to California before resuming her visa application.

The three returned to California. Fiona moved back to her rented apartment in West Hollywood with SJ, while Rusher was camping on a friend's couch in nearby Westwood. They commenced a four-month battle – a war, really – in the courts for custody of SJ. That first trip to Hobart, in which the true nature of Fiona's new living arrangement had become clear to Rusher, had enraged him to the point where he told friends he would 'scorch the earth' to stop SJ going to Australia. Steve Rusher, a good-looking, physically imposing, bronzed Californian with a lifelong addiction to 'positive thinking' and a vocabulary indebted to the self-help industry, was given to making big statements. Once he talked himself up – his natural gifts, his self-described business prowess, his innate ability to get others to do his bidding – Rusher had no doubt that he would prevail. He began to see himself as a crusader not only for SJ's welfare, but as a representative of all men who have been betrayed by women. He believed he had the swell of history on his side.

Fiona's new friend, with whom she planned to raise SJ, was a Tasmanian woman called Terri Maxfield. Fiona and Terri had met in the mid-1980s when Fiona, then twenty, was backpacking around the world. Terri Maxfield was a large woman, a public servant who was as robust and plain-speaking as Fiona was slight and genteel. Terri had been married and divorced by the time she met Fiona in a Salamanca Place pub. Opposites attracted. Their 1980s affair in Hobart was short, and Fiona would consign it to the back drawer of youthful experimentation. For Terri, also, it was early days in the new path she was cutting herself. But their brief encounter was sweet enough for them to remain close confidantes over the following years. They kept in contact, over the phone and by writing, during the decade of Fiona's subsequent marriage to Steve Rusher. As she was splitting with Rusher in 2000, Fiona started to wonder if she had taken a wrong turn when she'd left Tasmania years before. The lifting of Rusher's oppressive, almost dictatorial presence from her day-to-day activities freed up Fiona's spirits in an unexpected way. Although she had not seen Terri in 13 years, although she had not been with another woman since Terri, Fiona became convinced that Terri occupied centre stage in her future. It would not have helped Steve Rusher's cause that the public servant living in a renovated Hobart worker's cottage was about as far as Fiona could get – literally and figuratively – from him. By late 2000, Fiona and Terri were making plans.

Rusher never suspected that Fiona and Terri had remained in close contact. Why would he? When he'd met and courted Fiona, Rusher was on top of the world. Born in 1957 in Long Beach, a white working-class area of Los Angeles, Rusher had achieved some success in the 1980s as a film producer. It was at a time when any young man who had a vague determination to get into movies wanted to be a 'producer'. Earlier, they'd wanted to be writers or directors: film-makers. But by the 1980s, the prized art was the art of making money, or getting a film made without spending money – persuading people to trust your promises – and so producers, formerly characterised as shifty used-car dealers, were by now the glamorous Hollywood players. Steve Rusher was in his element. He had not one creative bone in his body except a gift for cutting deals, in selling. He did all right. By Hollywood standards, he was a midget mogul, running a small production company that made low-budget police thrillers selling straight to television and video. Rusher put up his own money for his early productions, got young actors and crew to work for the experience alone, and increased his bet the next time. He began to leverage his profits, leasing a Beverly Hills office which he would line with movie posters (only some of them his own movies, but that was a mere detail) and inviting prospective investors to hear his pitch there before driving in his leased Mercedes coupe to the Polo Lounge at the Beverly Hills Hotel where he would wink and raise a thumb to passing stars. Thinking he was someone they knew, sometimes they grinned and waved back. In the patented American style, Steve Rusher was able to parlay his self-belief and David Hasselhoff looks into the appearance, and to some degree the reality, of a genuine career as a film producer.

In 1988 Rusher moved into a $US1.5 million house in Benedict Canyon, a movie-star gulch north of Hollywood where, just up the road, Roman Polanski's wife Sharon Tate had been murdered by Charles Manson's Family in 1969. Steve Rusher would take friends for what he called 'history drives' around the canyons, his own fantasy version of the stars' home tours conducted in LA and which he himself had taken as an ambitious youngster. Often he would invent sightings with a gossipy edge – any house would be Rock Hudson's gay pad, or Nancy Reagan's astrologer's house, or Don Johnson's bachelor flop. As with much of his life, Rusher made it up as he went along. At this stage nobody was going to pull him up on his exaggerations. He was a high flier. His house wasn't as opulent as the real studio producers' homes overlooking the city or in Beverly Hills, and it was shaded most afternoons by the overhanging hills; but it wasn't bad either, with a pool, a cabana, a jacuzzi, and a three-car garage. Steve Rusher, whose father still worked on the docks at Long Beach, had fulfilled his own American dream.

Hollywood replicates itself in its different social strata. Rusher's low-budget, on-the-up scene had its own self-serious pretentions to glamour. In 1988, Rusher hosted several friends, agents, B-movie actors and investors for a party in Benedict Canyon. One of the young women brought along for the party – an executive assistant for an actors' agency – was Fiona Emery.

Fiona and Rusher had met once before, in 1984, when Rusher was still married to his second wife, Anna. (Rusher's rich and varied romantic history had yielded two wives – not to mention countless flings and one-night stands, according to him – and two children. Rhonda was a childhood sweetheart he'd married at 19 and left at 21. They had a son, Pete, in 1977. Anna, the daughter of one of Rusher's first backers, had lasted four years in Rusher's mid-twenties. Nicky, their daughter, was born in 1984. From the mid-1980s on, Rusher was only in Christmas- and birthday-card contact with his ex-wives and children. Foreshadowing his custody battle with Fiona, he had fought and lost court cases with both ex-wives. Both times, once he lost, he washed his hands of the children, dedicating his energies, in one of his favourite phrases, 'to checking out and moving on'.)

Fiona, seven years Rusher's junior, caught his eye – she was slim, attractive, long-haired and had a natural refinement that Rusher must have envied as well as admired. Brought up in wealthy Orange County, Fiona Emery was an aristocrat to Rusher's self-made man. He built a new fantasy around her, idealising her as the perfect complement to his glad-handing, opportunistic, edge-of-the-seat business style. She embodied his most cherished ideal: 'class'.

When they met again at the 1988 party, Rusher seduced Fiona. She moved in with him that very week, and left her job to join his production company. They were good business partners; as Rusher focused on making deals and selling ideas, Fiona ran the logistics and administration tasks for which Rusher had no patience or concentration.

The next two years were their best together. They married, on Santa Monica Beach, in 1990. A magazine named Steve Rusher as one of the highest-flying young independent producers of the day. A newspaper photographed him in Benedict Canyon in mirrored sunglasses and Hawaiian shirt, the model Californian go-getter. He told a friend that some little boys want to be train drivers when they grow up, but he'd always wanted to own a movie studio.

Yet Rusher's empire was built on hope and hot air. He owned nothing. His house, car, even his chrome-and-leather furniture were all leased. What he had, he gambled on new enterprises, multiplying the risk with heavy borrowings. His problem was impatience – he wanted to own that movie studio sooner rather than later, and to do so he needed to take big risks. In the early

1990s the management of TV and movie studios, Rusher's customers, changed when they were consolidated under new multinational corporate owners like the French company Vivendi, Japan's Sony, and Australia's News Corporation. In his business – doubling up on each winning bet – Rusher needed to be lucky not just once, but all the time. In 1991 he produced his first movie for cinema, a US$3 million adventure about a motorboat racer. It was never released, not even on video or TV. Rusher had stepped up a weight division and been knocked out. His backers panicked and called in their chits. Rusher, overcommitted, filed for Chapter VII bankruptcy.

If image was everything in Rusher's business, that could be said as much for the downside as the upside. Just as actors can run hot and cold, so can producers, and through the 1990s, Steve Rusher was ice-cold. He tried to rebuild through increasingly risky schemes – branching out from movies into Ponzi schemes, dabbling in property development, 'inventing' a memory-enhancement product to sell on home shopping TV – and sailing close to the limits of accounting probity. As a couple, he and Fiona moved to a cheaper rental apartment in Hayworth Street, West Hollywood, and survived largely on donations from Fiona's parents. Fiona stuck by Rusher, and it was during this tough period that she decided she wanted a baby. Rusher didn't, and when Fiona fell pregnant in 1995 their relationship began to unravel. After giving birth to Steven Orson Rusher on 1 December 1995, Fiona ceased her sexual relationship with Rusher. She stayed at the West Hollywood apartment, while Rusher slept on the couch in a friend's apartment at Santa Monica four nights a week and came home for weekends. Later, he stayed in a series of friends' houses before renting a one-bedroom apartment in Westwood, 15 minutes' drive from Fiona and SJ. There was a continued deterioration over the next three years, during which Fiona resumed and intensified her correspondence with Terri Maxfield in Australia. The pair discovered that they were, once again, in love. Fiona resolved to take SJ to Australia to live with Terri. She told Rusher she wanted to move overseas, and the separation, which Rusher had hidden from his business contacts for four years, became public.

For a man like Steve Rusher, fuelled by self-confidence and the presentation of a certain image, sexual prestige was almost more important than financial. His charisma and good looks were his consolation: when he was broke, he could look at wealthier men and say to himself: 'No matter how much money they have, they'll still be ugly.' Steve Rusher was always able to turn female heads, and as his business affairs foundered he compensated with love affairs. But this only masked his insecurity, and his sexual self-esteem must have been shattered by the discovery that his wife had left him for another woman. Never mind that the marriage was in trouble without Terri Maxfield's involvement. Rusher flew into a rage when he discovered that Fiona had been staying in touch with Terri, and when he learnt that she was planning to take SJ to live in Australia, the final strut holding up Rusher's ego was knocked out from under him. A February 2001 court decision, reducing Rusher's access to SJ and paving the way for Fiona to move to Australia, seems to have been the last straw. He obtained two passports under false names and took SJ on his second trip down-under.

A frantic Fiona, still in Los Angeles, found photocopies of the false passports and told the police. The FBI put out a warrant on Rusher. On the run up and down the east coast of Australia, 'Warren Huck' and his son 'David' stayed in motels and short-term accommodation until renting a flat on the Gold Coast. Well-groomed, optimistic, handsome, a caring (and apparently single) father, Rusher was able to charm the Australians he dealt with.

It was about then that Rusher and SJ turned up on the Gold Coast. Rusher came every day to send emails to Fiona and check if she was replying. She wasn't. He befriended the council's information officer, Les McAtee, a reserved, shopworn-looking Queenslander with shaggy brown hair, three children and the voice of a pack-a-day smoker. Les, a movie fan, liked the smooth American producer and ate up his Hollywood stories. Rusher found out that Les was a single father of three and assumed Les was divorced, not widowed. Rusher believed he'd met a kindred spirit, and when he wasn't name-dropping about the movie business, he was griping about modern women and the desperate lot of the honourable man who just wants to raise his children morally. Les didn't take any of this too seriously – he got used to the American's big-noting ways and was happy for the variety and colour Rusher brought into his life.

Rusher soon trusted Les McAtee enough to ask him to help send anonymous emails to Fiona. Les suggested Rusher just set up a Hotmail account, but Rusher said he wanted to conceal the emails' point of origin. He confided that he was on the run and on a mission to protect his son from abuse. Abuse? Les was sceptical, but he could understand that Rusher was a man of conservative moral views, and sympathised, up to a point, with Rusher's wish to keep SJ out of a house with 'two Moms'. Les wasn't quite as disgusted as Rusher, and didn't quite see this as 'abuse', but he could see where Rusher was coming from.

What Steve Rusher didn't know about Les McAtee was that the council information officer had, in an earlier life, been a reporter for *The Gold Coast Bulletin*: a police roundsman, what's more, with contacts in law enforcement. Les had given up journalism when his wife died and he needed to spend more time with his children. The old gumshoe instincts didn't leave him, however. Snoopily, he broke into Rusher's emails and found that he was sending coded messages to the US under the name Harvey, the name of his favourite actor – whom he'd once met – Harvey Keitel. Rusher seemed to be enjoying the fantasy life of a man on the run.

At the same time, Rusher saw Les as a fairly hapless, starstruck hillbilly. Having secured Les's complicity in concealing the emails, Rusher asked for his help in obtaining other false documents. Les – torn between suspicion and sympathy – agreed to offer some help if Rusher told him who he really was and why he was in Australia.

Rusher confessed. His mission, he said, was to 'serve documents' on Terri Maxfield to stop SJ being put in Fiona's custody. Rusher wanted to open new Family Court proceedings in Australia, because the law here, he said, gave him more hope than in America. He said that once he had 'served the documents', he would turn himself and SJ in, take the rap on the false-passport problem, and commence his new court case.

Rusher told McAtee he'd been down to Tasmania on his earlier visit to Australia, and met a family friend of Terri Maxfield's ex-husband, Robert Brennan. This friend went onto Steve Rusher's payroll and linked him up with Brennan, who told Rusher that Terri had been physically and verbally abusive during their marriage. What about children? Rusher asked. They hadn't had any, said Brennan, but as Terri started to come out as a lesbian, Brennan felt she 'got a set against' all males, including young boys. Once Terri had hit a nephew. Rusher dug up an old court statement Brennan had made against Terri during their divorce proceedings, in which he'd mentioned perverse sexual inclinations. Rusher's eyes lit up: if Terri was some kind of sexual deviant, the prospect of leaving little SJ with her would surely alarm any Family Court judge. Rusher sniffed and ferreted for evidence. But Brennan couldn't really help him. All Terri's 'deviancy' turned out to be was that she admitted to having had affairs with women.

Rusher told Les McAtee all of this, appealing for Les's agreement that this was a sound basis on which to build a case that living with Terri Maxfield and Fiona posed a danger to SJ's upbringing 'as a normal guy'. Through the Hobart friend, Rusher had employed a private investigator to trawl the gay scene for information on Terri Maxfield. But apart from rumours of her sleeping around, Rusher had been able to dig up no incriminating evidence on the woman.

He didn't tell Les McAtee the full extent of his failure, instead referring to Terri Maxfield bitterly as a 'dyke pervert' and stressing the danger for SJ.

Although he felt sorry for Rusher, whom he liked, Les McAtee also worried about SJ. From his *Bulletin* days, Les had retained contact with a retired Federal Police officer called Brian Mellon. When Les told Mellon about this flash American, Mellon had an ex-colleague look up Rusher's name and found the FBI warrant out for his arrest. Reluctantly – but certain it would be for SJ's benefit – Les McAtee turned Rusher in to immigration authorities.

Back in Los Angeles, Fiona was waiting for news. When Rusher was turned in, Fiona flew back out to Australia and took care of SJ. Together they flew to Hobart and moved in with Terri Maxfield.

Steve Rusher never knew that his new mate Les was the person who turned him in. The day after his incarceration he called Les and asked him to look after some details – collect money, the car registration, and other effects from his rented flat. Before long, he was phoning repeatedly to ask for Les's help with his 'document serving'. He asked Les to call the Hobart friend and offer Robert Brennan money if he could 'remember' any more sexual or physical abuse by Terri Maxfield against boys. Les McAtee, who was beginning to like Steve Rusher less and less, never made the call.

Among his effects, Rusher had got Les to pick up a letter detailing how Terri had 'brutalised' her young nephew. Les read it, and believed it a forgery. He threw it aside.

Rusher was suffering in the heat in a Brisbane immigration detention centre, and became desperate to be moved to Sydney. His requests fell on deaf ears, so he pulled a typically inventive legal stunt. After fleeing America, he could be charged with kidnapping SJ. No-one had laid charges, so he decided to do it himself. He launched an application, as SJ's father, against himself, as SJ's kidnapper, in Sydney, where he'd landed in Australia. So that he could appear in this bizarre matter of *Steve Rusher v Steve Rusher*, he was moved to Silverwater jail, in Sydney. The upcoming Family Court hearings would be in Sydney, and Rusher wanted to be there to argue that, if left with Fiona, SJ would be in 'grave danger'. Fiona won custody – there was no blemish on Terri's record, although a rather old-fashioned judge made remarks sympathetic to Rusher's distaste for a same-sex couple raising his son. But, these humiliations aside, Fiona was free to take SJ back to Tasmania and start life with Terri.

According to Les McAtee's later testimony under oath, Rusher had been phoning him every night from Silverwater saying he wanted to kill himself. But then, enraged at losing in the Family Court, he told Les: 'The dyke's got them both now.' Rusher seemed to have convinced himself that Terri Maxfield was an evil sexual predator who had overpowered and brainwashed Fiona. He redirected his suicidal urges outwards: he decided to have Terri Maxfield killed. His problem was that he was now in jail, but he had a way around that. He'd often talked big about his connections in the Los Angeles underworld, and now asked Les to call a friend of his in America called 'Atillio', and tell Atillio it was time to repay a favour.

Les McAtee, increasingly reluctant to help Rusher yet unable to bring himself to abandon the man – he was, after all, Rusher's only friend here – pretended to try calling Atillio for a few days before finally doing so. Atillio told him Rusher still owed people for past 'favours', so he might as well forget it.

With that avenue closed off, Rusher asked Les to phone a Tasmanian woodcutter whose name he said had been supplied as a potential hitman. The conversation between Les and the woodcutter was short: the man was going on holidays to Thailand, and would have nothing to do with it.

Up to then, Les said he'd been helping Rusher because he felt guilty about dobbing him in, and because the poor guy kept phoning. There was another link between them: Les had 'lost' some of the money Rusher had left with him. After he went into detention, Rusher asked Les to sell his car and look after US$10,000 for 'legal bills'. Most of that money, Les said, he left in a computer disk box at home. Rusher told him to move it to a safe in his office at the council, and shortly afterwards the safe was robbed. Les said he suspected a disgruntled council ex-employee called 'Jodie', who disappeared at the same time as the money. But there were no formal records of a 'Jodie', and Les didn't put in a formal report of the theft to the police.

In July 2001, with his Family Court hopes going south, Rusher called Les and told him: 'God's given me an early birthday present.' Rusher had met a Greek-American in Silverwater named Yanni Diamondopoulos, who had agreed to kill Terri Maxfield and Fiona for him. Both of them now? The 'favour has been doubled', Rusher told McAtee. In disbelief, Les asked him how it would be done. Rusher said the plan was to make it look like a burglary gone wrong.

Diamondopoulos was in remand on a robbery charge, and hadn't been able to meet his $15,000 bail. Rusher put the money up. But Rusher apparently did not want to be identified as Diamondopoulos's benefactor. He took elaborate measures to distance himself from the money. The parcel of cash was left at the front desk in Silverwater in Les McAtee's name, picked up by a courier, and taken to Diamondopoulos's Australian de facto, Christine Farragher. She banked the money in her own name, and picked up Diamondopoulos from jail.

Les had not known whether to believe Rusher's threats that he was going to kill anyone, let alone both Terri and Fiona. The guy was, after all, a chronic bullshitter. But after the 'early birthday present' conversation, Les realised Rusher was serious. 'Up to then I'd thought he was dreaming, and I never swallowed the whole Atillio thing,' Les would tell the court, 'but not anymore.

Diamondopoulos was real, and sounded like an authentic piece of work.'

Les told the Queensland police, who got the NSW and Federal Police involved. For safety, Terri Maxfield, Fiona and SJ were moved out of Maxfield's Tasmanian house. The police caught up with Diamondopoulos and Christine Farragher at Sydney Airport. They needn't have worried. Yanni and Christine were on their way to Chicago, courtesy of Steve Rusher. They were pinching his money and running. Interviewed by police, Diamondopoulos admitted Rusher had given him the money but he couldn't remember why. The police arrested him, and he was eventually acquitted of the robbery charge. He and his de facto went to America. Under the terms of Diamondopoulos's bail, the $15,000 reverted to the person who'd banked it – Christine Farragher. It never went back to Steve Rusher.

If the police believed Steve Rusher was trying to kill Terri or Fiona, they still didn't have enough evidence to prosecute him successfully. Diamondopoulos was an unreliable witness, and the case then boiled down to Les McAtee's word against Rusher's. Les wasn't prepared to do that, but he was sufficiently concerned about Rusher's intentions that he agreed to help the Federal Police set up a sting on Rusher.

Willingly deceiving him now, Les told Rusher he'd contacted a waste contractor in Tasmania who carried out hits. Rusher was agreeable to the idea. Les told Rusher a go-between for these people, known only as 'Spike', would come and visit Rusher in Silverwater to arrange the hits on Terri and, now, Fiona, upon whom Rusher had turned his sights.

Late in the afternoon of 19 July, Spike arrived to meet Rusher in the remand centre. Spike was fitted up with a listening device, and it was on the basis of his two taped meetings and two taped phone conversations with Rusher in the next week that Rusher was charged with soliciting to murder Terri Maxfield and Fiona Emery.

When Rusher met Spike for the first time, he greeted him with the words: 'Welcome to the asshole of the earth.' Regularly mustered for roll call, subjected to poor food, cramped conditions and incessant noise, he was understandably despondent. He was placed on suicide watch. Sometimes he took Valium to sleep.

Yet he didn't want to leave. His Family Court appeal was coming up. To buy himself some more time against deportation, he applied for refugee status on the grounds that he would face persecution in the form of his anxiety over SJ's welfare. It was a long bow, and met with a predictable refusal. But the process kept him in Australia. No matter how far he had fallen from his high-flying days as a telemovie producer, no matter how acute the humiliation, no matter how unlikely his chances of gaining real evidence against Terri Maxfield, he was desperate to stay.

As always, there's another version of the story. The facts are much the same, but the interpretation is turned on its head. This is Steve Rusher's side, as he put it to the court, and it is a story of a father's overpowering will to protect and care for his son.

By this version, Rusher had been, in his own words, 'crapped on by the world for a very long time'. Yes, he'd made a few mistakes in business, but Hollywood is a shark pool and his enemies hastened his demise. Fiona had been drawn to him when he was a wealthy man, but her love faded as the money dribbled away. Moreover, she was secretly betraying him with this Australian lesbian. Even though Steve had given her a wonderful life in their heyday and continued to provide for her, Fiona was – there's no other way of putting it – morally unfit for motherhood. She was a weak character, abandoning him when his business turned sour, and was probably being brainwashed by this depraved Tasmanian.

Amid all the gloom, little SJ was the one ray of light in Steve

Rusher's life. Then, the bombshell that Fiona was going to take SJ not only to Australia, but to a gay relationship, broke Rusher's heart.

He knew he was violating the law by taking SJ to Australia, but he was desperate to protect his boy. Time was running out. He planned to come to Australia and win joint custody of SJ. He didn't want to take him away from Fiona. If Fiona wanted to live with Terri Maxfield, fine: but she couldn't have it both ways. She could explore her new 'identity', or be a mother. But not both. SJ needed a male role model in his life. A boy needs his dad.

To bolster his Family Court case, Steve needed evidence on Terri. Fiona, Steve thought, seemed 'programmed' by the woman, refusing to investigate her true character. Well, that was Fiona's problem. Rusher's mission was to ensure it didn't become SJ's problem, too.

He admitted he'd made a mistake: bringing SJ here under the false names. But all the dice were loaded against him, and he'd had to take desperate measures. This was the way he lived, in business and in life. He rode his luck. But his intentions were pure. He was a father doing no more than trying to stop his son being stolen from him and exposed to a depraved way of life.

Rusher had no idea he'd been dobbed in by Les McAtee, whom he'd thought of as a pal. He'd been taken for a ride by McAtee. Rusher was vulnerable, needing to trust people, and McAtee seemed to be a man who understood another father's plight. But McAtee had discovered that Steve Rusher had some money, and he manipulated Rusher into giving him his cash and possessions when Steve went to jail. The bait was too much for McAtee, who was now showing his true colours. McAtee's plan was to pocket all the money he'd got his hands on, and the car, and make sure Rusher never came back out to retrieve them.

So McAtee, this shady, down-at-heel gutter journalist, discovered that if he put a certain twist on events and helped the police set up a trap, Steve Rusher could go to prison for a long time. Yet again, Steve Rusher's vulnerability and love for his son had been exploited.

Les McAtee – Steve's only friend, or so he thought – started taping his phone calls. He got Steve talking about his plans to serve documents on Terri Maxfield. Rusher, depressed and lonely, spilt his guts to Les: he was absolutely frantic to protect SJ, and would do anything – legally – to keep Maxfield from harming him.

Meanwhile, poor generous Steve was being ripped off by people in Silverwater. Yanni Diamondopoulos had lied to him about his de facto being pregnant. Rusher, always generous to a fellow sufferer, lent him $15,000. But now Yanni seemed to have shot through with it. Rusher was suicidally depressed by the time McAtee suggested to him a waste contractor might be able to go to Hobart and do better than the $40-an-hour private investigator Rusher had previously used to 'serve the documents'. Reluctantly – but what were his choices? – Rusher agreed. It was the worst mistake he could have made.

These two versions of the one story – the Crown's and the defence's – meant nothing less to Steve Rusher than the difference between prison and freedom. A jury was empanelled in the District Court in Sydney to find out, as best it could, the true version of the Steve Rusher story.

Jurors can't be trusted. This is one of the guiding rules of our legal system: certain evidence must be kept from the jury's view, because it will distort their minds against the accused. The exclusionary rules of evidence are complicated, but one of the main principles is the 'Christie discretion', from a 1914 English case, which states that a judge may conceal evidence from the jury if it is factually only slightly probative but may cause great prejudice against the accused. If Fiona wanted to say certain prejudicial things about Rusher's past, we jurors weren't allowed to hear them. Such evidence could stamp Rusher in our minds as a dishonest or violent character, yet would have no direct bearing on the Crown's case.

Hearsay, past convictions or rumours of this kind couldn't be admitted. The District Court judge would have ruled on this kind of evidence in the 'voir dire', or the pre-trial hearing before the jury came in.

Some of the above account we were allowed to hear. But much about Steve Rusher was kept hidden from us and I have only found out about his background since the trial finished.

Would it have helped us to know more about him? Would more background have prejudiced us against Rusher in a solicit-to-murder trial? I don't know, and the court wasn't going to give us a chance.

CHAPTER TWO

PANEL BEATING
OR
HOW JURORS AND LAWYERS CULL THE POOL

The jury system is actually bizarre. Where else in our society would you invite disparate laymen, novices with absolutely no experience or previous information in a given field, to be the ultimate judges about issues in that field, with almost no restrictions on their qualifications except direct, personal bias, willingly admitted? Bizarre, yes? They've never been to court, know nothing about trial procedure or the law. They hear the case just once – orally. They may have little schooling and little information about most aspects of our society, let alone expertise in the subject in question. They may be innately bright or slow, interested or disinterested, privately prejudiced or not. They're recruited and pressed into service, not even willing volunteers. And then, this motley crew, this questionable 'board', is given ultimate authority to judge crime and punishment, life and death, right or wrong. Why? What did our tribal elders, our societal sages have in mind when they designed this system?

– Sonya Hamlin, *What Makes Juries Listen?*

Growing up in the suburbs of Sydney, a trip into town was an exotic event. My earliest memories of city shopping excursions with my mother and grandmother involve dressing up in our best

– my grandmother wore matching gloves and handbag for a day in town – and ploughing through the department stores of David Jones, Farmer's and Grace Brothers with their wooden escalators, concertina-door lifts operated by ancient attendants and, best of all, top-floor cafeterias where my brother and I would gorge ourselves on egg-and-lettuce sandwiches and scones with jam and cream, exploring the camphor-scented chaos of self-service while Mum and Gran rested their bone-weary legs.

We rarely ventured into the southern CBD, where by the 1970s the department stores had gone to seed. Gran reminisced about the grand days of Anthony Hordern's, Marcus Clarke's and Mark Foy's, the most opulent emporia of the inter-war years. By my childhood, Marcus Clarke's and Anthony Hordern's had been flattened. Only Mark Foy's remained, though it closed in 1980 after years of neglect and would lie vacant for the next decade.

Built in 1908 to a design by Arthur McCredie and Arthur Anderson, modelled on the Bon Marché store in Paris, Mark Foy's had once boasted Sydney's first escalator and first outdoor cafe. Brothers Francis and Mark Foy had expanded the family business from their Drapery Palace in Oxford Street to three department stores on Elizabeth Street, of which the Emporium at the corner of Liverpool Street was the flagship. Francis Foy used to work his shopgirls for 100-hour weeks, a sin for which he was punished when he dropped dead on a train returning to Sydney from the 1918 Melbourne Cup.

Mark Foy's long decline started with the Great Depression. The stretch of land from Circular Quay to Central Station was too long to support a concentrated shopping district, and the construction of Museum Station beneath Mark Foy's was not enough to save it and the other big stores south of Brickfield Hill (Town Hall) from the more successful stores towards Wynyard.

The Foy family also met with misfortune. Juanita Nielsen, the heiress, disappeared in 1974, presumably murdered for her role protesting the demolition of terrace housing in Potts Point. When the NSW Government decided to redevelop the

Mark Foy's Emporium as a courthouse in the late 1980s, it renamed the building after R.R. Downing, the Justice Minister and Attorney-General from 1941 to 1965, the salad days of the corrupt politico-legal cartels that are believed to have conspired in Nielsen's death.

I grew more familiar with the city during the 1980s, and remember passing by Mark Foy's, wondering if the white glazed-brick building with the turreted mansards, fancy gold cornices and green pressed-metal awnings would fall under the same wrecking ball with which Sydney stamped out most of its architectural past.

The carapace of the Foy building did survive around the refurbished interior of the Downing Centre. When I entered the building on an overcast morning in winter 2002 I noticed a circular mosaic crest – MARK FOY'S LTD – on the foyer floor. Along the exterior walls, mosaics proclaim the wares for which my grandmother went to Mark Foy's: Hosiery, Silks, Millinery, Shoes, Laces, Gloves, Corsets, Costumes and Flowers. One day it may preserve its legal inventory in the same way: Arsonists, Robbers, Rapists, Murderers – oh, and don't forget Barristers and Judges.

And Jurors, whose number I was about to join. Beyond the metal detectors, walls of glass bricks and grey paint transformed the glorious exterior into the institutional drabness of a government building. Following the signs, I went downstairs to the Jury Assembly Room, an auditorium with a few hundred seats administered by blue-uniformed officers of the NSW Sheriff's department who asked me to present my summons as identification.

I didn't have my summons. I'd sent it back, inscribed with a story that had been good enough to get me off jury duty in 1999: as a journalist with *The Sydney Morning Herald*, I might be required to travel out of Sydney at any time, and moreover had written at times on law-and-order issues. (Of course, had jury duty involved, say, a month's sequestration in a five-star hotel with poolside massages interrupted only by calls from the restaurant asking whether I'd like the duck or the salmon, I'd never have thought my profession would in any way invalid me out.) Instead of my summons, as my identification I flashed the letter the Sheriff's Office had sent in reply to my begging-off request. It said: No.

My attempt at shirking seems lame against the baroque backdrop of a 2004 NSW Sheriff's Office report on 'interesting excuses'.

One shirker claimed: 'I'm a clairvoyant and therefore I would know whether a person was guilty or innocent. I would be concerned that I may not be able to convince my fellow jurors.'

Other statements listed in the report included:

'My friends are criminals so I wouldn't be able to help.'

'I have to stay home and mind my sick budgerigar.'

'I couldn't come in because I was pissed and stoned.'

'I am a night person.'

'I hear voices that tell me I shouldn't attend'.

'I can't leave home due to the impending holocaust.'

One shirker had even enlisted a shirker doctor, who wrote:

'This person should not do jury duty as he has a mind like a computer; sometimes it is overloaded and crashes, then he needs to reboot, sometimes causing his thoughts to be scrambled.'

Little wonder the Sheriff's Office fobbed off my limp attempt. Not only had I tried to shirk – a form of failure in itself – I had failed at failing.

I arrived at the court, then, a double-failure. Which probably suited me perfectly for the role of juror. I've heard it said that you wouldn't want to be tried by 12 people who can't get off jury duty. Certainly my hunch was that only the retired, the unemployed and housewives served on juries, as well as the odd blue-collar worker who preferred a few weeks in court to a few weeks in a production line. This impression – that the clever get out of it – was reinforced when, in the Jury Assembly Room, I met an acquaintance, Andrew, an executive at a publishing house. Andrew was also keen to get off, but rather than send in a speculative letter, he planned to beg off in person.

He asked if I was going to try again, but I figured I'd had a good shot at getting off, and now that I was here I may as well do it. I mumbled platitudes about civic duty and making the best of a bad thing. I felt much the same as an American juror, Graham Burnett, had at the same point:

> *At the start, I decided to treat the unwelcome interruption of jury duty as something like a vacation, a brief visit to a foreign country of bureaucratic languor and vast waiting rooms ... Plus, I could get some reading done ... The criminal court began to look like an opportunity to hide in plain view.*

I opened up a novel and settled down to hide in plain view. There were about 200 prospective jurors in the Jury Assembly Room, a windowless space with the ambience of an airport departure lounge. People's behaviour in this situation must have a certain universality, because Burnett might as well have been talking about my own fellow jurors when he wrote: 'In the twice-exhaled air of the jury waiting room, about two hundred disgruntled New Yorkers had arranged themselves like a tray of magnetic monopoles: maximum space between each particle and its neighbours.'

Mind you, Burnett also observed that the Manhattan jury assembly room 'secreted an unexpected libidinous energy' as the magnetic monopoles began to attract and jurors started to eye each other off. I couldn't detect such energy in the basement of the Downing Centre, which is not to say that it didn't exist; but the nervousness in the room was more irritable than libidinous (although a male Federal Police officer was later to tell me, 'You always hope there's one or two nice-looking girls on the jury. It keeps you interested. Um, human nature, I s'pose.').

After half an hour's inaction, about 30 of us were taken on a ten-minute tour of a courtroom, where a sheriff's officer named Theo explained briefly where the judge, jury, accused and lawyers sat. I told Andrew that if he failed to get off, he could try what a lawyer friend had told me a few days earlier:

> *When they call you up from the back of the court, go the wrong way to the jury box – around the wrong table, or in the wrong direction – the prosecution will always challenge you if they see you can't follow the simplest direction.*

Theo, meanwhile, was warning us not to get 'intimidated or panicked' if we got called into the jury box. Silently, I scoffed. Why be intimidated? There was nothing at stake for a juror: you didn't have to perform, like the lawyers. Your future wasn't on the line, like the accused. You had no axe to grind, like victims and witnesses. You didn't have to watch your step or be appealed, like a judge. You were just a blank. The juror had the easiest job in the court.

After we were led back into the Jury Assembly Room, Andrew tried his excuse on the sheriff's officers. Whatever it was, it worked. I noticed a lot of others working: a self-employed man I heard saying: 'I can't go back to the job in four weeks; in four weeks, the job will be gone'; and, coincidentally, I saw a man I'd been trying unsuccessfully to interview recently for a story. I'd filled up his voicemail with messages, and he'd never called back. He got off jury duty, too.

Getting out of jury duty has a distinguished history. Burnett, an academic historian, was told that he need only mention that he studied 'philosophy', and he'd get off. But in America jurors are assessed by a verbal interview process. In big cases, jury consultants are employed to research jurors' backgrounds and grade them on a scale of how favourable they will be.

That's the first of the many ways our system diverges from

America's. In Australian courts, a juror's anonymity is protected and we are known only as numbers. So strategies for getting out of jury duty revolve around pre-trial applications, statutory exemptions, and if all else fails the tricks you can pull when you go into the courtroom.

The statutory exemptions apply to people like lawyers, doctors, pharmacists, emergency workers, senior public servants, politicians and their staff, pregnant women, students in the middle of exams, and convicted criminals. This already reduces the pool. Also missing are the two million or so Australians who are not on the electoral roll, from which juries are drawn. Then there are those who just don't turn up. According to the NSW Sheriff's Office, of the 90,000-odd people summoned for jury duty in NSW every year, more than 10,000 don't show, risking fines of up to $2,200 which are enforced by debt collectors. About 2,000 of those no-shows end up having to pay.

A juror sitting recently in NSW told me about 'the unfortunate statistics of jury duty':

> *For my panel, 80 potential jurors were selected from the roll. Twenty-nine were immediately disqualified . . . Out of those remaining, about a dozen or so did not appear on the day nominated. About half the people that did appear wrote out reasons for not wanting to stay.*

That left something like one in four potential jurors being available to serve – and this was before the lawyers got to work on them.

One of my work colleagues, David, also went on jury duty around the same time. For his empanelling, 14 of 40 jurors didn't turn up. I have a self-employed friend who preferred to pay the fine than waste a day. Some employers will cover the fine rather than lose a worker for a month or more.

It's not as easy for country jurors. One juror in Narrabri, where the Jury Assembly Room was nothing more than the shade of a tree outside the courthouse, told me it was 'much tougher to get excused in the bush.'

> *Unwilling and unavailable jurors had to go to the front of the court and give their excuses in a loud voice, prompted all the while by extra questions from the judge. Sydney jurors only had to ring a court officer with a halfway-reasonable excuse.*

There's always an injury to feign. In the comic movie *Jury Duty*, Pauly Shore arrives on the courthouse steps to find a man tying a bandage around his head. 'Couldn't get out of it,' the man says. 'At least not yet. Give me a hand.' The twist in that movie is that, perversely, Shore is desperate to get on a jury. He's lost his job and his mother has moved to Las Vegas, so Shore has nowhere to live unless he can get himself onto a long trial and be sequestered in a hotel, meals supplied. It says something about the regard in which jury duty is held that only the comically desperate would make serious efforts to perform it.

About an hour after I arrived in the Jury Assembly Room, two panels had been called out and we'd done our courtroom walk-through. People stared into space, listened to Walkmans, read, made calls on their mobile phones, or converged on a snack trolley whenever it appeared.

By the second hour I'd lost Andrew, and was happily reading my book when our attention was called to a short video, titled *Our Juries – Our Justice*.

I watched curiously. My wife, who trained as a film director, makes a living from writing and directing videos like this. I was interested to see its effect on the jurors. I knew, from her work, that the big trend in educational videos is to dramatise the subject, create characters rather than lay out dry information. In *Our Juries – Our Justice*, the two main characters are a middle-aged businessman, annoyed at being called up, and a wholesomely dutiful housewife. The businessman is empanelled, and puts himself forward as jury foreman. Humiliatingly, he's outvoted in favour of the housewife. But, as the trial goes on, the businessman begins to appreciate the experience, and by the end is glad he's done jury duty. As he leaves the court, reformed, we're told 'No Juries – No Justice'.

My fellow prospective jurors seemed attentive enough, though there was little else to do but watch. When the jury video finished they watched, with equal or perhaps closer attention, a morning TV segment about an elephant that could paint with its trunk.

What struck me was that *Our Juries – Our Justice* was honest enough to concede the irksomeness of jury service. Usually official videos put a gloss of 'positivity' over reality. But getting out of jury duty is such a national pastime, censoring it would be an act of Soviet absurdity.

One juror told me:

> *. . . the attitude of many friends and colleagues regarding my inability or lack of desire to 'get out of' jury duty really surprised me. It's as if one has lost one's marbles if one doesn't at least try to come up with some laughable excuse to put to the sheriff!*

American figures show that we're not alone – up to 31 per cent of jurors there get off without turning up to court. In colonial Virginia, no-show jurors were fined in pounds of tobacco.

As jury historian Jeffrey Abramson writes:

> *Then, as now, persons occupied elsewhere were not keen to interrupt their daily routines and travel to court. In short, we should not romanticise the virtues of the past or exaggerate the vices of modern life. The American jury survived the days when colonists were too busy to serve, and it will survive today's oft-expressed indifference.*

As with most of our attitudes towards civic duties, our indifference to jury duty evaporates once we have a personal stake. We try our best to get out of jury service, but by God, if we're accused of a crime, we demand the right to a fair jury trial. (And we demand good hospitals when we're sick and better public transport when we need it, but run like scalded dogs from paying for them.) What's uniquely pressing about the jury system is that the relationship between what we put in and what we get out is so direct: if we don't serve on them, we simply won't get them.

After two hours in the Jury Assembly Room, I was called into court with two dozen others. We sat in the public gallery, separated by glass from the judge and barristers. The glass alone set an intimidating scene, as if the public had to be protected from the goings-on in there. Any jurors who'd been joking or swaggering suddenly put on a solemn mask, standing with their hands clasped and lips pursed as if we were now on trial. The judge's associate drew the numbered juror cards from a box (not a spinning barrel, as in some places, nor, as was the case in 17th-century South Carolina, by a blindfolded child).

My number was about the seventh called, and Theo was right after all – it was intimidating. In shock, I entered the court and promptly lost the feeling in my legs. Had I planned some stunt like walking around the wrong side of the courtroom, I'm not sure I could have pulled it off. My automatic pilot said: Obey. My feet took me the right way around the right table and into the right chair. My hands shook, and I felt as if the whole world could see through to my core. The respectable citizen inside me – which lies dormant most of the time, I've got to say – reared its bland, law-abiding head and took hypothetical umbrage against anyone who might challenge me. The air in the courtroom turned me into a teacher's pet; I felt an entirely unexpected rush of responsibility. One of my fellow jurors would say later: 'I wanted to be called up – right up to the moment when I was called up.' Well, I had the opposite reaction. I didn't want to be called up – until I was.

The box was filled with 12 jurors. What followed happened over a period of two or three minutes, and I was too frazzled to take much in.

This was the challenge period. The jury box was to the judge's left, opposite the accused. The Crown lawyers were at the bar table nearer us, and the defence near the accused. One by one, we were asked to stand and take a Bible presented by a sheriff's officer. As we stood, the barristers from either side could say 'Challenge', and immediately the juror would be excused and replaced by another. Each side was limited to three challenges, though they could take an unlimited number of challenges agreed jointly. I can't recall who challenged whom, but we lost three or four jurors at this point. All were men. One was Asian, another Middle Eastern, and one was obese. It seemed, for reasons unclear, a kind of ethnic streamlining had taken place, where the only jurors left were, like me, nondescript and Caucasian. For their challenges, the lawyers didn't have to offer any reason. If they didn't like the look of you, you were gone.

Tricks of the Trade

Every trial lawyer uses hunch, bias and instinct to try to engineer a favourable jury. But really, they're just hoping for the best. They judge us by our appearances, and most of the time, they acknowledge, they get us wrong. We jurors are the greatest and most powerful mystery to the lawyers; we people their nightmares; we will determine their success or failure. We have replaced gods and oracles as the dispensers of justice, and lawyers are trying to appease, interpret and second-guess us for their clients.

The only time lawyers can indulge fantasies of trying to create a jury is in the challenge phase. But their powers, and the structure of the challenge, vary.

There is a famous line about the difference between Anglo-Australian and American trials: with us, the trial starts when jury selection is over; with the Americans, when the jury is selected the trial is already over. It's more than just a snappy saying: one study has found that in NSW the average time spent selecting a jury is 30 minutes, whereas in California it is up to six weeks.

Trial lawyers know how much is at stake. A Victorian judge and former barrister, Liz Gaynor, has portrayed how counsel feel about the jury at the end of a trial, when it has retired to deliberate over its verdict:

> *What are those idiots (the jury) doing? Oh God, oh God, what have I done? . . . My poor, poor client. A life ruined. That stupid solicitor. I told her I wanted no jurors over fifty and what do I get? A swarming crowd of desiccated old men who look as if only the re-introduction of whipping in the stocks would bring a smile to their withered lips. No, it's my fault . . .*

American jury selection has spun off a mini-industry of jury consultants, whose job it is to build profiles of jurors and advise on challenges. In 1982 there were 25 jury consultants in the US; that number was 250 by 1994, grossing an estimated US$25 million a year. One trial attorney said it had 'gotten to the point where if the case is large enough, it's almost malpractice not to use them.'

As far back as the 1970s, jury consultants were analysing jurors' handwriting and body language. By the 1980s, they were polling the jury district for opinions on high-profile trials, and carrying out surveillance on jurors' lifestyles (in John Grisham's book *The Runaway Jury*, where the case is a tobacco tort suit, the consultants spy on a prospective juror sneaking a ciggie behind a tree). For the 1972 trial of the Harrisburg Seven, a group accused of attacking an army draft office, defence jury consultants ranked 46 prospective jurors on a scale of 1 (best) to 5 (worst), and challenged from the bottom up.

American lawyers have been candid on the subject. Clarence Darrow, who appeared in the Scopes 'Monkey' trial where the theory of evolution itself was at issue, wrote a 1936 article which concluded:

> *Favourable to defendants were Irish, Jews, Unitarians, Universalists, Congregationalists, and agnostics. The ideal prosecution juror had high regard for the law and a religious attitude toward sin and punishment, qualities found among Scandinavians in particular but also among Lutherans, Baptists, and Presbyterians.*

A 1935 trial manual advised: 'If a party's case was primarily emotional, the advice was to go with Irish, Jews, Italians, French, Spanish and Slavs. If the strategy was to combat emotional appeals, then the nod went to Nordic, English . . . and German jurors.'

Jeffrey Abramson continues: 'In medical malpractice cases, however, the plaintiff was warned away from Jewish jurors because "most Jews want their sons to become doctors . . . and they want their daughters to marry doctors."'

In 1963, lawyer Melvin Belli wrote that farmers favoured the State but waiters and bartenders were more forgiving. In civil trials, good plaintiff's jurors according to a 1989 article were 'cabdrivers, union members, secretaries, social workers, salespersons, [and] retired government employees'. Good defence jurors included 'physicians, engineers, architects, executives, supervisory administrative personnel, unemployed people, and . . . insurance adjusters'.

F. Lee Bailey, one of O.J. Simpson's defence team, wrote that 'heavy, round-faced, jovial looking persons' made the best defence jurors, while 'the undesirable juror is quite often the slightly underweight and delicate type'; and a Los Angeles judge concluded that 'women are often prejudiced against other women they envy, for example, those who are more attractive.'

In NSW trials since 1997, jurors are anonymous, so all the lawyers have to go on is a gut feeling from our dress, body language and appearance. Hoping to be challenged, my colleague David wore a suit. He was unchallenged, but a guy in boardshorts was sent home. Another juror recalls:

> *I took the opportunity of a day off work to do some shopping in town before fronting up at the court, and I was so sure I wouldn't be chosen as a jury member when I learned the case was a rape case that I left my shopping bags by the seat I originally occupied [at the back of] the court, and had to ask for them to be retrieved when I found myself a member of the jury. To this day I feel I was only sworn in because the defendant's lawyer had run out of objections. He was unlucky that I was the next in line – I was a feminist from way back, raring to go.*

Compared with American lawyers, Australian barristers have few opportunities to challenge. In 30 years at the NSW Bar, Malcolm Ramage has seen the number of challenges whittled down, and identification of jurors disappear. He laments the change:

> *The challenge has ceased to be a part of the barrister's armoury. You used to have up to 20 challenges for a murder trial. But now, they don't even give you the names or occupations of jurors. So when I appeared for a Turkish accused, I didn't know if the jurors were Greek, or Armenian. I've appeared for a Palestinian client but didn't know if there were any Jewish persons on the jury. So it's pot luck now. It's to protect jurors' anonymity, but it leaves us with the merest indicia of juror behaviour.*

But even within their three challenges, lawyers will still try their best. Adam Morison, a defence specialist, prefers young women: 'My instincts say it's best to go for younger, open-minded people. I also prefer more females than males, because they're more likely to debate issues amongst themselves rather than accept the Crown case at first blush.'

Youth, in general, is positive for the defence, Morison thinks:

> *Because police corruption has been exposed a lot in recent years, younger people are more likely to take police evidence with a grain of salt. It's harder to educate older people if you're wanting to convince them that the police are lying.*

Yet Morison's tutor, Phillip Boulten, goes by the opposite intuition:

> *Young girls, I think, are more likely to be unquestioning of authority. I prefer people who have a bit of life experience . . . It's visceral, not scientific. The number of challenges you're allowed is so small now, you can't do much to affect the gender or age balance of the jury, but having said that you do develop established ideas about particular types of people that influence how you challenge . . . If it's at a court in Campbelltown, say, you may want young, rough-and-tumble types who have an open mind about the accused. If it's in Sydney, you try to weigh your jury with people who look like* Sydney Morning Herald *readers rather than* Daily Telegraph *readers. You do go for the wildcards. I used to think a lot more about who to challenge on juries, but now I think it's random. In the end, whatever they look like, you can't tell what they're thinking.*

There are the obvious moves – defence lawyers challenge RSL and Rotary types, while prosecutors challenge unkempt hippy types. Often it depends on the nature of the trial, as one lawyer notes:

> *You go for a jury that you feel come from the same background as the accused, so you can say to them in your opening, 'Look, these two guys had a fight, and the one who lost is the accused.' You can say that sort of thing to a jury, but you wouldn't try it to a judge.*

Sometimes a potential juror can dress and act in such a way as to disguise his or her prejudices. This was the case in the Bjelke-Petersen trial, where Luke Shaw turned up for empanelling in scruffy clothes, unshaven and pony-tailed. He looked like anything but a National Party supporter, and his trick worked: the prosecutors let him onto the jury.

An experienced Sydney barrister says this kind of disguise is common, and tends to work against the defence:

> *Conviction-oriented, law-and-order types can effectively disguise themselves in normality; while the hip, the counter-culture, the rebellious don't dress up and so they get knocked off.*

One agreed area is that both sides challenge jurors who look as if they don't want to be there. 'If someone looks like they don't want to be there, they're huffing and puffing and looking at their watch, you get rid of them,' says Morison. 'Businesspeople also you don't want, because they give an impression of having already made up their mind and wanting to get out quickly.'

And then there's the 'wildcard juror'. A senior Crown prosecutor says, somewhat pessimistically, that '12 people selected from anywhere will include at least one oddball.' What to do with the unusual-looking juror? Barrister Murugan Thangaraj observes that the unknowability of the jury presents a quandary from the challenge stage onwards:

> *I had a murder trial, and among the jurors there was a woman who looked distressed – not like a normal person, but as if she had a psychiatric illness. We had a tough case to defend, and I wanted jurors to be as clear as possible about the evidence and who would not make their minds up early. So we challenged her. As it happened, we lost, and I wondered afterwards if I'd made a mistake. The case was so overwhelming against us, it might have been better to have a disruptive influence in the jury, a wildcard. When you have a strong case against you, you like to see divisions in the jury.*

But who is the wildcard? The person, says Morison, 'who laughs and giggles at the wrong times and acts contrary to what you'd expect'. But 'overall it's a total lottery, and just a warm-up for the trial. If a certain juror gets on, I think "Oh no" – but that person can end up being the one who pays you the most attention.'

Another Sydney barrister, Tom Molomby, takes a different tack: 'I don't go for the wildcard juror. I believe in reason, and hope reason will win.'

Mostly, though, lawyers know that the peremptory challenge is a stab in the dark. 'I've given up on trying to work out who to challenge,' says Crown prosecutor David Arnott.

> *I don't lean towards people I might consider as wildcard jurors. If the person is not guilty, I don't want to resort to anything to put him in jail. If he's not guilty, I'm more than happy to see him acquitted.*

That winter day, I and 11 other 'ineddicated, vulgar, grovelling wretches' were handed the scales of justice. Five minutes earlier

I'd been reading, idly and complacently, in the Jury Assembly Room. Now I was part of a jury, indistinguishable from the others.

Or was I? When the Bible came around, I decided to take an atheist's affirmation instead of the Christian oath. I was the only one to do so. This left me feeling alone and sweatily conspicuous. All 11 of my new colleagues stood and said 'So help me God' together, and then I had to stand on my very own and say something like 'This I do solemnly swear.' I wondered if either side would have challenged me had they known me as an affirmer rather than an oather. Were the lawyers watching me now? Did a little mark go down against my number? Did my non-religious stance make me a potential wildcard, or voice of reason?

Lawyers do notice. Affirmations seldom happen, and Phillip Boulten says, 'If someone takes an affirmation, I don't forget it. That person sticks in your mind.'

Morison uses the oath/affirmation debate in a different way:

> *Sometimes I say to jurors, 'You took an oath, but I bet not all of you went to church on Sunday or believe in God or the second coming.' I point this out to show that if a witness is nervous, or my client stumbled in his interview, sometimes it's because he's said something to go along with what's expected, and hasn't intentionally lied. The jury can relate to that.*

Advocacy teacher Sonya Hamlin puts the 'lone affirmer' into the wider context of lawyers guessing the jury 'opinion leader':

> *The jury will be a group. They will function as any group of people does. There are leaders, followers, opposers and bystanders . . . Is the obvious leader type on your side?*

Are there too many followers or bystanders waiting to be led? Keep a lookout for the nonconformist. Who is the opposer? How strong will that opposer be? Is the group strong enough to overturn him or her?

Was I going to stick in their mind? Perhaps I would follow the tradition of the most famous non-oath-swearer in legal history, a juror named Edward Bushell. Called up in the 1670 trial of Quakers William Penn and William Mead, Bushell refused to kiss the Anglican Book of Prayer at the jury swearing-in. Penn and Mead were accused of breaking the law by preaching Quakerism in the street. Bushell led a group of four jurors wanting to acquit Penn and Mead, not because they hadn't broken the law, but because the law was a bad one. The jury came back with a verdict of 'guilty of speaking on Gracechurch Street', which was not, actually, the charge. It meant nothing.

The judges sent them away to reconsider, abused them, threatened to starve them and to slit Bushell's nose. That was enough to sway the entire jury to Bushell's argument. They voted not guilty, and the judges threw them in jail.

Bushell won, eventually. The King's Bench overturned the conviction of him and the other jurors, upholding the jury's power to 'nullify' laws that they believed wrong. This was affirmed in 1697 by Lord Chief Justice Holt, who said: 'The King could dismiss judges and discipline lawyers, but jurors were impregnable.'

Was I to be an Edward Bushell, or just another atheist? Jurors are icebergs, and the players in the case only see our very tip. As Molomby says:

Many people whose true allegiance is for an affirmation will often go for the oath to stay with the crowd. Affirmation people may be more likely to stand on their own, so you do register that. But that doesn't say which direction they will be strong-minded in. They could be strong-minded fascists.

That's right. I might have been a strong-minded fascist. I guess we were all about to find out.

CHAPTER THREE

CHALLENGING THE CHALLENGE

There was a lot happening in the courtroom of which I wasn't aware. The challenge period works on two principles. The court, on the one hand, wants an impartial jury, randomly selected from the local community, who have no problems accepting the job they're called for. The lawyers, on the other, want a jury that will help them win.

To secure impartiality, a list of witnesses had been read out and we were asked to excuse ourselves if we recognised any. (Faking this, of course, would be another way to get out. All you'd need to say is: 'Joe Bloggs! I have no problem with him, except that I lent him money five years ago and he still hasn't called me.') Also, we were told to avoid any media publicity surrounding the case. (A frisson in the jury: We could be famous!)

The general idea is that a jury comes into a trial as a blank slate. This was not, however, the way juries started out. Our jury system originated about 900 years ago in the trial by 'compurgation', when neighbours to the alleged crime were called up to swear testimony supporting the accused or the accuser. (Indeed, the word 'juror' stemmed from the Middle English 'juree', meaning 'oath' or 'inquiry', and prior to that 'jure' in French and 'jurare' in Latin, meaning 'to swear'.) The whole idea was that the neighbour knew the facts of the case. Jurors were more like witnesses. If the neighbour's testimony contradicted that of the person he was called to support, it was said to 'burst the oath'. Alternative modes of trial included battle and ordeal, where the accused would be thrown into a lake, or have his hand shoved in a fire. These trials were administered by priests. If the accused floated on the lake, the holy water was said to have rejected him, and he was guilty. If he sank, he was 'accepted', and innocent. (If he was lucky, he'd be fished out alive.) If he endured ordeal by fire, the verdict rested on how long his burns took to heal. If they got infected, this was a divine sign of his guilt.

After 1066, the Normans imported the 'inquest', where men would be summoned from the community to provide information under oath, or 'veri dictim' – a declaration of truth. In 1086, the Domesday Book was compiled from inquest registers. Royal Commissioners toured, gathered up inquest juries, and centralised England under one legal system. Henry II (1154–89) enforced inquests and made dispute settlement public rather than private. He also phased out compurgation and ordeal.

The Constitutions of Clarendon in 1164 ruled that land tax, eviction and eventually felony disputes could be settled by 12 sworn men, but only at the pre-trial stage. 'Grand' juries still didn't try actual cases, only whether the evidence justified a trial by battle. By 1215, Magna Carta proclaimed that:

> ... [n]o freeman shall be taken, or imprisoned, or disseized, or outlawed, or exiled, or in any way harmed – nor will we go upon or send upon him – save by the lawful judgment of his peers or by the law of the land.

Magna Carta often gets credit for the jury system, but the decisive reform was a separate one in 1215, when the Fourth Lateran Council barred the clergy from trials. The European solution was to decide disputes with an inquisitorial panel, while England stuck with the inquest. Ordeal and compurgation were banned. Royal Commissioners began calling up a second (petit)

Challenging the Challenge

jury to ask if it concurred with the grand jury's suspicions. If so, the suspect was convicted.

Often the same jurors sat on grand and petit juries. In 1352 a law allowed the accused to make 35 challenges to the petit jury. It was around this time that the number 12 was settled on. Nobody really knows why, though Lord Devlin once speculated that it owed to 'an early English abhorrence of the decimal system'. The US Supreme Court in 1970 called it 'a fluke of history', though 12 does have harmonious connotations in English and Christian cultures: the Knights of the Round Table, the apostles, the sons of Noah, the officers in the Book of Kings, and pennies to the shilling all amounted to 12. While the earliest recorded jury, the Egyptian 'kenbet', had eight members, in Greek myth Orestes was tried for killing his mother Clytemnestra by a jury of 12 Athenians.

(Yet, as Nicholas Cowdery says, 'there's no magic in the number 12, and there's some economic consideration for reducing the size of juries.' He's backed up by a recent University of Glasgow study that found that decision-making groups of eight or more were dominated by small cliques, whereas the most democratic results were achieved in groups of five, six or seven. So what's the optimal size? The jury's still out.)

Early juries were meant to be familiar with the details of the alleged felony. In the mid-1400s, the English Chief Justice John Fortescue defined:

> ... *a jury of twelve men, persons of good character, neighbours where the fact was committed, apprised of the circumstances in question, and well acquainted with the lives and conversations of the witnesses, especially as they be near neighbours, and cannot but know whether they be worthy of credit or not.*

Jurors were expected to be so knowledgeable that they could visit a witness at home, go to the scene of the crime, and conduct their own investigations. Their knowledge of the people involved was proof of their wisdom.

By the time the jury system was imported to the Australian colonies, this was changing. Of course the size and penal origins of NSW meant that at first military tribunals and then freemen-juries would know the accused and the details of the accusation, but, as the colony grew, so did the belief that jurors should have a more open mind – that is, be *unaware* of the very details that had formerly given them their expertise. The idea of local justice was turned on its head. Now, the appropriate juror was to be ignorant of the facts and even of the law, a notion Mark Twain lampooned in reporting jury selection in America in 1903:

> *A minister, intelligent, esteemed, and greatly respected; a merchant of high character and known probity; a mining superintendent of intelligence and unblemished reputation; a quartz-mill owner of excellent standing, were all questioned in the same way, and all set aside. Each said the public talk and the newspaper reports had not so biased his mind but that the sworn testimony would . . . enable him to render a verdict without prejudice and in accordance with the facts. But of course such men could not be trusted with the case. Ignoramuses alone could mete out unsullied justice.*

Since the late 1800s, Herbert Spencer's description of the jury as 'a group of people of average ignorance' has held. Jurors who are overly familiar with an accused or the case are asked to excuse themselves. The major transgression in the Joh Bjelke-Petersen trial was that Luke Shaw, the eventual foreman who engineered the hung jury and got the Queensland Premier off the hook, was an active National Party member and Joh supporter. He knew Joh too well – a quality that, 800 years earlier, would have made Shaw an ideal juror.

In the trial of Oliver North in America in 1986, the judge

allowed a juror who admitted he 'saw North on television but it was just like watching the Three Stooges or something'. In the obscenity trial of photographer Robert Mapplethorpe four years later, the trial judge dismissed the only potential juror who had seen the Mapplethorpe exhibit, the only one who said she attended museums regularly, while among those who survived challenges was a panel member who 'never went to museums'.

So the know-all juror has changed into the know-nothing juror. (Though some elements of local justice have survived. In Seymour circuit court in Victoria in the 1960s, a jury acquitted a man who was fighting overwhelming circumstantial evidence that he had stolen sheep. When asked why, the foreman said: 'We couldn't very well pot him, because the man who actually stole the sheep was on the jury.')

We were to discover, some weeks into the trial, the probable reason why three non-white and obese jurors had been challenged. In his taped telephone calls to Les McAtee from jail, Steve Rusher made a few jokingly disparaging references to non-white inmates, and also called a friend of his by the nickname 'Chub-a-lub'. Would these have offended the prospective jurors? Possibly. Would their impartiality, as jurors, have been compromised? That's a long bow. An Asian juror might dislike an accused if he thinks he's racist (though there were other instances of Rusher offering non-white prisoners a great deal of help) – but it's contemptuous and, I think, unfair to assume that that would prompt the juror to interpret all of the evidence in a hostile way.

As a result of the challenges, our jury was less representative of the community than it had been after the random draw. Judging by our appearances, we were whiter, blander, more 'mainstream'. This is a particular shame given the history in Australian juries of different groups' struggle for inclusion. Only since 1977 have women been able to serve on juries without making a special application. Only since 1947 have people without property been on jury lists. From the very beginnings of the jury system in NSW, there has been a contest for more inclusion. From 1788 to the mid-1820s, the only 'juries' here were six-man military tribunals sitting alongside the Judge-Advocate. As more and more convicts were freed and chose to remain in the colony, these Emancipists began to form a majority of the free population. Both the military and the free settlers, the Exclusives, held obvious prejudices against Emancipists and resisted the advent of jury trial: what military man would brook a land-owning ex-convict to sit in legal judgment? Exclusives were already opposing any recognition of ex-convicts as full citizens of the colony, stopping them from running for political office or practising as lawyers.

Emancipists petitioned the Colonial Office in 1819. The first jury trials were held between 1824 and 1828, but were only for minor Quarter Sessions trials and excluded Emancipists. Not until 1829 were Emancipists permitted to sit on juries. This right was expanded to Supreme Court trials in 1833, albeit allowing the accused to opt for a judge-only trial if he was an ex-officer or an Exclusive who didn't want to be tried by former convicts. This option lasted until 1839.

Not coincidentally, responsible and representative government soon followed. The advent of jury trial was all of a piece with these developments, forcing open the door of democracy against British and military authority, as it had in America 80 years earlier, when grand juries boycotted oppressive British laws and became forums for democratic sentiment that led ultimately to the American revolution.

Still, Australian juries have struggled to be truly representative. In 1981, Judge Martin of the District Court discharged a Bourke jury in the trial of a black man because the Crown had challenged all Aboriginal jurors – a common occurrence. Indigenous jurors are almost unknown in NSW, due to challenges and disqualifications. Aborigines are represented by 0.5 per cent of jurors, but 7 per cent of the prison population. They are arrested six times more frequently than whites and imprisoned

15 times more often, mostly on traffic, public order and minor property offences. Given the disproportionate number of Aboriginal defendants, their scarcity on juries seems, to put it diplomatically, less than fair.

Similarly, in 1990 the Queensland Supreme Court nullified a trial in which the male accused had challenged all women jurors because, he said, to be tried by women would be 'an abomination of God'.

These kinds of prejudices spread far beyond gender and race. A 1996 review of American trials showed lawyers challenging:

> *... social workers (likely to favour treatment over incarceration), health care professionals (too liberal and lenient), people in the arts (affinity to drugs), accountants and engineers (too meticulous), or people with Spanish surnames (likely to speak Spanish and not to feel bound by the official translations of the testimony of Spanish-speaking witnesses).*

As an American chief judge has said, the peremptory challenge 'allows the covert expression of what we dare not say but know is true more often than not'.

In other words, the challenge is a licence for racism, sexism, ageism, fattism and every other prejudice a lawyer and an accused can think of. But the second part of the dictum – 'what we dare not say but know is true more often than not' – is clearly contradicted by lawyers' own admissions about the unknowability of the jury. You can challenge women jurors on sexual assault cases, but women are just as likely to be pro-accused as pro-victim. The challenge gives licence to prejudice, not truth.

The main purpose of the peremptory challenge is for PR, or, as Nicholas Cowdery says, 'to provide the accused with a safety valve so he thinks he has some input into gaining a fair trial'. But it's purely cosmetic, and, at its extreme, can produce absurd 'proportional representation' juries, as has happened in America.

The convicted black killers of Yankel Rosenbaum, an Australian orthodox Jew murdered in New York in the early 1990s, were granted a re-trial because the trial judge unlawfully manufactured a 'proportionally representative' jury of blacks, Jews, whites and others.

The assumption in the peremptory challenge is that people can't vote across group lines; that if you're black you will vote for a black accused, or if you're a woman, you'll vote as a woman rather than as a juror. Experience suggests the contrary: jurors will render their verdicts as individuals, influenced by their own reading of the evidence and the specific dynamics of their particular jury. They don't always favour their own kind, whatever 'their own kind' might be assumed to be.

Jury historian Jeffrey Abramson argues that juries are about deliberation, not representation: 'By history and design, the jury is centrally about getting persons to bracket or transcend starting loyalties.' Because a unanimous vote is needed for a verdict, a majority can't just vote down a minority – jurors must produce arguments that persuade across group lines and 'speak to a justice common to persons drawn from different walks of life'.

'Peremptory' is, after all, a synonym for 'rude'. The peremptory challenge is an insult to jurors, an insult to democracy, and only panders to an accused person's superficial notion of a 'fair trial' while, his lawyer is likely to concede, possibly doing him more harm than good. Who knows – that fat man, or those dark-skinned men, might have been Steve Rusher's firmest advocates. 'Scientific' rationales for the challenge are also a throwback to an uglier time, when personality could be read from the bumps on one's head or the shape of one's brow. I remember studying at university the work of the turn-of-the-century Italian 'criminologist' Cesare Lombroso, who devised a complex system correlating the shape of a forehead and nose and chin and other facial features to criminal tendencies. A German psychologist,

H.S. Schmidt, said in 1934 that one could judge intelligence from a person's face with 70 per cent accuracy. Those sorts of ideas are best left in 1934 Germany, not perpetuated in our courts.

Abolishing the challenge has been mooted by several researchers, most notably New Zealand professor Warren Young, who has conducted the most comprehensive Antipodean juror survey. Jurors, he found, 'comment that the [challenge] process is a demeaning one which they resent'. Abolishing the challenge would preserve the randomness of jury selection. Lawyers should still be able to challenge for cause – for example, if a juror is physically incapacitated or knows a witness or has served in another jury in the same matter – which might slow the process down a little, Young says, but still protect jurors from the insult of stereotyping.

Impartial observers argue that the peremptory challenge as it currently exists is a waste of time:

> *It was difficult to see any logic behind many challenges made during the selection of juries. The overall impression was that the peremptory challenge was used by both Crown and defence counsel in a casual or even arbitrary fashion. Methods of challenge often seemed partisan, even haphazard . . . It is very difficult to see the challenge as resulting from any suspicion of 'bias' more substantial than the most random, unsystematic hunch . . . The gender, ethnicity and age of the jury seemed very often to be only minimally altered after the peremptory challenge process had run its course. As for the jurors themselves, they seemed either intimidated or puzzled by the experience.*

The UK Royal Commission into juries, moreover, found no link between the use of challenge and a lower likelihood of conviction.

Jurors, when asked, oppose the challenge. In the 1994 NSW study, a challenged juror said: 'I felt cheated that I wasn't even given the opportunity to be considered.'

Others said: 'The fact that both the prosecution and defence can challenge any member just on their looks makes the whole thing a joke'; and, 'Just pick names out of a hat, no challenging.'

Even defence lawyers have lost faith in the peremptory challenge as it exists. Ian Barker QC says, 'The current formula is little better than no challenges . . . In my view permitting but three challenges is absurd.'

If the challenge is abolished, to counterbalance any ill-effects of that move, many commentators argue that the jury pool should be widened and it should be harder for jurors to get off. At the moment, 42 per cent of potential jurors get off through automatic exemptions or disqualifications. This throws an unfair weight onto the remaining 58 per cent. It's inconvenient to do jury duty this month? All right, the court can allow jurors to nominate their availability period in advance. Barker thinks the 'criteria should be re-examined and expanded. I do not know why (for example) the spouse or partner of a member of parliament is not suitable for jury service.' Driver's licence and other databases should be consulted so that the two million Australians not enrolled to vote can't shirk jury duty as well. Financial hardship, rather than status, should be the principal consideration – why should a self-employed person have to do jury duty while schoolteachers, ministers of religion and senior bureaucrats are automatically excluded? And, to enable Aborigines to have a better chance of sitting on juries, the prohibition on people with criminal records should be raised to exclude only those with serious convictions. Why should a suspended sentence for shoplifting incurred in one's youth rule one out of jury duty? And why should politicians be excused automatically? In NSW, 93 per cent of people support the jury system and 75 per cent support compulsory jury duty – I reckon nearly 100 per cent would support the view that politicians should have to do jury service, to keep in touch with their constituents, at least once every five years.

Just as the lawyers in the Rusher trial were trying to decipher our blank faces, they were conscious of making a favourable impression upon us. Phillip Boulten says, 'You can't do anything without thinking, What's the jury going to make of this expression, posture, tone, the way I'm speaking? It's all calculated for its effect on the jury.' (How much should he worry about this? According to one survey, not much. The 1994 NSW jury study found that 4 per cent of jurors said the lawyers' attitude affected their verdict. By comparison, the accused's demeanour influenced 13 per cent, the witnesses' demeanour affected 9 per cent, the judge's manner affected 2 per cent, and 3 per cent said they were influenced by the probable sentence hanging over the accused.)

Among defence lawyers' first decisions is how chummy they should seem with the accused during challenges. Some say it's best to sit close to their client, even with their arm around the accused, to show the jury that the lawyer believes in his case. (This used to be unnecessary, as the law did not permit the barrister to take part in the peremptory challenge process. The accused or defendant was meant to make his own challenges. Lawyers got around this by devising a code – tapping their pencil on the Bar table, writing, adjusting their wig – to tell the client whether or not to challenge – and eventually the rules were adjusted to allow them to confer.) On my own account, I could have told them not to bother. I remember little of what was going on during the challenges, and least of all whether the defence barrister was sitting near Steve Rusher or not. Ultimately, as Tom Molomby says, it's the client's challenge, not the lawyer's:

> *I tell clients I don't have any magic system for selecting or challenging jurors. 'You want people who can make a contribution, so you should challenge anyone who looks*

> *not up to it, or out of it. Apart from that, if you just get a feeling that someone has the evil eye for you, it's probably best to get rid of them. Most clients will say that any honest 12 people will do, but then they'll lean forward and whisper, 'Get rid of the third from the left in the back row.'*

Of course, the argument for abolishing the challenge rests on the assumption that we do want jury trials. But do we? The fairness and usefulness of jury justice was to wrench me this way and that for the whole month of the trial. As I sat in the Jury Assembly Room before we were called into court, I'm not sure that I did support the jury system in principle.

Even a week ago, as I write, an English rape trial was aborted after several jurors, rather than participate in deliberations, watched the World Darts Championship on TV.

On the other hand, jury research tells a different tale. In the most recent survey in NSW of 40 trials, the judge and at least one counsel agreed with 95 per cent of juries.

In the 1950s, the biggest-ever survey of jury verdicts polled more than 500 judges to return data on 3,576 criminal trials. They agreed with the jury 78 per cent of the time. Some have interpreted this to mean juries 'get it wrong' in nearly a quarter of cases. But should judges be the yardstick of correctness? Not at all, a serving District Court judge told me: 'Very rarely do juries return a verdict that I wouldn't have given – and even then, who's to say I was right and they were wrong?'

In a case in Geelong in the 1950s, a 21-year-old man fell off scaffolding and was rendered sexually impotent by his injuries. A jury awarded him £75,000. The defendant appealed the amount to a court of three judges, aged 82, 77 and 68. One whispered to another: 'Don't you think that a jury of young men in Geelong would be better able to assess in monetary terms what impotency would mean to a boy of 21 than you or I?'

Who has a better grip on justice – judge or jury? English juror Trevor Grove weighs up Professor Glanville Williams's statement that 'There is no guarantee that members of a particular jury may not be quite unusually ignorant, credulous, slow-witted, narrow-minded, biased or temperamental.' Grove counters: 'But it would surely be easier to find a judge who exemplified at least the last three of those qualities than a dozen people on one jury who exemplified them all.'

As for the notion of 'rogue juries' administering their own brand of justice, that cuts both ways. As Abramson says, jury trial is about the best and the worst of democracy:

> *Jurors in Athens sentenced Socrates to death for religious crimes against the State, but in England jurors went to prison themselves rather than convict the Quaker William Penn. Juries convicted women as witches in Salem, but they resisted witch hunts for communists in Washington. Juries in the American South freed vigilantes who lynched African-Americans, but in the North they sheltered fugitive slaves and the abolitionists who helped them escape.*

The value of the jury system is not going to be decided on one or two persuasive cases. It's a matter of how deeply our society cleaves to the idea of common, as opposed to professional, wisdom. Jurors have always been heroes one day and villains the next. Which was I to be?

Chapter Four

The Foreman was a Storeman

Courts operate like the military: Hurry and wait. Wait and hurry. After staring into space for two hours in the Jury Assembly Room, within a few minutes our group was empanelled, sworn in, welcomed by the judge, who added some introductory remarks about our impartiality and not discussing the trial with anyone outside the court, and straight into the Crown's opening address.

We were to know the Crown counsel as 'Mr Crown', which was how the judge would address him through the trial. The defence barrister by contrast was to have a name – Mr Nisbett. This is standard for criminal trials, although in one that Michael Chesterman surveyed, the jury named the lawyers 'Mr Crown' and 'Mr Clown'. One of our jurors liked to give Mr Crown some personality, so she called him 'Thomas Crowne'.

Our Mr Crown was in his early forties with bouffant brown hair and irritable eyes, as if he suffered from allergies. His halting manner gave the impression of someone under whose skin others were often getting. Or maybe I was projecting my prejudices about prosecutors as hapless, school-prefect types. I've always been a kneejerk supporter of the underdog – any underdog – and prickle against authority. I'm told I inherited this from my father, who is a conservative, law-abiding, status-quo-loving citizen until someone tries to tell him what to do, when he turns into a Hell's Angel. Ordinarily he will not create a ripple, but if a policeman tells him not to burn down a house he'll go out and dynamite it. It's pathological, and genetic. Aside from this, most of the lawyers I knew were defence types, not prosecutors. This was one of the reasons I'd put on my letter asking to be excused, but I suppose the sheriff had concluded that a slight anti-Crown bias was no impediment in a system where, after all, the accused is presumed innocent and the Crown must prove its case.

Prim and wigless, Mr Crown summed up the story he was going to tell us during the trial. Steve Rusher and his wife, Fiona, had endured a messy split in California; Rusher kidnapped their young son and brought him to Australia where he undertook to have Fiona's new lover, Terri Maxfield, killed. Rusher was jailed for immigration irregularities, but while there he tried to have not only Maxfield killed but also Fiona. The Crown case would rely principally on taped conversations between Rusher and an undercover police officer, who posed as a 'waste management consultant' who would arrange the hit; and on taped conversations between Rusher and his go-between, Les McAtee. During these conversations, Mr Crown told us, we would not hear Rusher order a 'murder' or a 'killing'. Instead, he had used a code phrase, 'serving documents', which, the Crown submitted, was a pre-agreed term to mean killing.

Up to this point, I hadn't paid Rusher much attention. When I'd first heard the indictment, picking up that it was a solicit-to-murder charge based on events in Silverwater, I glanced at Rusher's glossy hair and Lothario good looks and assumed he was some kind of local thug, or a businessman involved in organised crime. Near Rusher sat a tired-looking woman and a teenage boy, who I'd assumed were his wife and children.

So much for first impressions. Rusher was an American, the location of the supposed crime was only Silverwater because he was incarcerated there, and we never saw the woman and boy again. Whoever they were, they had nothing to do with Steve Rusher. Perhaps they were just spectators.

Being a juror is a constant process of grasping impressions and then letting them go. After Mr Crown's address, the judge sent us off for lunch. The 12 of us marched down the narrow corridor outside the courtroom, where the sheriff's officer took us to the lift and up one floor and showed us into one of several jury rooms. We were kept away from the public areas at all times, to prevent recurrences of such situations as a couple of years earlier in the Downing Centre when relatives of the accused harassed jurors with cries of 'He's innocent!' or 'You look like the hanging jury!'

The jury room itself seemed okay – another false first impression. Two jurors went to the toilet cubicles inside the room, a few went to the kitchen alcove and made themselves coffee or tea, and the rest of us moved to the large circular table which, along with a dozen swivel chairs, was the only furniture save an empty water cooler and a low coffee table. On one wall was a whiteboard, on another a print of the forgettable kind you see in motel rooms. Other than that, nothing: not a single window. It might as well have been an interrogation room.

A sheriff's officer gave us statutory declarations to fill in, and distributed Popper juices around the table. I'd hate the participants in the trial to have seen us attempt to deal with either of these challenges.

The stat decs were to identify ourselves and give the Attorney-General's office our addresses so they could send us our allowances, which would start at around $70 a day and move up to around $100 by the third week. When some jurors hesitated at putting down their personal details, the officer assured us that this would be the only information identifying us and would be kept under lock and key. There was no way the lawyers or the accused or anyone else would know who we were. Unfortunately, the officer didn't show a ready acquaintance with the forms, and gave us a series of wrong instructions which left our stat decs scarred and smudged with crossings-out and amendments. By the time I'd finished with it, mine looked as if it was filled in by a two-year-old.

No more encouraging were our efforts to disengage the Popper straws from their plastic sheaths and insert them into the cartons. Thumbs muddled, straws broke, juice sprayed. Amid nervous laughter, somebody said exactly what I was thinking: 'God help us if the guy on trial saw us doing this.'

At this stage, the other jurors were still a blur. My colleague David, who was being empanelled the same week in the Supreme Court, would liken it to being 'cast off on a lifeboat together'. I had the feeling you get at the beginning of a group holiday – all these people are in black and white on the first day, all blended together, but as time goes by they will sharpen into living colour and you will know them better than you know your own family.

But that was all in the future. First we had to elect our foreman. This in itself is significant: before we knew anything about each other, before we knew how we'd relate to each other, before we knew who was dominant and who was submissive and who was a leader and who a follower, we were to vote for our spokesperson. Absurd and ultimately damaging to the jury process as this is, it was what the judge had told us to do first-up and what was done in the training video.

In these situations, my first instinct has always been to retreat. My relationship to authority, as I've said, does not make me a fit and proper person to be a jury foreman. No way would I put my hand up. And if there was one lesson from that video, it was *don't stand for foreman*. The middle-aged guy had been completely humiliated by his failed candidacy.

I was in the toilet when the foreman discussion started. When I came out, someone asked if I'd like to be foreman, and I said: 'Preferably not'. Immediately I blushed, feeling that my very phrasing – why couldn't I have just said 'No', or 'No thanks, mate'? – betrayed a kind of stiff shyness that I was determined to hide.

We went around the table twice, and nobody nominated themselves. A short period of silence followed. Then, as I'm sure must often happen, two people nominated themselves at once. One was a bleach-blonde woman in her fifties who had already let it be known that this was her third jury. The other was a 29-year-old guy who had the rosy meat-fed face of a butcher and a goatee beard turning prematurely grey. He told everyone he had four kids under five years old and looked to jury duty as a 'much-needed holiday'. At this point, with nobody knowing anything about anyone, either candidate seemed as good as the other. The woman deferred, and we had a foreman. As chance would have it, by profession he was a storeman who worked on the waterfront.

There's no manual for foreman selection – there's no manual for anything once you're in the jury room – and consequently, different jurors' methods of voting their leader varies. My colleague David recalls:

> *We went into the jury room, and there was dead silence. I said, 'Maybe we should introduce ourselves.' We went around the table and stated our names. Then there was more dead silence. I said, 'Who wants to be foreman?' There was more silence, then somebody said: 'Why don't you do it?' So that's how I became foreman.*

In some trials, the person elected foreman happens to be in the right (or wrong) place at the right (or wrong) time. Graham Burnett's jury foreman had dropped out, and the judge moved Burnett, who was sitting in the next seat, into the foreman's place. When the jury went into their room for deliberations soon afterwards, Burnett suggested a few moments of silence for jurors to collect themselves, then called for a vote on whether they wanted to keep him. But:

> ... at that early moment, when relief (that things were finally in our control) and excitement (something new!) were strong, people waved off the suggestion. It was clear that several jurors thought that reaching a verdict was going to be a matter of minutes, so procedural questions seemed quaint, irrelevant.

More comically, in the movie *Jury Duty*, the foreman's duty is seen as a poisoned chalice because the accused is likely to face the death penalty. Pauly Shore gets the job by default while he's in the toilet:

> Juror 1: *And tell that psycho he's going to the electric chair? Not me!*
> Juror 2: *It'll be like sentencing Satan himself. He'll give you that evil eye.*
> Juror 3: *It will haunt you until the day you die.*
> Juror 4: *The nightmares alone will have the supernatural powers to kill you. I'm out.*
> Juror 5: *Well then, who?*
> (Shore comes in from toilet.)
> Juror 1: *Kid, it's your lucky day.*
> Shore (looking at his trousers): *What, I didn't get any on me?*
> Juror 1: *No, you've been elected jury foreman.*

What research has been done on foreman selection suggests it is commonly done in just such a haphazard, almost flippant, way.

The New Zealand jury project found that on average, juries took four minutes to select their foreman:

> Few actually discussed it, and in only a few cases did more than one candidate emerge ... For many juries, with only a hazy idea of what the task involves and what prior experience is likely to be relevant to it, and under considerable pressure from the court and the court staff to make a rapid decision, virtually any indication of interest in the job or of some relevant skill is sufficient to seal the nomination. Not surprisingly, selection relied very heavily on people volunteering for the task: in 31 of the 48 cases in our sample, at least one juror described the foreperson as having volunteered for the job.

Other reasons a foreman nominated himself or herself included prior experience on juries or committees, neat appearance, being seated at the head of the table, being first to speak (like David), having a surname beginning with A, or being male on a predominantly female jury.

Men do, statistically and notoriously, have a habit of bullying their way to the head of the table. In the 1985 study, 72 per cent of NSW foremen were male. By 1994, this had fallen marginally to 66 per cent. Most were in the 40–54 age group, 75 per cent white-collar workers, 33 per cent chosen by election, 26 per cent self-nominated, 5 per cent nominated by others, 5 per cent picked by default or chance.

There is logic behind these patterns. American researchers have found that 'even though selecting a foreperson takes only a few minutes, the process is not as unstructured as it appears. Status in the jury room mirrors status in the outside world. More often than not, the chance of leading the jury is highest for a white male with a college degree or postgraduate work, in a high-status occupation, and with previous jury service.'

Stories abound of the domineering Alpha male taking charge from day one – indeed, this was the character parodied in our training video. A judge told the 1994 NSW survey:

> *I have had certain letters from persons who have served as jurors in which they have a complaint of lack of clarity as to the nature and extent of the role of a foreman. It seems that occasions have arisen when the person who has been chosen as foreman has taken to himself or herself various kinds of authority which do not in truth exist.*

Such expectations can lead to the opposite reaction. For instance an English juror, Anthony Barker, would not nominate himself as foreman because he thought, mistakenly, that the foreman had to be impartial and he wanted to be in among the arguments. In any case, the 1985 study found that only a minority – 19 per cent – of foremen dominated jury discussions.

For juries trying sex crimes, foreman selection can anticipate later jury-room debates between men and women, as one former juror told me:

> *The jury was made up of a classic mixed bunch. There were five women and seven men, and we included a retired storeman and packer, a (very) disabled woman, a hotshot young businessman, a housewife, a schoolteacher and a book editor. We ranged in age from barely twenty to retired, in IQ from low to high . . . When we were first in the jury room, well, there we were, twelve good men and women who'd never clapped eyes on each other before. And the first thing we had to do was elect a leader, a spokesperson! We all sat there looking nervously at each other, then people began talking and a rather obnoxiously loud and self-confident man identified himself as a schoolteacher 'used to public speaking', and put himself forward as potential foreman. The people around the room murmured agreement. My heart began to palpitate because I wasn't used to thrusting myself forward, but I felt very strongly that because this was a rape case the foreman should be a woman. So at the last minute*

> *I stopped the proceedings and explained my feelings, and I was amazed when I was voted foreman.*

While her motives were undoubtedly pure, others can push themselves forward as foreman to mask a nastier agenda. In the Bjelke-Petersen case, after an initial awkward silence, the unionist played in *Joh's Jury* by John Howard is about to propose himself when Luke Shaw, played by Malcolm Kennard, butts in: 'If nobody else wants it, I may as well take it.' As a suspicious narrator, played by Simon Bossell, observes in voiceover:

> *I was surprised at his eagerness, the way he rushed to throw his name into the ring. He seemed pretty sure of himself for someone on his first trial, like he had something to prove. He said he'd done debating at school. Anyway, for better or worse, we had a foreman.*

Once the foreman is elected, what does that mean? In our jury, Storeman Foreman played little role other than writing notes for us to send the judge. An affable, uncomplicated wharfie, he did not try to enforce his views on the jury at any time. As the trial wore on and we got to know each other better, we identified de facto leaders – of which Storeman Foreman wasn't one. He was our Governor-General, not our Prime Minister.

But inside the court, the selection of foreman is one of the earliest pieces of information the lawyers can grab hold of. It may be as pressing and dramatic as John Grisham makes out in *The Runaway Jury*:

> *[The lawyers] quietly pondered the great question, the one they loved to guess about. As they looked at the [juror] seating charts and studied the faces for the millionth time, they asked over and over, 'Who will be the leader?' Every jury has a leader, and that's where you find your verdict. Will he emerge quickly? Or will she lie back and take*

> *charge during deliberations? Not even the jurors knew at this point.*

Actual lawyers are ambivalent as to how much the selection of the foreman tells them of jury chemistry. To take four reactions from four lawyers:

> *There's a common perception that the foreman is an influential person, but I don't know.*

> *I don't assume the foreman is a leader. I assume that they might have been on a jury before, and that's why they're the foreman.*

> *I know there's no system of selecting a foreman, but we know that person has some gumption, because he or she is sufficiently on the front foot to take responsibility.*

> *You do assume that the foreman has a disproportionate influence. In recent years it's surprised me who gets chosen to be foreman. It used to be middle-aged aggressive businessman types, but now there are more women as foremen.*

Those poor lawyers – they still don't know anything about us, and if they focus their efforts on Foreman Storeman, they're wasting their time.

Yet the foreman can be the real leader, forcing a decision on the other jurors or, as Luke Shaw did in the Bjelke-Petersen trial, misrepresenting them. In *Joh's Jury*, after he asks the judge questions about the definition of 'commonsense', questions unauthorised by the rest of the jury, they return to their room, furious at him. (I'll refer to the characters by the actors' names.)

> Penny Cook: *What are people going to say? My children are going to think I'm crazy. I know what commonsense is.*
> Noah Taylor: *Dickhead!*
> Julie Hamilton: *I don't believe you could have asked that question!*
> Malcolm Kennard (Shaw): *I thought he'd give us a better idea.*
> John Howard: *It's as plain as the nose on your face!*
> Kennard: *I can't see the nose on my face!*

After some heated argument, Kennard says: 'Okay blokes, I think we'll have a break now.'

> Taylor: *Yeah, break your frigging neck.*
> Hamilton: *Why? We've just had a break.*
> Kennard: *It's getting a bit heated, that's all.*
> Howard: *No, no. I think what we need is a new foreman. Everyone else agree?* (They agree.)
> Kennard: *I've been the foreman since the beginning of the trial! You can't change me now!*

They vote 'Kev', played by John Jarratt, as the new foreman, yet Kennard (Shaw) must still occupy the foreman's seat in court and represent the jury to the judge. When they return to court for more questions, he again misrepresents them. This time they have found evidence that he and another juror, 'Val' (played by Elaine Hudson), are actively conspiring to block a verdict. A scene follows where the jurors show that they do not know their rights in the matter:

> Hamilton: *We should tell the judge.*
> Jarratt: *What are we going to say? 'Excuse me, your honour, Luke is a pain in the arse and he's not representing us correctly'?*

> Cook: *Luke's the foreman. He should be representing us.*
> Hamilton: *But if we have a problem, we should be able to talk to the judge.*
> Cook: *We should be able to sort it out ourselves.*

One important conclusion from the Bjelke-Petersen fiasco was that the jurors had not known of their right to tell the judge Shaw was misrepresenting them. The television script, based on interviews with the jurors, shows them pondering an approach to the judge but fearing a mistrial.

This fits into the wider context of jurors not knowing their rights, but also adds weight to the New Zealand jury project's proposal that the foreman not be selected until after the evidence is heard and deliberations are about to commence. 'By then,' the authors say, 'the jurors will have had a chance to assess each other's qualities.'

Shelley Saltzman (nee Hampton), who interviewed the jurors in the 2001 NSW study, found that 'the general tenor was that forepersons should be elected after the jurors have spent some time together [and] come to understand something about each other.'

The hasty model applied in our courts leaves:

> *. . . no time to introduce themselves in any detail or to deliberate. Given that the jurors do not know each other, the lack of consistent or detailed guidance on what the task of foreman involved and the pressure to decide quickly, the choice is inevitably almost random.*

As a result, the New Zealand project authors say:

> *[I]n a significant number of trials the foreman is largely ineffective, and in a number of cases the decision-making process either produces errors or is unduly prolonged because of the foreman. This could be because the*

> *foreman either has no real understanding of his or her role, and so does not behave appropriately, or discovers that he or she is not suited to the role and is unable to fulfil it.*

If the foreman were selected after evidence, Luke Shaw would not have been the Bjelke-Petersen foreman. He might still have hung the jury, but he wouldn't have been able to misrepresent the group in court. It's hard to imagine any disadvantages in selecting the foreman later, and it would avert the many foreman-related problems the New Zealand study found.

Uniquely, the New Zealand research tried to identify and analyse 'successful' and 'unsuccessful' foremen. Unsuccessful foremen clustered at two extremes – overbearing, intimidating, and misrepresenting the jury in court on the one hand, and too weak on the other. These latter were described by fellow jurors as 'just one of the group' and 'not generally effective'.

> *Some of these forepersons had the necessary 'people' skills for the job, giving everyone a chance to have their say and allowing only one person to speak at a time. But they lacked leadership skills, and their failure to structure the order in which points were raised, and to organise the way in which evidence was discussed, led to deliberations which were disorganised, lacking direction and, in the perception of other jurors, even 'chaotic' . . . This was exacerbated where forepersons were under the illusion that they had performed their role satisfactorily.*

A weak foreman led to the same result as an overbearing one: 'The vacuum created by an ineffective foreperson could easily be filled by strong personalities who took control of and dominated, rather than facilitated, the deliberation process.'

Comparing 'unsuccessful' with 'successful' foremen, the New Zealand study found that men were more successful than women, highly educated people more successful than less-educated, and there were no differences in age or ethnicity. (But, they added, it was a small study and the typing of 'successful' was the subjective judgment of other jurors.

As alarming as the stories of rogue, domineering and idiot foremen are, there are as many foremen who are a powerful force for good. Graham Burnett wrote (unsurprisingly) that as foreman he maintained impartiality and never showed his opinion. When he finally came out for an acquittal, to break a deadlock, it was a trump card that swayed the waverers.

A real heroine of jurors' rights is Mary Timothy, the foreman in the murder-kidnapping trial of Angela Davis in the US in 1972. Her election as foreman, which happened after the evidence was heard and the jury retired to deliberate, is one of the best examples of sensitive jury-room politics:

> *No one wanted to sit down. No one knew how to get started. With all the others milling around the room, I wondered where I should sit. . . I went over to get a drink of water and when I straightened up from the fountain the rest of the group had moved en masse to the table and were pulling out chairs and taking seats. I joined them and found that the only empty chair was at the head of the table. Each of the jurors had instinctively avoided that seat. I hesitated. I didn't want it to appear that I was assuming that I would be selected, or that I wanted the job, or that this was a fixed election. As I stood looking around the table, trying to avoid sitting in the only empty chair, Bob (an elderly juror) called out: 'Mary, come sit here!' and he stood at the head of the table pulling out that chair for me to use.*

Bob then made a short speech proposing Mary as foreman. Another juror objected and nominated Jim, an airport flight controller. They held a secret ballot, which Mary Timothy won

8-4. She then said Jim should sit beside her and be deputy foreman, to help out with ticklish issues. Jim accepted, leaving us with a nice story of coalition government that works.

Anyway, for better or worse we had our foreman. The other candidate, the woman I'll call the Old Hand, took it okay. She'd been on other juries, and knew that it didn't always run smoothly. She'd read John Grisham's *The Runaway Jury*, in which a blind man, Herman Grimes, forces his way onto the jury despite his disability, and then becomes foreman. The lawyers hide their consternation. But the judge is:

> *. . . relieved that his jury was able to reach this routine selection without apparent acrimony. He'd seen much worse. One jury, half white and half black, had been unable to elect a foreman. They later brawled over the lunch menu.*

CHAPTER FIVE

THE DEFENCE OPENS

After we'd elected Storeman Foreman and eaten lunch, the conversation turned to the one thing we had in common: what we'd just been told about Steve Rusher. Some jurors were rubbing their hands at what a juicy case we had. We might have been unlucky and got some dreary fraud or, worse, a stomach-turning sexual assault or murder. Rusher's case was both clean – no dead body – and stimulating. It was also convoluted, and as jurors tried to piece together the story we'd heard while still recovering from the shock of being empanelled, there was one conversation that went something like:

'So if he's American, why's he being tried in Australia?'

'They're saying he committed the crime here.'

'He's an illegal immigrant, then?'

It did seem unfair that the Crown was able to get the opening shot in, and we weren't able to hear the defence reply before we broke and convened for the first time.

But just as I was wondering whether to butt in and say something – like, 'Hi, I'm Malcolm, nice to meet you, and by the way he hasn't committed the crime, we haven't heard any evidence yet' – thus introducing myself as the Burden-of-Proof Nazi, someone else spoke up. This was the Old Hand, the woman who'd been on two juries and had deferred to Storeman Foreman. When she heard people gossiping, she said: 'You can't say he's committed the crime. He's innocent until proven guilty.'

She got up and wrote on the whiteboard: INNOCENT. She turned around and said: 'He's innocent.' Then she wrote '+ EVIDENCE' and said, 'If the Crown gives us enough evidence, then he's guilty.' And she wrote: '= GUILTY'. That line – 'INNOCENT + EVIDENCE = GUILTY' – remained on the whiteboard through the trial, a constant reminder of our duty.

The others assured everybody that they didn't really mean Rusher had committed the crime, they were just trying to piece together Mr Crown's story. I admired the Old Hand not just for setting the ground rules but, more, for having done what I'd been afraid to do.

She earned even more respect a short while later. She was chatting with another juror, a wizened little bachelor in his sixties, who took great pride in being a Justice of the Peace. They were joined by the Stickybeak, a raven-haired spinster of around 60 with a busy manner and a magpie face, in a conversation about the barristers and their wigs. They'd noticed that Mr Nisbett was wearing a wig, but Mr Crown wasn't. They offered up all sorts of theories why – maybe Mr Crown had yet to earn one, maybe only defenders wore them, or perhaps Mr Crown was hot.

Then the Stickybeak (who was, as it happened, a hairdresser) said: 'But I don't like the judge's wig at all.'

'Me neither,' said the JP.

My ears twitched at this conversation, because as far as I could remember, the judge wasn't wearing a wig.

'Yes, the judge's wig is all wispy and silvery and thready, it's just not nice,' said a third participant, a woman of around 40 whom I came to know as our Christian Mother.

The Old Hand, who had a German accent and came from Switzerland, interrupted: 'Are you sure he's wearing one? I thought he was without.'

'Oh, no,' said our Christian Mother. 'He's definitely wearing one. It's a horrible thing.'

The Defence Opens

The Old Hand remained sceptical, and as others were getting involved, she called for a vote.

'Is the judge wearing a wig? Raise your hand.'

Eight voted that he was wearing a wig. Four of us said he wasn't.

After a further hour-and-a-half for lunch, the sheriff's officer took us downstairs to the court. As we waited in the corridor outside, Storeman Foreman said: 'Now, everybody, make sure you're not all staring at the judge's head when you go in.'

Just as our laughter burst in the corridor, the door opened. This wasn't the last time our growing camaraderie, our ability to share a joke, might have come across as inappropriate to those inside the courtroom. But, as Lord Chief Justice Holt said 300 years ago, not even the King can tell a jury what to do.

(These kinds of speculations are not unusual in the jury room. Tom Molomby recalls a conversation with a sheriff's officer in which he was told: 'Barristers would never guess the type of things juries were curious about. The jury wanted to know why none of the barristers were wearing wedding rings.')

As it turned out, our judge wasn't wearing a wig. He was a slim, fifty-odd, Mr Bean lookalike with a monotonous voice but a reassuringly straight, helpful manner. One of the jurors said he looked like Mr Humphries from *Are You Being Served*, but the clipping of his speech was meticulous rather than camp. His voice came from the speakers above and behind us. The only annoyance was that he was typing constantly onto his laptop, the sound of which was picked up by his mike and projected into the jury box as a staccato clicking, like a mouse scuttling about on floorboards.

Anyway – our powers of observation were 8-4 to the bad. Later, a retired judge told me that perhaps the jurors mistook our judge's hair for a wig because they were focusing so intently on his instructions. Maybe. The rule on wigs is that if the judge declines to wear one – a rare instance in District Court criminal proceedings – then the wig is optional for the barristers, too.

But it wasn't a good look for us to be roaring away with laughter when we were let into the court. As in airports, jokes are generally a no-no in the courts. In April 2004 – April 1 – a drug trafficking case in the Downing Centre was aborted after a juror came into the jury room and announced: 'We don't have to sit today. They've pleaded guilty.' As the looks passed around the room, he said: 'Ha, ha. April fool.' It doesn't sound like an especially funny joke, but despite (or because of) this, he decided to try it again with a court officer. Unamused, the officer told Judge Ian Dodd, who discharged the jury and aborted the trial.

After lunch, it was time for Mr Nisbett to open. If Mr Crown was almost a caricature of the dry, colourless prosecutor, Mr Nisbett played up to his archetype equally. When he opened Rusher's case, Nisbett came across as engaging, impish and, at least in his own eyes, suavely charming. He modulated his tone more than Mr Crown, deployed the dramatic pause to good effect, and made twinkling eye contact with all of us individually. Olive-complexioned, with darting dark glances, he came across as the street-fighting naughty boy to Mr Crown's aloof patrician (which he was – Mr Crown was a private-school boy from a wealthy industrial family). Mr Nisbett was what film directors would call more 'actorly' than Mr Crown.

Nisbett painted Steve Rusher as a loving father whose sole ambition was to save his little boy, Steve Junior, from Terri Maxfield. 'A boy needs a male role model in the house. A boy needs his father, and if he can't have his father, then he needs *a* father. This was all that concerned Mr Rusher.' Rusher's breakup with Fiona Emery had been unfortunate for both of them, but Rusher was not out for revenge against her. 'It was all over. He was happy for Fiona to lead her own life, but she wanted more than that. She wanted to take SJ to Australia to live in a lesbian . . .' Nisbett paused to examine us, 'a *lesbian relationship*. A so-called *gay marriage*.' Rusher came to Australia unlawfully – Nisbett said that his client admitted that – but he only wanted to 'increase his knowledge' of Terri Maxfield's unsuitability as a parent, which he would use in Family Court proceedings to support his claim to shared custody.

I'd tried to avoid looking too much at Rusher until now, when we were hearing his story from his own side. His hair was indeed, as the Stickybeak had said, 'magnificent'. He was one of those men about whom the first thing you notice is this great flowing mane. If I'd never seen Rusher again, and someone had asked me about him, I'd say: 'The guy with the hair'. Most of the time its thick mass was pointed right at us, as his face was angled down, while he wrote notes. The box in which he sat was glassed in, though the sliding window was open in front of him. He wore a dark-blue suit, a white shirt and a 1980s-style tie with horizontal stripes. Behind him dozed an officer.

Like his barrister, Steve Rusher was a performer. Whenever his love for his young son was mentioned, Rusher blinked away tears. He'd remove his reading glasses and dab a handkerchief to his eyes. He'd blow his nose. He'd wipe his eyes with the back of his hand. He'd snivel loudly. And then, when the talk passed on to other matters, he'd pull himself together. I wouldn't have felt so sceptical if the waterworks didn't come on like clockwork at the mention of SJ's name. It was quite a show. It didn't turn me against him – after all, he was admitting he'd do just about anything to save his son – but I was fascinated by his lack of effort to hide his emotions. It said nothing about his guilt or innocence. Either way, it was in his interest to show us how much he loved his boy. An innocent is under no obligation to preserve a stiff upper lip.

Then something unsettled me. Every time Rusher looked up, he seemed to be looking at me. No-one else. Just me. I looked away, then back. He'd look away, caught. Then he'd snag my eye again. No emotion passed between us – on my part, thanks to some effort to present an impassive face. But I wondered what he was looking for. Perhaps he'd remembered my heathen affirmation.

The Crown case was going to rest on taped conversations. But we couldn't tell, from his barrister's opening statement, how Rusher was going to rebut this. Was he saying the conversations hadn't happened, or that he'd been entrapped? Was he going to say he'd just been mouthing off about killing Terri and Fiona, just bignoting? (I think of this as the Lawrence Dallaglio defence, after the England rugby captain who was caught telling journalists he'd buy them ecstasy and other drugs. He said he was just making empty boasts.)

The crux of the case, in those first hours, was already taking form. How was Steve Rusher going to address the tapes? As far as I could see, the defence was hoping that some of the jury would have such a violent reaction to the word 'lesbian' – Nisbett's eyes darted around the jury box as he said the word, apparently with great delicacy and reluctance – that we'd put Maxfield effectively on trial and excuse anything Rusher might have done.

These were, I stress, only my own reactions. Among the jury I was the Silent Sentinel – not anti-social, but shy. I wanted to get some reading done in the jury room, and didn't really join in the forced sociability that most of the others apparently enjoyed. It was one of those groups where, if the conversation lulled for a few moments, someone would invariably crack: 'Hey, everyone's gone silent all of a sudden!' That was fine. We were pretty tolerant of each other. But when I recall my running assessments of the trial, they're mine alone. I don't know what the others were thinking.

Getting a Foot in the Door

The tactic of an opening statement from the defence is a relatively recent development. Traditionally, the Crown would open its case and go through its witnesses, with the defence's only input its cross-examination of that evidence. Then, the defence would either offer up its witnesses or simply address the jury.

The Defence Opens

The advent of the defence barrister is interesting in itself. In 1692, the English Parliament introduced laws offering Blood Money to citizens who arrested highway robbers, thieves and deserters. But the bounty was also incentive for police and accusers to concoct evidence. The defence counsel entered the trial as a means of protecting the accused against this corruption. In 1696 their powers were widened, the Treason Act allowing defence counsel to examine and cross-examine witnesses and address the jury.

By the early 1700s, the defence counsel was winning so many acquittals that, to even up the contest, more prosecution counsel came in. But it wasn't until the end of the century that defence barristers really got their hooks into the criminal court system. The proportion of ordinary felony trials where a defence counsel appeared increased from 2.1 per cent in the 1770s to 36.6 per cent by 1795. Thus trials changed from 'the accused speaks' into the 'testing the prosecution' model we have now.

This evolved into the defence counsel speaking for, and instead of, the accused. Defence counsel were able to tear down Blood Money charges, and because the accused could win without taking the stand it became common for him to refuse to testify, which in turn evolved into his so-called 'right to silence'. The expectation that the accused would speak disappeared. A French observer of English courts wrote: 'In England the defendant acts no kind of part; his hat stuck on a pole might without inconvenience be his substitute at the trial.' On the Continent, by contrast, the defendant had to respond directly to questions from the inquisitorial panel of judges.

Some say defence counsel have hijacked the criminal courts, but before their intervention, trials had been shamefully short, one 18th-century observer writing that 'a full two-thirds of prisoners, on their return from their trials, cannot tell of any thing which has passed in court, not even, very frequently, whether they have been tried.'

The defence opening – an address at the trial's beginning – didn't develop in New South Wales courts until the 1990s. An expatriate American barrister, Henry di Suvero, and Tom Molomby were among the first to use it.

Until then, di Suvero recalls, 'I attempted on a number of occasions to open right behind the Crown opening and was denied whenever the Crown opposed, which it often did.'

Di Suvero, who had practised the opening submission in America until he left in 1979, continued to campaign. After a letter from di Suvero, Nicholas Cowdery, who succeeded Reg Blanch QC as DPP, directed prosecutors to allow a defence opening. But judges still limited its extent, preventing di Suvero from bald statements such as 'We will show the prosecution witnesses to be liars' or 'The presumption of innocence means your starting point is that the accused did not do what he is charged with. That is the beginning point.' One judge, di Suvero says, would not allow the defence to open unless he could vet the statement beforehand.

Molomby, who followed di Suvero's lead, says the defence opening is all about the jury:

> *I try to give a clear outline of our case, and make sure to mention new points I'm confident we can prove early. If you show the jurors you have something to say and can deliver on it, they're more likely to stay open-minded.*

Murugan Thangaraj, a barrister who was a pupil of Molomby's, says:

> *I almost always open, so the jury can get a feel for who I am, even if I'm not saying much. I don't want to give too much away. If media are present, I always try to present something to counter what the Crown has said, so that the next day's papers won't all go one way. If the jury has heard both sides at the beginning, we don't know how*

> *that will affect the dynamics inside the jury room but we know it'll give us a better chance than if we don't open.*

The virtue in a defence opening is that it's like a job interview: you humanise and dramatise your story, get the audience on your side. The argument against an opening address is that the defence may want to keep its aces up its sleeve. Often a defence case will rise out of cross-examining Crown witnesses, so the counsel won't know beforehand what opportunities he'll be able to exploit. Yet there's nothing to stop a defence barrister from opening up with boilerplate instructions on legal principles, as Adam Morison says:

> *If you're unsure how your client's case will proceed, you might not open. But when I do open, I stress the legal principles that might be counter-intuitive, like putting the burden of proof on the Crown, and not convicting unless it's beyond reasonable doubt.*

The New Zealand jury project found that juries appreciated clear opening statements from judge, prosecutor and defence. As a juror, I concur – the first day of a trial is such a blur that you don't retain very much unless it is stressed and repeated and, if possible, tattooed on your arms.

The New Zealand project recommended that the jury be given a break immediately after empanelment, to get over the shock, to get to know each other, to make arrangements for childcare. (Not to mention aged care. Shelley Saltzman recalls one juror in the 2001 NSW study who 'sought an exemption because his parents were elderly and had become very ill prior to his empanelment and relied upon his care. He was so distressed by the conflict between his need to care for his parents – and travel to see them – and the pressure of the trial . . . that he did not feel that he had served as well as he might otherwise have under less stressful circumstances.') All these matters should be taken care of before the jury settles down to hear these crucial opening submissions.

The New Zealand study also called for a systematic identification of issues in dispute at the start of a trial, preferably in writing as well as orally:

> *Although the [opening] address is generally well received by juries, it is not always well recalled. This could be for a number of reasons, including the obvious one that the actual evidence in the trial 'overprints' memories of the address. It is clear, however, that jury recall and comprehension is aided by access to written and tangible materials. Crown counsel should be encouraged, when opening the Crown case, to make available to the jury copies of the indictment, the list of Crown witnesses, and non-controversial exhibits such as maps, plans and photographs.*

As for the defence opening:

> *Jurors sometimes find it difficult to assimilate, evaluate and interpret the evidence in a case because they do not receive an adequate factual 'framework' at the start of the trial. They are forced to sift the evidence and to determine what weight to place upon it without knowing what the issues in dispute are. This is because, to the extent that the defence has a 'story' or narrative which it wishes to present, this only emerges towards the end of the trial and even then is, or is liable to be perceived as, incomplete. Even though most jurors are willing to change their view in the light of evidence presented by the defence, their version of events is inevitably based on a partial recollection of the earlier evidence.*

THE DEFENCE OPENS

In the 1994 NSW survey, nearly all jurors said an opening address immediately behind the Crown's opening was helpful from the defence. At the same time, it had little or no impact on their final verdict.

What if the defence chooses not to open? A Queensland judge asks:

> *If a formal invitation is made by the trial judge and the invitation is not taken up, is there a risk that a jury may consciously or subconsciously think that there is no substantial defence? A warning cannot effectively be given against making any such assumption without highlighting the situation.*

Looking back, my own view is that although Mr Nisbett's opening address seemed to give Steve Rusher a motive to kill Terri and Fiona and therefore didn't do him a lot of good, it was probably better than nothing.

'I try to explain the fundamentals at the start,' says Tom Molomby. 'Cases are lost because the defence hasn't been able to show that it has a case, before little doors have shut in the jurors' minds.'

By the end of day one in the Rusher trial, the defence opening had kept those little doors open.

CHAPTER SIX

MEET YOUR NEW FAMILY

We had been frog-marched into a world we knew nothing of, speaking a language we sometimes barely understood, governed by regulations that made us feel we were back at school again. And when we got home from this topsy-turvy working day, we weren't even allowed to talk shop with our nearest and dearest . . . Then, after four months of this, we had been abruptly abandoned and ordered to resolve our confusions as best we could on our own. We were like the befuddled lovers in A Midsummer Night's Dream, *after Puck had scrambled their wits and left them sleeping on the forest floor.*
– Trevor Grove, *The Juryman's Tale*

Most of the first two days were taken up with legal argument, which meant that we were sent off to our stuffy little room. Why couldn't they have got this out of the way before empanelling a jury? It was quickly emerging that the convenience of jurors was the court's last consideration. On our brief excursions into court, the judge would apologise to us and say, 'There have been some matters I've had to attend to', in a matter-of-fact way that brought to mind picking up his dry-cleaning and returning videos; but from the tense faces at the Bar table I knew that in our absence the most important battle in Rusher's trial – what evidence would be excluded – was being fought.

As a juror, it's exasperating to know that so much is happening behind your back. Our absences reminded me of the blindfolded woman holding the scales of justice. We were meant to have an intuitive grasp of truth and fairness, but we were also blinded to certain assertions, facts and biases. (Trevor Grove puts it another way: 'It made us feel like children forced to leave the room while the grown-ups discussed something supremely interesting behind our backs . . . On reflection, I thought crossly, it is not blindfolded Justice with a set of scales in her hand that should symbolise the impartiality of the law: it is a blindfolded juror holding a styrofoam coffee cup.')

We had to be both perceptive and ignorant. It's a delicate mix. And frustrating. I used to be a cricket writer, and a trial is similar to a Test match. During delays, you itch for the real action to get under way. The play may be tedious at times, but at least it propels the drama towards its climax. What's frustrating is when you have to fill in time in-between – while it's raining in cricket, while you're sent out of the court. I could sympathise with Pauly Shore in the movie *Jury Duty* when he approaches the bench alongside the lawyers for their secret chat with the judge.

> Judge: *What in God's name are you doing here?*
> Shore: *Your Honour, I don't think it's fair that you guys get to have your own little pow-wow over here while we can't listen. We have to hear too, for information.*
> Judge: *You're a juror. Get back in that box!*
> Shore (retiring): *Just trying to do my job.*

We did see flashes of court action. The first witness was Fiona Emery, Rusher's former wife and the mother of his son. Mr Crown walked her through the history of her relationship with Rusher. During their early days together, they led what she admitted was a good life. Fiona administered the production business while Rusher schmoozed actors, agents, writers and studio execs. 'He was the ideas man in the partnership,' she said. 'I was the nuts and bolts.'

Fiona came across as a strong witness. Well presented and articulate, she was manifestly upset to be in the same room as her husband. In cross-examination, Mr Nisbett tried to paint her as something of a gold-digger, a mere adventuress attracted to Rusher by his money and glamour. But Fiona pointed out that she remained with him for several years after his fortunes turned south. Indeed, it wasn't until 1995 that she fell pregnant with SJ, and it was this, not Rusher's dry run, that broke their relationship.

Fiona testified that Rusher hadn't wanted the child as much as she had. SJ was her baby, Fiona said, and her relationship with Steve deteriorated during and after the pregnancy. Their sexual relationship ended – Nisbett tried to probe her on whether she 'couldn't' or 'wouldn't' sleep with Rusher anymore – and after SJ was born Fiona and Steve led separate lives. She lived in the West Hollywood rental, and re-established her relationship with Terri Maxfield. By 2000, she was ready to move to Tasmania to start a new life with Terri. That had been nearly two years before the trial. Was she still with Maxfield? 'Yes.' Was she in love with her? 'Yes.' Mr Nisbett shot us a look, intentionally bland, like an actor attempting to restrain his disgust.

Testing Fiona's evidence against a statement she had made the previous year, Nisbett tried to find contradictions in her story. There were minor ones – such as whether or not she 'hated' Rusher, and on the true extent of her relationship with Terri Maxfield, as in, how often they had spoken on the telephone or written to each other while she was living with Steve. But Nisbett was smart enough to accept that Fiona would be possibly the Crown's most sympathetic witness, so he didn't overdo it. In fact, Nisbett's main endeavour seemed to be to stop her saying things. At one point she said she was 'terrified' of Rusher, at which point Nisbett cut her off and we were sent out of the court. There were several points in her written statement that Nisbett made sure we didn't hear – frustrating but, I assume, fair enough.

The nub of it was, though, Fiona was only there to give us background. As a target of the alleged hit, she couldn't be of much help telling us what Steve had been planning. She wasn't in contact with him, except through lawyers, and hadn't been alone with him since 2000.

What was perhaps most interesting in her testimony was that she was asked to identify Rusher's voice from the tapes that would form the heart of the Crown case. This meant we could hear him for the first time. Everyone in the court donned headphones connected to a CD player operated by the Federal Police officer who had headed the Rusher investigation. Some jurors had problems operating the headphones, but once we were under way we listened to the tapes up until the point where Fiona raised her hand to show she recognised Steve's voice. Again and again, we'd hear his greetings – chirpy, cocky, sometimes testy, but always quite distinctive. He had a classic Californian Beach Boys accent. No doubt some Henry Higgins could come in and identify Rusher's place of birth, education and parentage. But that hardly mattered. After hearing 25 short grabs, even I'd be able to pick out Rusher's voice from a crowd.

In the first few days, these moments of drama were raisins in a stale loaf of inaction. Some jurors complained of feeling drowsy in court, and had trouble maintaining concentration. (In every jury, drowsiness is public enemy No 1. One American juror, Joanne Duke Gamblee, says her group organised 'concentration shifts', where each juror took responsibility for rolling eight-minute shifts, so that they knew at least one of them was concentrating at any given time.) Luckily, the Rusher trial was compelling enough to keep us on the alert. Nonetheless, the very nature of jury duty makes jurors feel, in the New Zealand project's words, 'bystanders rather than participants . . . frustrated by the sense of powerlessness it engenders'. Accordingly, once we were back inside the jury room and free to talk among ourselves, a jolly esprit de corps grew.

A juror correspondent told me later, in a comment that probably reflects the rest of my group's perspective:

> *The jury room became such a home from home! Being closeted there all day, day after day, turned into a huge relief from the tension of the courtroom. I have read about people being horrified and affronted by sounds of laughter coming from the jury room, but we only laughed because that was our way of releasing tension. Everyone treated the whole experience very, very seriously. We concentrated so much during the hours in the courtroom that when we got to 'our' room we relaxed – perhaps too much, made silly jokes, but boy, did we need that release. My memories of the jury room hours are very happy, even when we were at our most serious and intense. We worked together very well, and everyone played a major part in deliberating and discussing. I was so impressed by the whole procedure.*

What were the jurors like? This is the most common question non-jurors ask, as if jurors are some kind of secret society with special characteristics. Had I been on a four-week cruise with these 11 strangers, I doubt anyone would care what they were like – we all make assumptions about the type of people who go on cruises. Jurors, on the other hand, are a completely random selection of the community, and that's why, I think, they are objects of such curiosity. Jurors are the community itself – and none of us really knows what our community is.

What did we have in common? We were all too stupid to get out of jury duty, I guess. I've mentioned the Old Hand, our Christian Mother and the Stickybeak, all women aged between 40 and 60, either retired, part-time or volunteer workers. The Old Hand was Swiss-German, used to work for Australia Post, and was now retired with her husband. She caught the train between home and the court with the JP, who lived in the southern suburbs with his elderly mother, and had had such a severe nicotine addiction that he claimed to have once overdosed on patches. The JP's voice crackled through his smoke-ravaged throat. A devout lawn bowler, he took on an immediate familiarity with the rest of us – 'Hi, Mal!' he'd say to me, or 'Ah, ya cheeky bastard!' if one of the young guys told a risqué joke.

Those four made up the older generation along with the Retired Gent, a late-sixties ex-real-estate agent from Sutherland Shire. Gregarious and traditional, he was very impressed with Fiona Emery's personal presentation and found it 'very, very sad' that her life – and Rusher's – had come to this pass. The Retired Gent seemed struck by the extent of Rusher's fall – 'Imagine,' he kept saying, 'a big Hollywood producer, and now look at him! It's very, very sad.' The Retired Gent placed a lot of store in witnesses' personal presentation – with his experience, he trusted his ability to judge books by their covers.

Coming after those five in age, there was a small intergenerational pair: myself – about to turn 36 – and the Mechanic, a likeable, golf-playing married father of about 40. He fixed trucks in the eastern suburbs and brought a *Sydney Morning Herald* to the court every morning. One of the more thoughtful and peaceable of the jurors, he was to take on a mediating role.

Then there was Generation Y. Storeman Foreman confessed very early that he didn't mind how long jury duty went on, because it was better than going back to night shifts on the wharf. Friday Night, a 19-year-old customer service representative, didn't say much but didn't mind jury duty as long as it didn't impinge on her plans to go out on Friday night. A statuesque redhead, she kept everyone on their toes by wearing a translucent white spandex leotard top one day and a six-ply black polo-neck jumper the next. Particularly attentive were Storeman Foreman and the two other men in their twenties.

One, Shut The Gate, was an Italian-Australian part-time pharmacy student who, despite his immigrant heritage, was the quickest to announce his radical political views, saying Australia should 'shut the gate' on all boat people. Borderline, 22, was one of those guys who you can see exactly how they're going to look at 50. He had a mop of prematurely grey hair, two scar-like wrinkles across his forehead, piercing green eyes and a stooped gait. He stumbled in every day, claimed varying incidents had happened the previous night – such as 'I was run over by a cement truck' or 'I was beaten to a pulp by five naked lesbians' – and promptly fell asleep. He said he was a vigneron, but it later turned out that he worked in a bottle shop, which he made tolerable by smoking 'traffickable' quantities of dope before, during and after his shifts.

Finally, there was X-Files. To the end of the trial, nobody knew what X-Files did or where he lived. He didn't seem consciously secretive – more shy than elusive – but there was something enigmatic about him, if only because of his silence. He dressed trendily, the neo-skater look with checked short-sleeved shirts and cargo pants, giving rise to speculations that he worked in the visual arts. Sometimes he wore black. He had an up-to-the-minute haircut. He said little about the trial other than that we should keep an open mind and wait until we'd heard all the evidence before we made our minds up.

During the first three days of the trial, we spent eight or nine hours locked up together. On day two, people were still going around the table checking names. We didn't exchange surnames.

The jury room also became a hotbed of wild speculation about the trial process. The Old Hand assured everyone that the barristers earned 'at least $5,000 a day' and that the court costs would add up to $50,000 a day, which would be paid by whoever lost the trial. There was general agreement that Rusher must be a very wealthy man to afford such an accomplished barrister as Mr Nisbett, and that the cost of Fiona Emery's flight to Sydney and overnight accommodation would be 'added to her bill' – all nonsense. Criminal trials are funded almost entirely by the public purse, that is to say, cheaply. Our collective lack of education is not unusual. In the 1994 NSW survey, some jurors thought the instructing solicitors were secretaries.

We went back into court to hear the second witness, Terri Maxfield. What was stunning about Maxfield was that she was the last woman you'd imagine hooking up with the refined, fragile-looking Fiona Emery. Terri shambled up, smirking like a bad girl called into the headmaster's office. She was a blocky 5'8" and 14 stone, with an open face, unmade-up, and iron-grey hair. She hunched forward in the witness box and answered each question with the bare minimum, suspiciously, as if everything was a trap. She didn't have much to say other than reaffirming what Fiona had said – although Terri said they'd kept in more frequent contact during Fiona's years with Rusher. It was in cross-examination that the fireworks started.

Terri Maxfield was not the most eloquent of speakers. We'd already heard of Rusher's claim that Terri was some kind of sexual deviant, and the woman was clearly angered to be dragged through this ordeal. Mr Nisbett did his best to provoke and confuse Terri Maxfield, asking fiendishly complicated questions and putting suggestions in double and triple negatives. Terri was an easy target, shifting in her seat, exasperated if not bamboozled by the gibberish. Nisbett wanted to draw out information about Terri's alleged sexual perversions by asking her if her former husband, Rob, had ever made a court statement about her 'predatory lesbianism'. Partly due to Nisbett's tortuous language, partly because she was so damn furious about the whole thing, Terri Maxfield misinterpreted the question as an accusation. Instead of hearing 'Did your husband ever say you were a sexual deviant?' Terri heard: 'You are a sexual deviant, aren't you?'

Feeling pinned, she sneered: 'What rubbish! Like all lesbians have to be predators?' She didn't want to talk about it anymore. When Nisbett pressed her, Terri Maxfield said: 'What, I've been to bars to try and pull straight women? If that made me an unsuitable parent, you'd have to take the kids away from half the men in the country.'

Nisbett thought he'd seen an opening. His eyes darting towards us, he said:

'You go to bars to – as you put it – pull straight women? That is, you try to corrupt women who are not, ah, lesbian?'

Terri snorted. 'Past tense, buddy. Ancient history. Anyway, who doesn't do that?'

While this might have given us some insight into the Hobart dyke scene, such as it was, it didn't seem to progress the case. In the end, losing her cool completely, Terri jabbed a finger towards Steve Rusher and spluttered: 'This rubbish is all dreamt up by that man over there to justify his stupid actions!'

After that, Nisbett – eyes flicking to the jury box, lizard-like, to check our reactions – was finished with Maxfield. Terri lumbered out, looking as if, Incredible Hulk-like, she was going to burst out of her trouser suit and tear down the nearest skyscraper.

Back in the jury room, there was much excitement about Terri doing her block. Jurors love drama. Many saw the Nisbett–Maxfield stoush in the same way they'd see a middleweight bout, and afterwards gave commentary and scores.

'Jeez, she's stupid, that Maxfield!' said Shut The Gate, who had, that morning, cheerfully informed us that the reason the barristers did not come and approach us in the jury box, as they do on TV, 'is because we've got the Westminster system'.

The Retired Gent shook his head soberly. 'God, how could Fiona end up with a – a woman? And a woman like that?'

While Terri Maxfield blowing her stack was a defence victory of sorts, it did seem just a curtain-raiser to the main event. So what if Terri had been promiscuous? So what if she was a lesbian? So what if Rusher thought she was a threat to SJ? It didn't matter: we were here to find out if Steve Rusher had tried to have Terri and Fiona killed. We weren't testing his motive.

You could believe every point the defence was making – that this Maxfield woman was some kind of evil witch – but it still made no difference. The real evidence still lay ahead of us.

Yet I could see what the defence was trying. By making such a big deal of Terri Maxfield's sexual proclivities, Nisbett was seeking to press emotional buttons in the jury box. Maybe someone in here had been molested as a child. Maybe someone nursed a lifelong grudge against lesbians. Maybe someone thought the whole concept of gay marriage, or gay parenting, was such an abomination of nature that they would sympathise totally with Steve Rusher. You never knew, and for the defence it's always worth a shot.

ANCHORS AND WANKERS

The tactic of going for 'psychological anchors' in the jury box is as old as advocacy itself. As Phillip Boulten puts it, 'There's always a tension between presenting arguments in a logical and intellectually rigorous way, and spinning emotions, pulling the heartstrings. You can't ignore either.'

Even though this wasn't a sex abuse trial, bringing in the merest shadow of sexual deviance – especially where a child might be affected – was going to increase the potential for jurors to respond unpredictably. In a Canadian survey, 36 per cent of jurors said they couldn't bring an open mind to child sex abuse trials, and many more said they couldn't apply the presumption of innocence to a defendant in such a trial. Lorana Bartels's study of NSW prosecutors found that the prosecutors believed 47 per cent of hung juries occurred in child sexual assault and sexual assault cases. While Terri Maxfield wasn't the defendant in this trial, by hovering over these deep emotional buttons we all have, the defence was blatantly trying to sway our focus from the real accused.

Lawyers love telling stories of how personalities can override evidence in jury sex trials:

> *I had a case where the accused said he was going to kill the man who was sleeping with his wife. The jurors took his side, because he was clearly a nice man. His second wife had just died of cancer. They were in tears throughout the trial. Technically, I suppose he might have been guilty of manslaughter, but they acquitted him on self-defence. Some of them hugged him later. I think they probably got it entirely right.*

> *There was an article written by an ex-juror in a rape case. The complainant and accused lived in the same block. The man got in through the milk delivery hatch. The jury hung. Those who voted for an acquittal considered the man and woman were having an affair – even though that never came up in the trial.*

What those jurors had enacted was a brand of 'jury equity', or taking the law into their own hands because they carried some fundamental idea of justice that is particularly potent in, but not exclusive to, sexual assault trials. The 2001 NSW study of the effect of publicity on jurors found that 'generic publicity' can be more influential than publicity specific to a trial. Jurors can easily discard newspaper reports on their trial, because they know the facts more closely than a newspaper report, but they can't as easily negate the type of publicity that is in the very air they breathe. Defence lawyers (the study found) had a bad time because they are portrayed negatively in TV drama; same with accused heroin traffickers and accused corrupt cops. A judge told the authors:

> *If it were a drug case I might say, 'If you've got strong views about drugs, you should let me know now.' I tell them that they won't be automatically discharged and that they might be required to serve somewhere else, so it's not a way of getting out of jury service.*

Similarly, race is a powerful 'psychological anchor'. A barrister told the NSW study:

> *I believe that juries in [country town X] are too ready to convict black people because there is continual publicity about the strife created in town by bad relations between blacks and whites . . . Sometimes I've referred to the racial characteristics of my client in an attempt to point out how he or she may be disadvantaged by publicity, but this is a risky tactic. It can easily backfire on you.*

In courtroom dramas, much is made of the emotional pliability of juries. In *A Civil Action*, John Travolta plays a plaintiff lawyer specialising in insurance damages claims. In the opening scene, Travolta wheels the paralysed victim into court, helps him drink, sits him up, all in front of the jury. The insurance company's lawyers scan juror reactions. As the first juror starts weeping, the insurance lawyer offers $1.2 million. Travolta shakes his head. As more jurors cry, the offer goes up to $1.5 million, and finally $2 million, before Travolta agrees to settle. He's won, using the jury's emotions, without even starting the trial.

In the made-for-video drama *We The Jury*, Lauren Hutton plays a television presenter accused of murdering her philandering husband. She admits to killing him, but pleads extenuating circumstances that bring out the gender-based psychological anchors among jurors. A man says, 'If we let her off for shooting her husband when he's getting a bit on the side, I'd better move to another country.' But a woman counters, 'You gotta ask what you'd do if your husband was running around. I'd do it in a shot, and I say all power to her.'

Lest this be taken as movieland hooey, the emotional breadth (or narrowness) of the jury is one of its defining real-world traits, as Jeffrey Abramson recalls from his early days in the law when a trial lawyer went into the judge's chambers and put a cogent argument in his client's favour.

> *When the lawyer finished the judge focused a knowing glance on him and said simply, 'But you know if this case ever goes to a jury, you'll lose.' A short time later, the client agreed to settle . . . Evidently, the law was one thing and jury justice was another; I remember being outraged by the difference. In my law school, there were no courses on jury forecasting. In fact, there were no courses on the jury at all. If juries introduced a disturbance into the legal system such that verdicts were not predictable from the law, then that disturbance was a proper study for psychology but not for law school courses. I was therefore able to graduate from law school and pass the bar examination without once having considered the role of the jury in our legal system.*

Is this a good thing or a bad thing? For Abramson, ultimately, it was the strongest reason to believe in the jury system:

> *To resent the intrusion of such popular conceptions of justice into the judicial process now strikes me as a resentment against democracy. In a democracy, the legitimacy of the law depends on acceptance by the people. And the jury today remains our best tool for ensuring that the law is being applied in a way that wins the people's consent.*

Be that as it may, the researching and exploitation of 'psychological anchors' in America is both sophisticated and costly. The 1955 Chicago Jury Project surveyed judges on what emotional factors swung juries to acquit. The highest factor was the accused's youth (47 cases), the accused's illness or disability (24), the accused's family's testimony or presence (23), the accused's physical attractiveness (23), the accused being a woman, a mother or a widow (22), the accused being a serviceman or veteran (20), the accused being old (12), a policeman (12) or emotionally repentant (10). Bear in mind, though, that these were just the judges' impressions.

American research quoted by the New Zealand jury study said:

> *If jurors like the defendant, this may predispose them to acquit; Physical attractiveness (of witnesses or counsel) is generally an asset . . . ; Authoritarian jurors appear to be most heavily influenced by the similarity of the defendant to themselves. If defendants have different values to the jurors, they will be judged more harshly; Jurors who assume responsibility for their own actions may be more punitive than those who attribute the cause of events to external factors; Jurors who wish to please the judge may be influenced by the judge's demeanour, and may attempt to decide the case in the direction in which they perceive the judge to be moving.*

A pioneer of the multimillion-dollar jury consultancy business, Donald Vinson, taught advocacy as a sub-branch of market research and advertising. He urged lawyers not to try to change jurors' minds through facts and argument, but rather 'anticipate which of the jurors' basic beliefs are consistent with, and which conflict with, various views of the case. The lawyer should adopt a view linked to the jurors' attitudes . . . consistent with what the jurors already believe.'

The lawyer's work, then, should be like the advertiser's: provide the target audience (the jury) with a craving (to give a favourable verdict).

This is easier said than done, and could be described as just a new-fangled way of stating an old principle. But in America, the analogy with advertising goes deeper, because lawyers will also do their own market research.

In an antitrust suit in 1977, IBM recruited a focus group to act as a shadow jury before whom the lawyers rehearsed their arguments. The mock jurors were then paid to sit in on the actual proceedings every day and report their reactions to the IBM lawyers. These nightly debriefings enabled the IBM team to tailor the next day's cross-examination to revise their presentations.

In 1980, antitrust lawyers representing telecommunications giant MCI in a case against AT&T did the same, testing their arguments before a mock jury through one-way glass. The key question was whether or not to specify the damages sought. First the lawyers specified US$100 million against AT&T. The mock jury awarded exactly US$100 million. Next night, with a new mock jury, the lawyers tried mentioning no dollar amount. The second mock jury awarded US$900 million. When it came to the case, then, the MCI lawyers specified no amount and the jury awarded $600 million. (It came to little: ultimately an appeals court overturned the $600 million award as excessive, and a second trial jury awarded $37.8 million.)

By raising the spectre of Terri Maxfield as a corrupting influence over a vulnerable young boy, was the defence hitting our 'psychological anchors'? This would depend on what kind of people we were. But the appeal to emotion made even more of a mockery of the peremptory challenge on day one. How can lawyers spot a juror so traumatised by the idea of a lesbian household that they are prepared to (a) react in Rusher's favour and (b) sway the jury in the same direction? How can they spot a juror who's a David Hasselhoff fan and therefore could never put Steve Rusher in jail?

That's the thing – they can't see our psychological buttons. And even if they could, would it do them any good? Possibly not. Jurors are swayed by their emotions, but, as the 2001 NSW jury survey found, most jurors' sense of responsibility will override even the most powerful sympathies:

> *[Jurors said the accused] was very, very charming and smiled at and made flirtatious eye-contact with some women jurors during the trial. Indeed, some of the male respondents in that trial also expressed the opinion that the accused was a likeable man. The accused's charm did not win him a 'not guilty' verdict, but the jurors definitely expressed some minor regret that such a nice bloke was involved in such a terrible crime and that they had no choice other than to find him guilty.*

After Terri Maxfield's testimony, we filed back into the jury room. The Retired Gent was still muttering about how Fiona had 'better get out of that relationship'. We sat around, and our Christian Mother, looking up from the paperback Seventh-Day Adventist tract she'd brought in to read, suggested that if we were going to be spending so much time together we should all bring in family photos. She might have wanted to offer, or seek, subliminal reassurance: let's all remind ourselves of the purity of the mother–father nuclear family. There was talk of bringing in games, and packs of cards. The Mechanic promised he was a 'mean Scrabble player'. The Old Hand replied: 'I play a lot of Scrabble, and I never lose.' (The spectre of a grudge match must have put everyone off, because Scrabble was never to make its appearance.)

After Terri's cross-examination, we were out of the court for more than a day. As in airports, when nobody explains flight delays until afterwards, in the jury room no-one gives you any idea of when you might be back in court. An apologetic sheriff's officer poked his head in to ask if we were all right, but could give us no answers on when we'd be needed. Sheriff's officers are not allowed to discuss cases with jurors. Ours complied strictly, though there was a case where a sheriff's officer was suspected of trying to sway a jury to acquit an accused cannabis dealer. The sheriff's officer himself was later charged with cultivating cannabis.

Someone suggested Hangman, which set off a burst of laughter. The Stickybeak tested the group with a pop quiz from one of the women's magazines that had been left on the side table. It turned out that Friday Night, who barely said a word otherwise, was the pop quiz whiz. This day she was wearing a jade butterfly clasp in her flaming red hair and a tight lime-green turtleneck. Borderline decided to try his luck chatting her up. He rocked back in his chair, arms folded like a middle-aged popinjay, and told her how much he enjoyed his 'profession', and how working in the wine business had given him a great education in how to get drunk with dignity. I admired his pluck. But before he could get too far, Friday Night leapt for cover into her *Who Weekly*.

Shut The Gate, the muscular Italian who wore perforated athletic shirts and was proud to tell us about the 'Westminster system', had gone quiet for a while, obviously mulling something over.

During a rare moment of silence, he took a deep breath and said: 'I have a question for the ladies in the room. I'm just asking this for my own curiosity, so I hope yous don't take it the wrong way. Okay? Um, when Fiona says she had, like, "difficulties", like, having sex after childbirth, what's that mean?'

We all looked at Shut The Gate. He'd been married since he was 19, to 'a good Calabrian chicky'. Now she was pregnant. He looked around at the four 'ladies'. Finally, the Stickybeak broke the silence:

'Tearing.'

'Oh,' said Shut The Gate, blinking hard. He waited for more, but nothing came. 'Right.'

What kind of people are on juries? Intuition and jury critics tell us that only the unemployed, the retired, housewives and bored unskilled workers will have the time or dimwittedness to sit on juries. But it just isn't so. We had three retirees, one volunteer worker, a housewife, a student, a customer service representative, a mechanic, a journalist, a vigneron-cum-bottle shop worker, a storeman, and one, X-Files, of unknown occupation. Eight men, four women. Age range 19 to 67. Mostly Anglo-Australian, but one Italian and one Swiss-German. One was soon to tell us about having been adopted. Five were married, seven unmarried. Five or six had tertiary education. Were we stupid or smart? In Glanville Williams's terms, we were probably the standard 'twelve people of average ignorance'. We weren't the dregs that jury critics make of us, we weren't over-burdened with the unemployed and the unemployable. Nor are most juries. The 2001 NSW jury survey found that of 480 jurors, only 22 per cent were aged 56 and over, only 4 per cent were unemployed and 4 per cent retired. Six per cent were students, 7 per cent housewives. Sixty-three per cent had a tertiary education (and in any case, education was not found to be a significant factor in jury deliberations), and one in four earned more than $50,000 a year. One respondent to that study, who had served on juries over many years, commented that a greater community cross-section was represented now than in the past. The 1994 study of NSW juries said the average age of jurors was 34 and education levels were marginally higher than for the general population. The gender mix was 4:8 or better in nearly all cases, and a 6:6 gender split was the most common. The only significantly under-represented groups in both studies were the unemployed and men aged 18-30, which is unfortunate because both groups are over-represented among criminal defendants.

What we did have in common was a thorough unfamiliarity with court procedures and a certain timidity in the face of the court, which added up to an ignorance of our rights and powers as jurors. I buried myself in the book I was reading, but when you read a book in groups like this, paranoia can set in. You worry they'll think you're a snob. (I wasn't being a snob – I just wanted to read.) You worry they'll ignore you when your turn comes to speak. But something was bugging me, so I spoke up.

'I wonder if we can ask the judge a question,' I said to Storeman Foreman.

'What's that, Mal?'

'I don't know about the rest of you, but the sound of the judge tap-tapping away is really getting on my nerves. Does anyone agree?'

Everyone agreed. But everyone also said that we couldn't dare send him a note. He was the judge, wasn't he?

'I don't want to get him offside,' I said. 'But if we just ask him to move his microphone away from the laptop, we won't hear it on the speakers in the box.'

'That noise is really giving me the shits,' Friday Night added in support.

'I dunno, Mal,' the Retired Gent said. 'It's a bit cheeky asking the judge!'

But I pushed it through. He's the judge, sure, but he still puts his pants on one leg at a time. I've met judges. Most of them seem nice people, reassuringly dull.

Emboldened, the Mechanic piped up: 'Well, my chair's stuck, too. I wouldn't mind seeing if they could get it fixed. Is that something we can ask the judge?'

I looked at Storeman Foreman: 'No harm giving it a go. The microphone and the chair.'

'Really?' He looked as if I'd suggested an armed uprising, with him nominated as Braveheart in the front line.

'What's the worst he can do? Say no?'

Reluctantly, Storeman Foreman wrote the note. The next time we were in court – as it turned out, for another short flurry before being sent out again – Storeman Foreman had the note passed to the judge. We all watched the ghost of a smile play on the judge's otherwise firm-set lips.

He addressed the lawyers, as his regulations, or bench book, instructed him: 'Gentlemen, I have two questions here from the jury. The first is, could I please turn my microphone away from my keyboard because the sound of my typing is distracting them? The second is, is there any way we can have the right-hand chair in the front row looked at, as it is stuck? Ladies and gentlemen of the jury, the answer to your first question is yes. The answer to your second question is, this is the District Court. However, I shall see what I can do.'

He turned his microphone away from his laptop. The sound of scuttling vermin distracted us no longer.

Jurors' rights one, intimidation nil.

The only problem was, now we couldn't hear him very well. Next time we were out, we'd have to write another message telling him he'd gone too far, and could he move the microphone back a little.

Chapter Seven

Let Them Eat Fruit: How Juries Subsist

What really makes me mad is that right now the Judge and all the lawyers and their clients and the witnesses and the clerks and the spectators and everybody else involved with this trial are sitting down to a nice lunch in a nice restaurant with real plates and real glasses and forks that don't snap in two. And they're ordering good food from a thick menu. That's what makes me mad. And we, the jurors, the most important people of the whole damned trial, we're stuck here like first-graders waiting to be fed our cookies and lemonade.
– Jury leader Nicholas Easter
in John Grisham's *The Runaway Jury*

*The hungry judges soon the sentence sign
And wretches hang that jurymen may dine.*
– Alexander Pope, *The Rape of the Lock*

One of my favourite jury stories comes from a friend, John, who served on three juries in another State, where it was customary for a carton of beer to be delivered every lunchtime at a ration of one bottle per juror.

All three of John's jury appearances were minor crime trials lasting days rather than weeks. On the first two, he was foreman, but he stepped aside on the last, which was a petty theft trial against a young Aboriginal man. When the jury retired to deliberate, there was little discussion – the foreman was talking football with a few others. John interrupted them to ask if they shouldn't start their deliberations.

'Why bother?' the foreman replied. 'We all know he's guilty. We just have to hang around in here for a while, then go back into court and put him away.'

John asked for a vote. It was 10–2 for guilty. The two holdouts were John and an old army veteran who figured most, if not all, police were fascists and he'd never believe their evidence.

But the task for John was an uphill one. Most of the jury would not countenance an acquittal of an Aboriginal accused. So John got up and looked in the fridge. He turned back to the jury and made the telling speech: 'They've been delivering beer to us all week. Not all of us drink, so there's quite a few left over. Plus, they'll be bringing in a case a day. Now, I've got nothing else to do. I'm happy to sit here and drink as much beer as I feel like until you lot agree on a not-guilty verdict.'

Something about John must have told them he could drink beer for a long time. Shortly after, the vote was 12–0 for an acquittal.

Mmmm, beer. Since my jury service, I've become greatly interested in the peripheral conditions of different jury rooms – precisely because they're not peripheral at all. Every aspect of the environment, from the courtroom to the jury room, shapes the way jurors make their decisions.

Food has long had a key influence on juries. Until 1870, English juries were starved and left without fire while deliberating, so they wouldn't be exposed to bribery or poison, and so they'd get on with it. An indecisive 1688 libel jury was left to deliberate all night without food and water. In the morning, water bowls were sent for them to wash their faces. They drank it instead. A juror named Austin held out, saying: 'Look at me. I am the largest and strongest of the 12; and before I find such a petition as this to be a libel, here I will stay until I am no bigger than a tobacco pipe.' There were some records of 'boot-eaters', or jurors who would 'eat the leather of their boots before agreeing to a verdict favoured by the remainder of a jury'. By the 19th century, jurors were caught smuggling in food, which caused verdicts to be overturned. When in 1870 jurors were finally allowed fire and food, they had to pay for it.

In *Joh's Jury*, the Bjelke-Petersen jurors can be seen drinking beer every lunchtime. Their jury room has windows (luxury!) and they are allowed to go to a separate cafeteria for lunch (those lucky, lucky bastards). In *12 Angry Men*, the steamy summer weather plays such a vital symbolic role in the plot – the storm breaks just as the critical mass of jurors swings to Henry Fonda's side – only because their jury room has windows letting the heat and rain inside.

The windowless, spartan room in which we were placed is more typical. The New Zealand jury project found that in 29 of 47 cases one or more jurors:

> *... complained that the jury room was cramped, claustrophobic, and/or lacking in natural light. In three cases, jurors complained of extremes of temperature and a lack of air-conditioning. In five cases, adverse comments were made on the layout of the room and inadequate furnishings; for example, a table with 12 chairs did not enable jurors to move around, take time out or defuse tension ... Tempers frayed, people developed headaches, and concentration lapsed. In a few cases, it was suggested that conditions in the jury room contributed to compromise verdicts or increased the pressure on dissenting jurors to change their minds.*

The authors went on to state:

> *Jurors who are thirsty, hot, tired and embarrassed about going to the toilet are unlikely to do their best, either in court or during deliberations. In long or difficult trials, in particular, poor facilities can not only distract jurors but also exacerbate conflicts between them and increase the pressures faced by dissenters. Just as significantly, the inadequacy of the facilities is liable to be seen by some as an indication of the justice system's lack of respect and appreciation for them and their role.*

Conditions in the jury room itself are just one stress on the juror's life. The daily routine is altogether new and, while not inherently onerous, reminds jurors that they are leading a completely different life now.

We had to turn up at the Downing Centre at 9.30am daily for a court commencement at 10.00am. We were to arrive not at the courthouse entrance but at another door down the quiet side of Castlereagh Street, near the back of the great concrete kitchen appliance known as the Masonic Centre. To identify ourselves, we had to flash our clip-on juror badges, which we'd been given on the first day and were constantly reminded not to keep wearing when we left the court and travelled home.

At the entrance, we had to hand in our mobile phones or anything else that didn't pass through the X-ray security system. In NSW in 2004, items picked up at security included 'knuckle-dusters, spear guns, Mace, hammers, knives, horseshoes and even a bottle of petrol', according to the Sheriff's Office. One man brought his guard dog (he agreed to tie it up in a carpark). 'Sometimes,' *The Sydney Morning Herald* reported, the confiscations 'end up doing the owners a favour. Like the woman who was surprised there was a blanket ban on aerosol cans but thankful she did not get the chance to use the insect spray on her hair.'

After we were X-rayed on arrival, we had to wait until a certain convenient number of other jurors from other cases had arrived – there are several jury trials running in the centre at any one time – and a sheriff's officer would escort us to the floor where our jury rooms were located. There we'd be handed over to another sheriff's officer who would take our mobile phones – all phone calls were banned – and tick off our attendance.

Our jury arrived in a more or less routine order. Some had further to travel than others, and were locked into train schedules. The Retired Gent and the Old Hand bonded over the purchase of weekly tickets and train travel from the southern suburbs. Likewise, Storeman Foreman and Shut The Gate caught the train home together.

I had a shorter distance to travel, and usually I'd arrive about five minutes late. Invariably I was the second-last to arrive. The only one who came after me – about 15 minutes late – was X-Files. Some of us began to take bets on what time he'd get in. It was a major scandal one day when he arrived on time and our Christian Mother was late.

When I entered the room, jurors would be chatting, reading the papers, or making tea or coffee. They'd greet me with a 'Hi, Mal!' I'd become Mal in the jury room, something I never am anywhere else.

As the days passed, I relaxed more with the other jurors. Sometimes I participated in the conversation, and sometimes dived into a book. My own reading habit licensed Friday Night to bring in a Marian Keyes novel. Our Christian Mother sometimes read her religious tracts, the Mechanic read his *Herald*, the Retired Gent his *Daily Telegraph*, and the Stickybeak brought in a Jumbo Crossword.

The very act of entering the jury room can be disorienting, a fact recognised by screenwriter Reginald Rose in *12 Angry Men* when, as the jurors walk in, the door is locked behind them.

Jack Klugman (ill-at-ease): *I never knew they locked the door.*

Ed Begley: *Sure they lock the door. What did you think?*
Klugman: *I don't know, it just never occurred to me.*

They never locked the door on us, but nor were we allowed to walk so much as down the corridor. If we wanted to communicate with anyone outside that room during the Rusher trial, we had to press a buzzer to call a sheriff's officer.

Most days our time in court would fail to start at 10.00am. On a good day, it was 10.15. Impatient as I was to get on with it, I couldn't believe a court couldn't get its act together by 10.00am. Possibly there were good reasons for these delays, but from the darkness of the jury room, of course, you can't see them.

Once in court, there would be a 20-minute morning tea break at 11.30 that rarely went for less than half an hour, lunch at 1.00–2.00pm but usually until 2.30pm, and then the judge would draw stumps by 4.00pm. I don't think we served our full four-and-a-half-hour day in court once. On Fridays, the judge would give us the afternoon off, like a teacher blessing us with an early mark.

How much were we paid? For the first five days, our jury allowance, paid by a cheque in the mail, was about $75 a day. For the next five days, it was $85. From day ten onwards, it was about $95, plus a travel allowance calibrated to our address. For the month-long trial we were paid almost $2,000 each.

Australian law stops employers from punishing you, in any way, if you do jury service. Many let you pocket the allowance and top you up for your full wage; if your employer is paying you in full, you forgo the court's allowance. For those who have no employer, our jury allowances are not too bad by world standards. In America, jury allowances range from $5 to $40 a day.

It was alarming to learn in 2005 that the Australian Government intended to take jury service provisions out of the federal awards system. This means employers won't be bound to compensate workers who go on juries. Politicians' contempt for jury duty has rarely been so brazen.

The New Zealand jury project found that employment and financial issues were the greatest inconvenience for jurors, and in most trials at least one juror had some kind of problem with work:

> *These 'problems' varied in seriousness . . . Employers could get 'tetchy' about the uncertainty of whether their employee would be on a jury that day. In longer trials employers could be described as 'becoming aggro'. Some jurors worried about their work during the trial, or were concerned about it building up because they would not or could not be replaced.*

Jurors did not know that they could ask for their allowance to be raised if they faced hardship as a result of jury duty. Some had to work before and after court, some had employers who required them to make up for lost time, self-employed jurors lost money, and none was compensated for lost overtime.

It's easy to forget that every juror has an outside life, as an American juror, Johnathan M. Carter, realised when one of his jury group in a 1998 murder trial in Wilmington, Delaware, was suddenly released without explanation:

> *As I wondered why, I realised that I was a single man, no family to take care of, and most of my time was spent thinking about what was going on in the courtroom. Imagine having a wife and children to take care of, and thinking the same way I was. It would be possible to become emotionally distant to a wife and children.*

In his self-published book *Johnny Nine*, Carter is a keen observer of every nuance affecting juror conditions. Most American jury rooms don't even have toilets, so a juror must ask a bailiff's officer for permission.

'That is a strange situation for adults to be in,' says Carter, 'having to signal someone that one has to go to the bathroom.'

Juror deprivation is common around the world. Carter was curious and frustrated about delays in court, and in the jury room hung on the faint ringing of the bell in the corridor which may have been the court calling the sheriff's officer to call the jurors back in. In our case, every time that bell rang, the Retired Gent would give a start and say: 'Here we go!'

Most often, it was a false alarm. It was always frustrating. I began to speculate, like Carter, that they had forgotten about us.

Cabin fever starts to set in. During Carter's six-month trial, jurors (including Carter) fell sick, and a general sense of madness took hold. As he recalls:

> *Out in the narrow, yellow corridor I heard Dan [another juror] say something about hyperventilating, so at least the majority of us were experiencing the same thing.*
> *I suppose there is some kind of twisted comfort to take in the knowledge that I was not suffering alone. Still, one cannot help but wonder at what point the first juror will be hauled out, screaming and drooling in a straitjacket, and when the others will follow.*

But when it comes to food and drink, I envy Carter. Until deliberations start, American juries are allowed to go outside for lunch. We had to stay inside for lunch. The food we ate conformed to a pattern just as strict as the jury allowance. For the first five days, it was a tray of triangular 'gourmet' sandwiches. They weren't too bad until day three or four, when we realised they would always be the same sandwiches from this day to kingdom come. By day six, we were served hot meals. Some of the jurors liked the food, and some would just peck. One day they'd be cooked by someone with rudimentary knowledge of the culinary arts, and the next day they'd seem to come straight from the Long Bay slophouse. You couldn't predict anything, except that they'd be heavy and unhealthy. By the third day of this, some of us were longing for the return of the sandwiches.

This may not seem a big deal, but what bugged us was how the food symbolised the court's overall treatment of jurors. An American juror, Mara Taub, recalls:

> *From time to time we were told how important we were, but our treatment did not reflect that. We were controlled, isolated and uninformed. Nothing in our treatment indicated trust in or respect for us. Only lip service was paid to our physical comfort and convenience. The judge was concerned that we like the pastry left every morning in the jury room. But when we mentioned that we would like something healthier, it was explained to us very firmly by the courtroom deputy that the court had a contract with a bakery and that was what we would get. We were welcome to bring our own.*

A judge told the 1994 NSW jury survey: 'I am of the view that jurors and jury panels should be waited on hand and foot.' Another judge in that survey went to greater length:

> *I am not suggesting that jurors should receive a multi-course à la carte meal provided by one of the leading chefs in Sydney. I do think, however, that the fare which they are normally served is bland, unappetising, unimaginative and not at all appropriate for people who have been plucked from their ordinary homes and occupations ... The whole question of the daily accommodation through a trial, particularly throughout a long jury trial, needs urgent revision. It is entirely exceptional, in my experience, to get these days a jury, all of whose members*

> *are of the same gender. This entails at least I should have thought a rethinking of such basic matters as toilet accommodation and the like . . . The whole physical disposition of the normal jury room is . . . unwelcoming, uncomfortable and positively intimidating to most jurors, especially if they are first time jurors. It is not at all unusual to find a jury room that is a totally enclosed and windowless space. Such jury rooms are, in my opinion, in the direct tradition of the Black Hole of Calcutta, and it is not only inconsiderate but it is positively insulting to ordinary lay persons to confine them in such a fashion. Every jury room should be required to have, as an absolute minimum, access to natural light and fresh air.*

It's nice to hear judges expressing their concern, but their motives may not always be purely neutral. Malcolm Ramage QC sees such speeches as dishonest judicial pandering: 'There's a judge who's always asking the jurors if they're comfortable, and how's their food, and all of this – but he's not going to do anything about it – he's just manoeuvring to appear to be on their side.'

The Downing Centre is notorious. The 1994 NSW jury study found:

> *Several respondents complained that the air-conditioning in the Downing Centre courts was either too hot or too cold, and therefore interfered with their concentration. Some said that the seats in the jury box were too hard. Others complained about the absence of windows and natural light in the deliberation room.*

Of all NSW courts, the Downing Centre got the lowest juror satisfaction rating (35 per cent). Only 42 per cent rated the food as 'good'.

Professor Warren Young, the leader of the New Zealand jury project, discovered for himself how jurors are treated as second-class citizens when, one day, he sat in the jury box. When the judge called for water to be served in court, glasses were filled and passed to the judge, his associate, the court workers, the sheriff's officers, the lawyers, the defendant, the witness and Young himself – but not to the jury.

Our Christian Mother decided to take matters into her own hands. She suffered from food allergies, and asked for a palatable vegetarian option. The vegetarian option she was given was roast beef and vegies minus the roast beef. So she brought salad and fruit for herself, and when she noticed others salivating she brought in enormous trays of fresh fruit. In a giant circular Tupperware container, she brought cut-up watermelon, kiwifruit, mangoes, pineapple, rockmelon, honeydew, oranges, pears and apples. She went to the fruit market every day and prepared this great feast for the rest of us. We pitched in with some money that she reluctantly accepted.

Her example began to prompt others to take initiatives, less wholesome perhaps, but equally welcome. On his 67th birthday, the Retired Gent brought bags of chocolates. Our Christian Mother brought in an orange cake to celebrate, even though her allergies prevented her from tasting it. I've been poking fun at her religious devotion and general naive niceness, but who knows – her fresh fruit might have been the crucial ingredient harmonising us as a team. Others brought lollies to share. We'd come a long way from not having been able to get our drink cartons open. My own birthday came up during the trial. I hate being the centre of attention and was determined not to tell anyone. But in conversation with our Christian Mother, I blurted it out somehow. She insisted on bringing a cake. I told her I'd bring one in myself. Everything was getting dangerously nice.

It wasn't, of course, because she was a woman that our Christian Mother provided for us in this way. But it's easier to imagine a woman doing this. Her provision of fruit and cakes made me feel sorry for those Australian juries, up to 1977, that didn't have women.

The jury was another area of democratic enfranchisement for which women had to fight. The English jurist Sir William Blackstone, an authority on so much else,

> *... thought it obvious that women were disqualified from jury service 'propter defectum sexus' ('on account of the defect of sex'). But the common law did impanel a 'jury of matrons' when a possible pregnancy affected an inheritance claim or the scheduling of a prisoner's execution. Loath to hang a pregnant woman, authorities turned to all-female panels to certify that the pregnancy was real rather than feigned.*

The first American jury with men and women was in Laramie, Wyoming, in 1870. But newspapers decried the appearance of women on juries, claiming that jury service took them away from their principal duty of child-rearing. One paper ran a rhyme: 'Baby, baby, don't get in a fury; Your mamma's gone to sit on the jury.'

Until 1977, women in New South Wales had to make a special application to sit on juries. Malcolm Ramage recalls that this was a good enough reason to challenge all women and have them removed:

> *The belief was that if someone desperately wanted to do jury duty, it was rarely because they were interested in principles of justice, but more likely that they had had property stolen, or were a policeman's wife, and wanted to get in there and convict someone ... When that changed, and women were on juries as often as men, we thought we'd see more acquittals. But the reverse was true. Those who had been beaten around by men all*

their lives relished the chance to be able to convict some other man.

When barristers are talking about women on juries, it's normally in the context of wondering which way they'll vote – as representatives of their sex. As we've already seen, there are conflicting homespun philosophies about which way women, as a bloc, vote in sexual assault and domestic violence cases. Federal Police officer David Laidlaw recalls 'a trial in Wollongong – a domestic dispute that ended up with slashed throats, punctured lungs, and so on. The jury hung. I heard later that the women on the jury just saw it as a domestic gone wrong, whereas the men were stronger for a conviction.'

Barrister Murugan Thangaraj says: 'I've often seen women on juries wink at the accused, as if to tell him he'll be all right. Women can show their feelings more.'

And women can intervene with their own brand of justice. American author Susan Glaspell's 1917 short story, 'A Jury of Her Peers', tells of a case where a woman was tried for strangling her husband. The jurors were taken through the couple's house looking for evidence. While the men searched in the main rooms and the cellar, the women looked in the kitchen, where they found a canary strangled in exactly the same way as the husband. It seemed proof that the accused had killed him. Yet the twist was, this man had regularly beaten his wife. The women jurors hid the canary from the men, and the battered wife was acquitted.

But do women act as women, or as jurors? As we've seen, women tend to submit to men when it comes to the choice of a foreman, although the case of Mary Timothy showed that there's no obstacle to a strong woman taking charge. It just doesn't happen as often. The historic bar on women jurors (as with women voters) rested on the assumption that women would indeed respond to the democratic challenge 'en bloc' – that they'd sway the judicial scales one way or the other, because they saw the world differently. Most of the jurisprudence on the issue comes from America, where anti-discrimination laws and constitutional insistence on equal protection have brought it to the surface. Jeffrey Abramson tells how the US Supreme Court, through a series of rulings, walked the fine line between recognising the 'sameness' and 'difference' of women. The two main arguments for including women on juries appear contradictory: on the one hand, women are no more or less intelligent or sensitive or perceptive or pro-conviction or pro-acquittal than men; and on the other, women were seen as necessary on juries because they did have something different to contribute.

The US Supreme Court trod this line delicately when it ruled on the 1943 trial of *Ballard v United States*. In *Ballard*, a mother and son were accused of mail fraud after they'd sent out deceptive religious material pleading for donations. As it happened, women formed the overwhelming majority of donors to such religious causes, and it was argued that women jurors would have a better understanding of the facts and should be specially included on that jury.

The Supreme Court said:

> *It is not enough to say that women when sitting as jurors neither act nor tend to act as a class. Men likewise do not act as a class. But, if the shoe were on the other foot, who would claim that a jury was truly representative of the community if all men were intentionally and systematically excluded from the panel? . . . To insulate the courtroom from either may not in a given case make an iota of difference. Yet a flavor, a distinct quality is lost if either sex is excluded.*

What did it mean by this 'flavor', this 'distinct quality'? How could it define this without insulting women one way or the other, either by recognising or ignoring their difference?

Abramson offers:

> I believe that the Court was trying to say that we can best understand the contribution women make as jurors by concentrating not on the act of voting but on the act of deliberating. The presence of women changes and enriches the deliberations for men and women alike. The 'subtle interplay' pushes each sex to consider facts they might have ignored in the absence of the other or to consider them from a new point of view.

Already we'd seen this in our jury – with the comforts that our Christian Mother provided, in the basic civics lesson that the Old Hand had given us, and in the Stickybeak's information that a woman might not be able to have sex after childbirth because of 'tearing'. Without that information, who knows – some of the men might have jumped to the conclusion that Fiona had chosen not to have sex with Rusher. It was not a significant fact in this trial, as things transpired, but the input of women as a counterweight to male ignorance can make all the difference. And the respect our Christian Mother had earnt for herself as fruit-provider – you never knew how important that would be with alliance-building later on.

Anyway – to settle the argument about women on juries, the reason lawyers are always surprised by women voting one way or the other is simply that women are no more predictable than men when it comes to verdicts and justice. As Abramson says:

> There is no evidence that women and men end up voting as blocs on juries. Research on gender and jury verdicts . . . establishes only two conclusions with any degree of certainty. First, women talk less frequently than men on juries. Second, female students on mock juries are more likely than male students to regard the defendant guilty in a rape case.

But overall, he finds, sex is no reliable predictor of jury voting, 'precisely because sex is only one factor among many that influence jurors'.

CHAPTER EIGHT

Undercover: 'Spike' in Silverwater

If you boiled it down, only three of the two dozen witnesses in the Steve Rusher trial were close to knowing the truth: Rusher himself, Les McAtee, and an undercover policeman known as 'Spike'. (During the trial he was known by his full undercover name, but this was later suppressed from publication.) After nearly four days' faffing about, the Crown was finally ready to present Spike.

As a cop in disguise as a waste contractor, the only problem with Spike was that he was too perfect. Built like a chunky lock forward, with a swarthy complexion and dark, distrustful eyes, head and face furred with black-grey stubble, he was the type of guy you wouldn't want to meet in a police station, let alone down a dark alley.

Still, there's something universal about policemen. American juror Graham Burnett could have been observing our man Spike when he wrote of a New York cop:

> *Many of these men share a manly density, a mass . . . [He] rolled his shoulders to settle his suit . . . [His] chest displayed the unlikely symmetry of an oil drum . . . head slumping forward on his bull neck, and his broad shoulders encroaching on his visage . . . there was a*

vulnerability about him here, in an arena where words would be the primary instrument of communication.

The Rusher indictment alleged that the offence had been committed when Steve had two meetings and two phone calls with Spike and arranged the killing of Terri and Fiona. Wearing a suit and speaking softly, Spike told us how he'd been wired up to meet Rusher. After meeting with the police officers running the Rusher investigation, Spike went to a surveillance van near the Silverwater jail and put on his wire, or listening device. It came as an earpiece with other parts concealed – the undercover cop didn't want to say too much about operational specifics, and was constantly asking the judge if he could guard his trade secrets.

We were to hear the main evidence on audio – the recorded conversations. We cleaned our earphones with alcohol swabs. The Crown tested the earphones on everyone in the court. Invariably someone's wasn't working, or the battery was flat, and the simple process of getting the jurors, lawyers, judge, judge's associate and Rusher rigged up took some time.

At around 7.00pm on the first day, Spike arrived in his car at Silverwater. He turned on his listening device and identified himself, the operation name ('Operation Wilko' – these names are randomly generated), the time, and what he was doing.

After a few minutes getting through the metal detectors, Spike came face to face with Rusher. As far as Rusher knew, Spike was connected with waste contractors Les McAtee had arranged to help 'serve documents' on Terri Maxfield and Fiona Emery.

'Welcome to the asshole of the earth,' Rusher greeted Spike in the noisy visiting area. On the tapes, Rusher's voice was cheerful but high pitched, as if nervous. After Rusher made a few genial complaints about the conditions in Silverwater, Spike asked if they could go somewhere quieter to talk. Rusher said that it was just another example of how terrible things were in there that they couldn't. There was a minute or two more of uncomfortable small talk, and then Spike said: 'So, matey, uh, what's the go?'

Rusher stammered: 'Well . . .'

Spike said: 'You know people and I know people, right, who've told me in a bit . . .'

'Yeah? Right?' Rusher spoke with a rising inflection, nervously but, through tone and, according to Spike, body language, encouraged him to go on.

'. . . bit of a roundabout way . . .'

'Right, uh-huh?' said Rusher.

'. . . through our mutual . . .'

'Yeah?'

'. . . mutual friend who knows you and me . . .'

'Right?'

'. . . this is that friend of yours.'

'Yeah?'

'Right now, as far as I'm concerned, my mate . . .'

'Mm-hm?'

'. . . and me are solid, pretty solid.'

'Right.'

'And he's quite happy, quite comfortable with your mate.'

'Great!' Rusher said.

'So if you've got any resolutions [sic] or any problems with me . . .'

'No, no problems.'

'. . . you may as well, you may as well say something now, because otherwise I don't want to waste my time, you know what I mean?'

'No, no,' Rusher said, 'I don't want to waste anybody's time.'

'All right.'

It was time for Rusher to say something. 'Hey man, it's all relaxed here.' (His tone suggested anything but. Here was the Hollywood schmooze-artist coming out.) 'We just gotta get square with everything, you know what I'm saying? And let's get this outta the way, like I said to my friend, I said, you know, we're not doing nothing illegal or nothing like that, you know what I'm saying?'

'Right.'

'It's all, like, above the line, y'know? I'm in enough trouble with the law as it is, man.'

'Sure, sure.'

'Y'see,' Rusher continued by way of explanation, 'I'm not exactly allowed to say everything that's in my heart here, like, the walls, the walls have ears . . .'

'Right.'

'Y'know, I got problems here, and we got family custody issues coming up, and I gotta get the documents served, y'know what I'm saying, the documents served and all the material I need, it's gotta be done by Friday at the latest, or even Thursday . . .'

'You would like things finalised by Friday?'

'That's when they're all comin' up from Hobart for, y'know, the court hearing.'

Having ascertained the timetable, Spike asked for descriptions of the people Rusher wanted him to 'serve papers on'. Spike said his mate – a man called 'Morgo' – was 'in Tassie, all set to go', but needed to make sure he was getting the right people. Rusher described Terri Maxfield's house, where he'd been on his earlier visit to Australia. Spike confirmed Morgo's sighting of a caravan outside the house. The cars matched up with Rusher's description. They definitely had the right house. (Terri, Fiona and SJ had actually been moved to another location, for their safety.)

Spike went on to confirm the arrangement: 'Well, mate, I suppose we're at the stage that my mate is basically waiting for a call from me.'

Rusher replied: 'Hey, I don't wanna know about it, man, you guys just do what you do.'

'And as long as I'm certain that you want them, you know, basically, put down . . .'

'Mm,' Rusher said.

'No ifs and buts here,' Spike continued. 'We don't want to do the wrong thing. So if you don't want them put down, like, put to sleep, you oughta tell me here.'

'Mm, well, those are your words,' Rusher said. 'C'mon, man, you gotta serve the documents . . .'

'I call Morgo tonight and tell him . . .'

'Uh-huh, okay . . .'

'I tell him what I just told you . . .'

'Mmm,' Rusher said.

Spike had definitely said 'put down' and 'put to sleep'. The judge had provided us with written transcripts to assist our hearing of these tapes, but told us that the tapes, not the transcripts, were the evidence. This was important to me. In a previous life, I'd worked as a subtitler for television programs, and I knew that listening to recorded words and transcribing them was not as simple as it sounded. The harder you listen to something obscure, the harder it becomes to hear it. All sorts of inaccuracies can creep in. Knowing that the transcripts had been written by law enforcement staff, I decided to keep my transcript folder shut and just listen to the tapes. I could come back and sort out any inconsistencies later.

But there was no doubting what Spike had said here. Rusher's response wasn't to correct him, or ask him what the hell he was crapping on about. Instead, Rusher just acquiesced without using the words himself. He obviously feared being taped, but he didn't fear it enough to contradict Spike. The opportunity had been there, and Rusher was clearly happy to let Spike do what was arranged.

Rusher didn't want to dwell on the action, though. He began to tell Spike about 'my history'. He said Terri Maxfield was 'a sexual deviant and I'd never leave my son with a pair of dykes, you know, all this gay marriage shit, it's not what a boy needs in his life.' Rusher told Spike about his flight from the USA, with SJ, under false passports to 'serve papers' on Terri Maxfield, but now, having been incarcerated for more than two months, he needed help.

'Your hands are tied,' Spike said. 'You need a good Samaritan.'
'Man, I need a good loyal friend,' Rusher replied.
'Morgo and I hopefully are your friends.'
'Hey, man, this gay marriage shit . . .'
'I've got a boy too. Boy needs a dad in his life.'
Spike described his mate, Morgo, in Hobart – 'been around, square deal, you know, done a bit of time, knows what he's doing.' Spike said that Morgo trusted Les McAtee 'with his life, so we know, we know you're okay with all this.'

After this second agreement of trust, the undercover cop said: 'So who do you want put down, two or one?'

Rusher said: 'Man, you know, it's like we say in the States, one man's opportunity is another man's, you know . . .'

'I, I'm not quite with you, mate.'

'Hey dude. If there's one it's one, and if there's two, you know, it's gotta be two. I mean, these women are planning to get married, like in a church! It's like, it takes two.'

'So you want two if possible?'

'Takes two to tango.'

Shortly after, Spike grew a little frustrated with Rusher's roundabout, semi-coded way of speaking. (As a policeman, he'd certainly have liked Rusher to be more candid, but also as a purported thug, he tried to urge Rusher to be clear on what he wanted.)

But Rusher complained: 'Man, it's not like I can say what I want.'

'Sure,' Spike said.

'Because, you know, I mean, you might be, like, FBI or something, you know what I'm saying?'

(Through this passage, Rusher often broke out into high-pitched, nervous, shrieking laughter.) Spike played it straight: 'That cuts both ways, too, both ways, I mean, I've got to be careful with you, I mean, it's only through our friends that we think we know who each other is.'

Rusher replied: 'Reminds me of negotiating with studios back in Hollywood. We're both out on the same limb.'

Some more cagey talk ensued, and then Rusher took up the thread again.

'In a perfect world,' he said, 'I'd say we gotta serve documents on these two women . . . but if I had a choice of one or the other, I mean, if you can only get one, it's the American.'

'Fiona,' Spike said.

'The American. The thin one. The one who doesn't look like a bull dyke.'

Having clarified the commission – 'serve documents' on Terri and Fiona if possible, but if it had to be one, only Fiona – Spike said he was concerned about SJ's welfare, because the little boy might be with Fiona when the 'papers are served'. So Spike got Rusher to describe Fiona in detail. Rusher said she was '5'4", no chest, droopy ass', but the giveaway was that she always had the boy with her.

'Like holding her hand?'

'Damn straight.'

'Right.'

'Damn straight,' Rusher repeated. 'So she's coming up here on Thursday.'

'Yeah, okay, that's all right, that's no problem,' Spike said. 'As I said, Morgo's all teed up, so . . .'

'Yeah.'

'. . . it's just waiting for me to call him.'

'Right,' Rusher said.

'And me . . .'

'Mm-hm?'

'. . . me being okay with that and then, um . . .'

'Cool!'

'. . . and then he goes and serves the papers, like, says nightie-night.'

'You gotta positively visualise it,' Rusher said.

'So all right,' Spike said. 'If you're okay with all that.'

Spike then asked for money upfront. He nominated a price of

'30 for the two'. Fifteen for Fiona, and another 15 'if the opportunity presents' for Terri Maxfield. Rusher said Les McAtee would arrange the payments.

Rusher was still treating Spike with great suspicion. Spike said: 'My foot's gone to sleep. It's got pins and needles.'

Rusher stuttered, and shrieked nervously: 'Is that a signal to the feds?'

'Eh?'

'A sign to the feds?' Rusher repeated, emitting a high-pitched laugh.

Spike laughed uneasily. For a second he must have seen Operation Wilko swirling down the plug-hole. 'No, mate, um, all right,' he said, realising Rusher was only joking.

'So,' Rusher said to put him at ease again, 'I'll be phoning our mutual buddy tonight.'

Spike reiterated Morgo's trust in Les McAtee, confirming that he would do the job. Rusher offered that if there was a problem with the money at Les's end, he'd arrange a withdrawal from his own funds at Silverwater.

Then Spike asked if Rusher wanted 'any, you know, above and beyond the expected, you know, inconvenience involved'.

'Listen,' Rusher said, 'my boy needs a dad. He doesn't need this perverse women's thing going on all day. I just need the documents served.'

'Right,' Spike replied.

'That's all I'm interested in.'

'It doesn't matter what type, which way it goes, with the papers?' Spike said. 'Like, a car accident, or a fire, or something we get into, you know, the food . . .'

'As long as it's legal.'

'Eh?'

'Nothing illegal, c'mon, man.'

'Oh. Right. I'm with you now.'

'Just the papers, get the job done, I don't care about anything else.'

Spike then reconfirmed descriptions of Fiona and Terri, saying he wanted to be sure Morgo didn't go for the wrong people or hurt the little boy. After which, Spike said: 'Have you thought about when these papers are served, right?'

'Mm?'

'That there could be, you know, someone might come to you here and ask questions.'

'Yeah, I'm the ex, right, the ex is always the first suspect,' Rusher said. 'I've been in TV long enough to know that.'

'What'll you say?'

'I'm in here! How can I have done it?'

'Yeah, sure,' Spike said, 'but there's visitor records. And I'm one person they will want to speak to. So if anything tracks back to any money changing hands or whatever, I've got to have some pretty good answer –'

Rusher interrupted him, helping him out: 'I'm commissioning you to serve papers, some legal stuff, for my court case. That's why I'm paying you, to serve legal papers so that my son can have a father. That's why you're visiting me. Because you're a father too, and, ah, you know how it is, and you share my views on, like, gay marriage and all.'

'The cops will do background checks on me,' Spike said.

Rusher jumped in: 'This is all about morals, man, a moral world for our children. Like, we know what this bull dyke has done, she cruises, she's got completely screwy ideas on the world, she doesn't believe in the family, y'know, and this is what I'm saying. You're here to help me because you share my, my views and you care about what happens to my boy, because a father-son bond, y'know, coz you're a dad too, you know how important this is to all of us.'

This apparently satisfied Spike. He offered Rusher his mobile phone number, but Rusher refused.

'I don't wanna know, dude, I mean, nice to meet you and all, but I could care less.'

'Sweet, fine, that's good . . . Cover my tracks . . .'

Again they discussed the money for 'two'. Spike said he wanted to be sure the money was paid.

'Listen, I've had problems before, in Hollywood, I know how things work,' Rusher said. 'If I screw up you'll kill me, right? That's what you do. Fine, that's my problem . . . I can handle it.'

On this savoury note, they farewelled each other, Spike promising to call, urging Rusher to get him the money, and Rusher again assuring him that Les McAtee would personally guarantee it.

'See you, mate,' Spike said.

For what was a key piece of evidence, the first Spike–Rusher conversation left me hungry for context. I could see, if 'serving documents' was a code for killing people, that the Crown story made sense. Rusher had been cagey, but had given enough away – or as much as you would give away if you were in his situation, meeting someone you've never met, in an insecure environment, to arrange such a thing. Yes, the Crown story made sense – and he'd definitely said that 'in a perfect world', he wanted the 'papers served' on both Terri and Fiona. We did have to keep both charges in mind.

But on its own, this tape didn't seem enough. What if there had been a terrible misunderstanding between Rusher and Les? What if Rusher seriously wanted Spike and Morgo to 'serve documents' and nothing more, and Les had mistaken this to mean a contract killing? Rusher did want to see Terri and Fiona hurt in the Family Court proceedings – he was desperate to prevent SJ living with Fiona and Terri – but he never actually said he wanted her killed. He repeated that he wanted everything done 'legally'.

There were problems for Rusher, though. If he wanted everything done 'legally', why did he have to keep stressing the possibility that they were being taped? Why did he flip out, nervously, about Spike 'sending a message to the feds'? If he was paying Spike for legal services, why did they discuss what they'd do if the police came knocking? Why would the police need to come knocking, if nothing illegal was being done? And why would he need to pay '15 to 30' for the serving of legal documents?

We were given a break after hearing this long and crucial tape.

More than anything, it was a fascinating insight into the lives of others. Whether Rusher was arranging a murder or something else, a conversation between a kidnapper and an undercover cop in Silverwater was not the kind of thing we jurors heard every day. Which is, for many, the prime attraction of courthouse stories: you are allowed to peep through the keyhole onto another side of life.

After a few heavy sighs, shaken heads and picking of ears, we 12 voyeurs filed back into the court to hear more. The cleaning of the earphones and leaving them on our seats meant that now we'd be sticking to our places. I was in the middle of the back row. Friday Night was on my left, dashing Borderline's chances of securing a regular spot by her side. He did ask me, during a break, if I minded swapping. I managed to convince him that his prospects were best served by playing hard to get. 'Yeah right,' he said. 'Like she's trying to "get" me.'

To my right was the Retired Gent, whom I could help with his periodic technical problems with the earphones. The back row was a good place to be, one row further from Steve Rusher. Now that we were getting to know him better, and immersing ourselves in the real nuts and bolts of the charges against him, I felt that further was better. He did, however, keep making eye contact with me.

The folder of transcripts of the tapes contained about 20 inserts, conversations between Rusher and Spike or Rusher and Les. We could see this from the front index page. The tape we'd just heard was the first recorded. The judge then instructed us to jump to insert number nine, a recording of a phone conversation between Spike and Rusher two days later, in the afternoon.

It was annoying to know that there were seven conversations between Rusher and Les McAtee between these two dates, and we weren't allowed to assess them yet. As a juror, you like to have a fluent narrative played out for you. But it would be too difficult for the court to have Les and Spike taking turns in the box, so Spike's evidence was consolidated at the one time, as would Les's be later. We'd have to formulate a full narrative once we'd heard all the evidence.

So – two days after they met, Spike called Rusher and said: 'Everything's in hand, but we've just struck a bump . . . I gave Morgo the green light, but he hasn't seen them.'

'Man, I told you they've gone,' said an audibly uptight Rusher.

'No,' Spike said, 'we've seen the dyke. But your missus Fiona and the kid aren't there.'

'They're in Sydney,' Rusher said.

'They're in Sydney?'

'Man, I *told* you. I *told* you they were coming up here.'

'Yes.'

Rusher was exploding now: 'I *told* you they were coming today!'

Spike tried to calm him, saying Fiona must have left before schedule. 'So okay, okay, I'll tell Morgo to give number two, the dyke, a miss, and hop on up to Sydney.'

To which Rusher, settling down, replied: 'All right then, you've got to go for number one.'

'We'll go for her. She'll be done, mate, no worries.'

Once again, following this edgy exchange, Spike raised his concerns about doing it in front of Rusher's son.

'Once my mate does the business, your boy'll be there just hanging around,' Spike said.

'I'll be on the scene before too long,' Rusher said.

'You?'

'I'm his father. I'll be contacted. It's not ideal, but it can't be helped.'

Spike said: 'So basically, what I'm saying is, you've got no problems with my mate doing it in front of your son? Doing the business in front of him?'

'It's the sad reality of what his mother has done,' Rusher said.
'All right, well, you know . . .'
'That's the end, that's the end of it. If I could wish for anything, I . . . but, y'know, it's her own fault.'

At this point, Spike suggested 'a car accident'. Rusher said he didn't care how, as long as it was done urgently. If it wasn't done immediately, he said, 'She could skip off, man, like anywhere, and she's gone, she's gone.'

Still mollifying Rusher, Spike guaranteed the job would be done once Morgo got to Sydney.

'I trust you, right?' Rusher said. 'But what I'm saying is, you have minutes.'
'Minutes?'
'Not hours.'
'You just relax.'
'Not days. Now listen, I mean, you've heard what I said, it's today, and if it's not today we have to reconsider our, you know, our deal.'
'You just sit back and relax, Morgo's on the case, all right? There's no problem.'
'Yeah, okay,' said Rusher.
'That's the only reason I've rung.'
'I appreciate it.'
'Someone'll give you a bell,' Spike said.
'I'll be here.'

We left our headphones on while the machine was cued up for the next tape. While there was still no explicit mention of 'knocking' or killing Fiona or Terri, this tape seemed to narrow down the alternative explanations for these conversations. I was still assuming Rusher was innocent, but it was getting harder. If it was only a matter of serving legal papers, what was the 'car accident' about? It did clear up one alternative for good – when Rusher had talked about 'serving documents' on 'number one', there was now no doubt he meant Fiona. He'd described her, and was now authorising Morgo to follow her up to Sydney.

Spike called Rusher again the next evening. In the morning, Rusher had been to the Family Court and seen SJ. Fiona was there, guarded by Federal Police officers. This time it was Spike who sounded agitated.

'Mate,' he said, 'what's going on with your missus?'

'You tell me,' said the ever-cagey Rusher.

'Mate, she's got a bodyguard, two of them. My mate thinks they're feds. Have you told me everything about your missus?'

'The feds think I'm going to kidnap her,' said Rusher.

Rusher, sensing Spike's unrest, assured him that Les McAtee still had the money ready, nothing had changed, but they only had the weekend to act.

Spike suggested poisoning Fiona in her motel.

'If God wills it,' said Rusher.

'So that's, ah, cool by you?'

'As I've always said, I want this done legally.'

'Yeah, sure, right.'

Rusher then chided Spike for not having done it 'three days ago'.

'Mate, chill,' said Spike, switching to the placatory role. 'He'll put her down, there's no problem, but he's just fucking a bit paranoid about these two blokes.'

Rusher said that he saw SJ that morning, and he was 'already damaged, and every minute you waste he's gonna be more damaged'. Spike showed no patience with this plea for sympathy, to which Rusher replied:

'I gotta lot of eyes on me here.'

'I realise that,' said Spike.

'And a lot of ears.'

'Right.'

'That's why I gotta tell you – make it all legal. Don't do nothing illegal.'

'Right, okay, matey.'

'Okay?'

'Rely on us, we'll get it done.'

As good as he looked in the role of hired assassin-accomplice, Spike didn't by this stage impress me as a very good hitman. Morgo's stuffed up the job in Hobart, has come to Sydney to arrange a car accident, but failed because Fiona has police protection, and is now saying he might poison her in her motel. I wouldn't be hiring Morgo for my next document-serving job.

But what was really happening? Was this a hit or something else? It certainly wasn't looking good for Rusher's 'legal papers' interpretation. He'd now authorised a full hunt for Fiona, in Sydney, and was implying that he had to 'make it all legal' because 'I've got a lot of eyes on me here'. No, it didn't look good at all.

Next we skipped through the transcript folder to two days later, when Spike visited Rusher in Silverwater again. Obviously some communications between Rusher and Les McAtee had been happening in the meantime – there were several inserts in the folder – and when Spike and Rusher met they had new subjects to discuss, principally the money.

'Morgo's just rung me,' Spike said. 'Now your old lady's in North Sydney at the moment. Morgo's got his tits in a knot.'

Rusher let Spike know, through a mixture of signals and words, that they should be careful because they were possibly being taped.

An apparently furious Spike complained about Rusher not having put the money up. Rusher said he had it all sorted out with Les. Spike stressed that the moment to 'do the job' was right now, with Fiona out shopping in North Sydney, and Morgo was out there waiting for the confirmation of the money. Rusher, ever the wheeler-dealer, said he was able to get money out himself from Silverwater, but had problems doing it immediately.

Spike grunted, apparently losing patience. Rusher continued talking, saying Fiona had filed an affidavit saying Rusher had hired hitmen, so Spike and Morgo would have to be very careful. Spike said Morgo was 'losing it' over the money. Yet again, Rusher assured him that he'd get the money through Les McAtee.

'You wanted this job done down in Tassie and now we're up here,' Spike said. 'But now, the problem is, we haven't had any chance to do it. And now we've got fucking problems because we've got no cash. So, mate, it's up to you, right?'

Rusher assured him again that Les would personally guarantee the money.

'We're still happy with thirty thousand,' Spike said, playing tough. 'But we can up it, you know, because of what's going on. Because, mate, Morgo has been chewing through the expenses, all this travelling round . . .'

'I know.'

'And he's got nothing to show for it.'

'He'll be paid.'

'And we're just fart-arsing about, you know, like, if you . . .'

'I've dealt with studio heads, I've dealt with top Hollywood agents, and it's always like this, it's just another business deal to me, you'll have to trust me . . .'

After some more talk along these lines, Spike raised the possibility of going down to Tasmania and killing Terri too.

'First things first,' Rusher said.

Spike wanted to talk more, but Rusher repeated his warnings about bugging.

'Enough of talking in codes,' Spike said. 'I'm trying to tell you what we're doing . . . Morgo's ready, he can do it. And it makes it easier for him because your little boy's not with her right now. He can do the knock easier.'

After Rusher excitedly talked about Les having the money – 'I'll call him and tell him to get it to you' – Spike added: 'What if it comes to, if we do the knock and come to you and there's no money? What happens then? . . . That's what gives me the shits. I don't know whether you're trying to double-cross me or what.'

'It's a two-way street,' Rusher said.

Well, maybe it was only a one-way street. The next day, the police arrested Rusher and charged him with soliciting the murders of Terri Maxfield and Fiona Rusher.

Reading these conversations now, it seems obvious that Rusher's code of 'serving documents' and doing everything 'legally' was a flimsy fig-leaf devised, by his own admission, out of a fear of being bugged. What else could he have meant, if not a 'knock'? Is there any way, from the conversations, he could have meant legal services?

Yet while I can't speak for the other jurors, I still had an open mind. I was waiting eagerly to see what the defence would do. The presumption of innocence angers a lot of critics of our legal system, who contend that the system 'favours the guilty'. Well, no – it gives the defence certain powers to counterbalance the powers of the State. There had to be another side to the story – why else would Rusher be here in court? – and I was looking forward to hearing it.

I had another reason to want to hear it. I came into this trial with an inbuilt distrust of police evidence. We'd had a massive Royal Commission into police corruption in this State, after which the commissioner, James Wood, said: 'I regard the manipulation of the criminal court process as the ultimate and potentially most cynical, arrogant and dangerous face of corruption that can exist.'

We'd all heard of police verballing, concoction of evidence, and so on. Coincidentally, I'd started reading a new book in the jury room: *Death in Bondi* by Darren Goodsir, a detailed account of the corruption among Bondi Beach police that culminated in the 1997 shooting of Frenchman Roni Levi.

Specifically, corruption by way of perjury has been explained as a way of balancing the scales against what police say is a defence-friendly court process – the time-honoured practice of 'doing God's work' and making sure the bad guys go to jail. After the Wood Royal Commission, a former judge and royal commissioner, Adrian Roden QC, said police had been fabricating evidence because they believed 'with some justification' that the exclusionary rules of evidence favoured the accused.

(Roden had also said in 1989: 'The rights of accused persons ... must be seen as part of a total body of rules designed to protect citizens from oppression, and to redress the imbalance in power between the State with all its resources and the otherwise very vulnerable individual.' These rules might protect the guilty, but they also protect the innocent.)

I'd grown up breathing the air of rumoured police, political and legal corruption. State Premiers of my lifetime had included Robert Askin, Neville Wran, and then one who actually lost office over corruption, Nick Greiner. The only High Court judge I could name when I was young was Lionel Murphy, the only magistrates Clarrie Briese and Murray Farquhar. If a lawyer suggests police or authority figures are corrupt, then I don't need a lot of convincing.

Sydney barrister Adam Morison admits to making a living out of exposing corrupt, sloppy and lazy police:

> *I'd say that 95 per cent of the cases I've won have been due to police incompetence or miscommunication or stuff-ups. I say to the jury, 'Why, if there's no doubt about this case, have they lied to you? Why is it acceptable for the police to lie under oath and cover up their incompetence? What are they trying to hide?' It never ceases to amaze me how police will stick to a ludicrous idea – sometimes I tell the jury that this policeman must have failed his evidence course at the police academy. And with the Police Integrity Commission hearings going on, it's a festive season for running these defences.*

Director of Public Prosecutions Nicholas Cowdery, whose prosecutors depend on police getting it right, agrees that 'there's much more critical examination of police witnesses by juries, which is not necessarily a bad thing, but gives the prosecutor a harder job.'

What's more, a juror can be openly contemptuous of police and sneer at them during a trial, with impunity. The NSW Court of Criminal Appeal held in the 2000 case of *R v Khoo* that a juror's anti-police behaviour did not mean the juror was violating his oath to give a true verdict according to the evidence.

As proud as we are of our own police scallywags, ours aren't the only ones. An American survey in 1992 found that only 41 per cent of jurors would trust police evidence, and among those, only 25 per cent of black jurors would. A District Attorney of Philadelphia once said that in:

> ... almost any factual hearing or trial, someone is committing perjury; and if we investigate all of those things, literally we would be doing nothing but prosecuting perjury charges ... The words of one 25-year veteran (policeman) still ring in my ears: 'They lie, so we lie. I don't know one of my fellow officers who hasn't lied under oath.'

There was a trial in Shepparton, Victoria, in 1980 where the barrister asked the policeman if he had been taught how to carry out an interview as part of his detective training.

'How do you mean?' the detective said. 'Physically, or verbally?'

If anything, the assumption that a policeman would be honest in the witness box has swung the other way, which is unfortunate for police but fairer for the trial process. The courts are not and never have been a level playing field. As jurors, we could feel it ourselves. The State could fine us or even throw us into jail for contempt if we disobeyed our instructions. Armed guards patrolled the courtroom and the corridors. The judge acted with the State's full authority. There's no stuffing around, when you get down to it: the State can do what it likes to any of us, and our ultimate defence is what we are allowed to say in the courts. The rights of the defendant, even if those rights are abused by the guilty, are all that stands between us and an ocean of State power. Who'd give away those rights, or let them be whittled away? Only, as far as I can see, comfortable people in their comfortable lounge rooms who'd never think they'd ever need to exercise their democratic rights; and the politicians, driven by a deep weariness with democracy's tribulations, who pander to this audience-jury.

Anyway – Spike was in the stand, and Mr Nisbett's rise to the microphone sharpened my senses. Here was Spike, a representative of State power at its outermost edge of legitimacy. He was a trained liar, a dirty plainclothed warrior. He embodied what Graham Burnett calls the 'large force waiting in the wings' of a criminal trial. And now the defence would have its chance.

Nisbett started off with a long string of procedural questions – how did the listening device work, where was the surveillance van parked, how long did Spike take to get from the van into Silverwater, who had written up the transcripts, and so on. Spike appealed to the judge when he wanted to keep his operational secrets, and the judge acted fairly, pressing him to give some answers but letting him refuse when it didn't really matter.

When Spike admitted that some of the jail staff were in the know about his mission, Nisbett shot us a sidelong look as if to say: 'What do you think of that?'

What were we to think of that? Apparently, we were just meant to be suspicious. Very suspicious.

Nisbett scored his first hit by questioning Spike on the timing of the first conversation. Spike had said, on the tape, that he was starting the recording at 7.00pm and finished at 7.30pm. 'Well,' Nisbett said, 'what would you say if I told you this tape had been timed at 34 minutes?'

Spike said his timings might not have been exact. He'd checked his wristwatch and his car clock, he said, and maybe they were out of sync.

Again, Nisbett gave us that look, implying that the four-minute discrepancy meant a lot – a hell of a lot.

(Incidentally, I'd been watching Rusher listening to the tapes. This was the first hardcore evidence against him, and I was interested in his reactions. He wore glasses and made notes. He looked constantly at the courtroom clock. This was one of those old clocks that has no second hand, the minute hands ticking over from one minute to the next – an unreliable clock indeed, if one is timing a tape. I had a theory that Nisbett's '34 minutes' were given him by the accused. Later, when we were able to listen to the tapes ourselves, I found that the precise length was 31 minutes, 50 seconds: an allowable margin of error between Spike's two clocks, and certainly not a four-minute Watergate-tapes mystery.)

Nisbett probed Spike on other bookkeeping discrepancies. The recorded timings were out a minute here and a minute there. Spike shrugged – they weren't doing all this by Greenwich Mean Time, were they? Then Nisbett turned his focus to the second tape, the phone call, which was muffled by several wonky electronic sounds, causing parts of the transcript to be completed from Spike's notes. Spike kept referring to his folder, which had the odd effect of making him look as if he'd come into an exam with cheat notes, particularly when other witnesses had only their fallible memories to go by. Nisbett attacked Spike's sloppiness but implied (in that confidential glance towards the jury box) that this was more than just sloppiness, possibly something approaching a conspiracy, and certainly an unwillingness, on the police's part, to carry out an unbiased investigation.

Which was where it was all leading – Nisbett put it to Spike that this was an operation with a predetermined ending: to catch Steve Rusher, to make him say things he wouldn't otherwise say. Spike dropped a dead bat onto this. No, he said, it was an investigation based on information he'd been given. He wasn't out to get Rusher. He was out to find facts. Nisbett countered that, as a trained undercover detective, Spike should have been able to get his watch synchronised with his car clock, and dot all the i's and cross all the t's. Spike had no response for this: a man can't be perfect. 'But,' Nisbett rejoined, 'you claim your notes were accurate enough to fill in the gaps on the second tape. Why should the jury believe you?' (Well, speaking for myself, I wasn't reading Spike's notes on the second tape, I was listening to the tape itself, and I heard the crucial bits clearly enough.)

Nisbett was scoring a few blows, but only flesh wounds. He might well imply some conspiracy from Spike's lazy bookkeeping, but that was all he could do – tickle some police-hating psychological anchor in the jury. He had nothing to back it up with. The substance of Spike's evidence – what was on the tapes – remained untouched.

There was one funny moment in an otherwise tense cross-examination. Nisbett had been going quite hard on Spike, but not so hard as to alienate the jurors. That's the line lawyers say they must walk when cross-examining police: you might try to catch them out, but you mustn't be cruel. Jurors pick up on cruelty, and they don't like it. So instead of cruelty, Nisbett fell back on the tactic that had worked so well with Terri Maxfield: if you can't bully them, confuse them. Nisbett was back to his double and triple negatives, and before long puzzled lines worked across Spike's brow. Nisbett asked him about 'Morgo', and Spike turned cagey. He thought Nisbett was forcing him to divulge some special secret police methodology on how to pretend to organise a hit. Nisbett kept asking him questions about Morgo, if Morgo was real or a lie, if Morgo was in Hobart or Sydney or not, and Spike kept hedging.

Finally the judge butted in: 'I think what Mr Nisbett wants to know is, were you and a man named "Morgo" or somebody else actually arranging to carry out a hit on somebody?'

Spike looked at the judge, blinking mutely.

The judge added, helpfully: 'I'd be very surprised if you were.'

A lot of us laughed. Even Spike's face cracked. The idea of there being an actual Morgo, employed by police to stalk Fiona, was very funny.

When I looked up, Mr Nisbett was laughing along with me.

CHAPTER NINE

CHILDREN OVERBOARD ON THE LOWER GROUND FLOOR
OR
THE WORLD AS SEEN FROM A ROOM WITHOUT WINDOWS

George Voskovec: *Maybe you don't fully understand the term 'reasonable doubt'.*
Jack Warden: *What do you mean, I don't understand? Boy, how do you like this guy? I'm telling you, they're all alike, they come over here, running for their life, and before you know it they're telling us how to run the show. Boy, the arrogance of this guy!*

– 12 Angry Men

Whenever something had happened during the trial that provoked a reaction – a chuckle, a frown, a grimace – Mr Nisbett was there with us. He had a sixth sense for it. Personally, I found this a little ingratiating, and I mentioned this to the jury after Spike's testimony.

'I like him,' said our Christian Mother, who liked to think the best of everyone. 'I like his smile.'

'He's very cheeky, the way he laughs along with us,' the Old Hand added.

'He's good value,' said Storeman Foreman.

Advocates are divided on the merits of making eye contact with jurors. Mr Nisbett obviously thought he could make a connection with us, especially given Mr Crown's studied aloofness. The jurors were beginning to look to Nisbett for entertainment.

In America, where attorneys can move around the courtroom, advocacy schools recommend eye contact. Teacher Sonya Hamlin writes in her book *What Makes Juries Listen?*:

> *Eye contact simply says to another human being, 'I see you. I notice you. I care about you. You are important in the process I'm now doing. What I say to you and what you think, matters. That's why I'm looking at you.' It gives the jury power. It enfranchises them. It gives them identity. It does another thing, too: it shows you are investing yourself, saying 'I'm committed'.*

Counsel make diverse choices about eye contact with the jury. Ian Barker QC says that, as 'advocacy concerns persuasion, the advocate has to make as much proper contact as is reasonably possible with the tribunal he or she is trying to persuade'.

Adam Morison says he uses eye contact, but only selectively:

> *I try to talk to them as 12 individuals, but if they're shaking their heads at me I'll focus on those who seem receptive. You want to create divisions in the jury room if the trial has been going against you.*

But many barristers resist this kind of connection.

'Jurors resent lawyers looking at them to see what they're thinking,' says Tom Molomby.

> *Jurors feel encircled anyway. I tend not to look at them now, except at the start, and I look at them very intensely when I address them. Asking a question in cross-examination, and then looking at the jury for their response, is something I find unprofessional. If it's a finely balanced case, that kind of thing can lose it for you. I try*

> to relate to the witness, not the jury, at that stage. I think what the jury's interested in is my relationship with the witness – that's where the tension and dramatic moment comes from, the spectacle that the jury will engage with. To break away from that would destroy what I've set out to do.

Malcolm Ramage has other reasons for not looking at jurors:

> I don't let jurors see my face. I keep side-on because I have a face that gives away despair and delight too easily. If my client is being cross-examined and makes a mess of it, I certainly don't want the jury to see me . . . Perhaps I lose jurors for the reason that I seem remote. Certainly you can't avoid eye contact altogether. But people don't like being stared at. They're like dogs in that respect. They only like eye contact if they want it.

A younger barrister says he tries to give each juror one-twelfth of his eye contact during his closing address, but generally doesn't make eye contact because:

> . . . sleazing onto them is exactly how I don't want jurors to see me. I don't want them to think I'm ingratiating myself with them. The risk of them thinking that is too great. If they're going to trust you, they will trust you without you trying to charm them.

In my researches after the Rusher trial, I heard several versions of a story about the male barrister who had established eye contact with a female juror early in a trial. All the way through, she acknowledged his winks and he always looked at her when the court was laughing at something. The barrister kept telling his team, throughout the trial, that he had this one juror onside. Then, late in the trial, the jury foreman passed a note to the judge, who read it to the open court: 'The jury asks counsel to please stop winking and making faces at them, as they find it an unpleasant distraction.' (Or, in another version, the jury gave a quick unanimous verdict against the charming barrister. Later, a juror told the barrister: 'She wasn't smiling at you because she liked you. She was playing with you because she thought you were a fuckwit.')

Australian jurors, when asked, have confirmed Malcolm Ramage's notion that, like dogs, they don't like being stared at. Jurors in the first Lionel Murphy trial said they hated the way Alec Shand's junior stared at them. (As well as other irritations – jurors disliked Shand's use of words like 'otiose' and 'moronic', and one juror sent a message to a solicitor telling her 'For heaven's sake, sit up straight!')

Overseas, too, staring at jurors is a no-no. Johnathan Carter, who had several months of evidence during which to form his opinions of the counsel, recalled:

At some point during the cross-examination . . . I felt like I was being watched and snapped my head around to see Connolly [the defence lawyer] staring at the box with his intense, dark eyes. Either it was that or the creepy lighting. Geez Poindexter, calm the frig down. He looked like a kid, smooth, polished, tall, thin, had his own special chair that he could lean back in. I guess the sun shone out of his asshole for him to have a chair like that.

Little methodical research has been done on whether or not jurors like eye contact with barristers, but the authors of the New Zealand jury project wrote: 'In two. . . cases, jurors felt intimidated by counsel staring at them, and a number of jurors also mentioned being stared at by the accused and by the families in court.'

'If I laugh at something in court,' says Molomby, 'I laugh to myself. I don't laugh to show the jury anything, and I don't laugh for the judge. If some jurors like to see you sharing the joke with them, I'd suggest that those are the jurors who are least likely to be the ones leading opinion in the jury room.'

I didn't know if I was leading opinion in the jury room or not, but I was definitely in the minority when it came to Mr Nisbett. The others lapped him up. I put my foot in it even further by saying we shouldn't be fooled by the wigs and gowns, the barristers on both sides were just trying to sell us a product.

'They're no better than real-estate salesmen,' I said, forgetting momentarily that the Retired Gent had spent his life selling houses in the Shire.

He kept a dignified silence.

You tend to forget, when you're in a jury, that there is a world outside. (This is no excuse for me – I was just tactless.) Beyond the four walls of the jury room, the world rolls on. Outside, my world was about to change. My wife was four months pregnant with our first child. But for the month of the trial, I ceased worrying about that. I was plunged into a world of suspended animation, a cryogenic state from which I would emerge not (as in science fiction) the same age as I'd gone in, but instead, many years older.

We jurors were barred from deliberating over the one thing we had in common. Twice, during the four weeks of the trial, Storeman Foreman made a tentative offer to the room to 'see how you're all leaning so far', but on both occasions the Old Hand quashed it quickly, asserting that we had to hear all the evidence before we took any votes or made any comments about Rusher's guilt or innocence. Her dictum, 'INNOCENT + EVIDENCE = GUILTY', remained on the whiteboard as an admonishment. Indeed, as Trevor Grove has pointed out:

> *Jurors pick up jury folklore very quickly in the coffee queue and it is conventional wisdom that trials always turn out to be less straightforward by the end than they seem at the beginning. The good juryman's motto is: 'I'm*

keeping an open mind.' I must have heard my colleagues use it five times a day.

If we couldn't talk about our verdict, we could talk about the other thing that everyone seemed to have in common, which was the state of the world.

For me, this made depressing listening. I found myself in a minority of one when it came to the terrorism–immigration issue. And it was a single issue. The ruling conservative coalition, which had won the last federal election, tried to revise history afterwards by saying they had won on the basis of their record. But while the campaign was happening, we all knew the real story. In Sydney, listeners to the radio announcers Alan Jones and John Laws had been softened up earlier in the year with a campaign against 'gang crime' in the south-western suburbs. Through July and August 2001, Jones and Laws pounded listeners with the evils of 'gangs', a euphemism for young Arab men and Arab-Australians in general. A white woman was pack-raped and allegedly told by one of her rapists that she was targeted 'because you are Australian'.

A latent racism had been stirred up, and the Federal Government brought it to the boil by turning away a Norwegian cargo ship, the *Tampa*, which had picked up mainly Afghan people from a boat near Christmas Island. Overnight the political landscape was transformed. For five years, the conservatives' backing had been eroded by the desertion of the right-racist fringe to Pauline Hanson's One Nation movement, who now came flooding back to a government they perceived as keeping our borders 'secure'.

And the terrorist attacks on New York and Washington seemed to provide an easily digestible link: let these Muslim immigrants into the country, and they will rape our women and bomb our cities. The Prime Minister said he couldn't rule out terrorists being on the boats coming down from Indonesia. Afraid of losing its own White-Australia support base, the Labor

Party tried to neutralise the immigration debate by falling into line behind the government.

Now is not the time for a political harangue. Nor was it the time in the jury room. I wasn't there to change people's minds. From my point of view, we were there for one thing, and that was to provide a just verdict on Steve Rusher. To that end, I didn't want to alienate my fellow jurors by arguing politics.

But it was hard. Every day, a vocal majority of the jurors damned Muslims and Arabs. America had bombed Afghanistan in retribution for September 11; jurors said the Yanks should bomb them back to the stone age – 'Not that that's such a long way!' Friday Night said the boats should have been sunk and the immigrants left to drown. Shut The Gate, a recent immigrant himself, said they should go back to Afghanistan and 'apply the proper way like the rest of us'. From his elder-statesman pulpit, the Retired Gent said: 'Islam is the most extreme religion! Whatever else you say about them, they're the most extreme people in the world. I mean, look at their praying, with the Koran and everything! I mean, it's just crazy what's going on!'

Whether or not racial prejudice, given oxygen by a desperate government, was gripping Australia, it sure was gripping the jury room. The Stickybeak came in one morning and said: 'I was on the train going home yesterday and the guard's voice came on, and I don't even think she was speaking English. It was 'Chingchongchingchongchingchong Regents Park chingchong Birrong . . . I grew up in Sans Souci, when Australians lived there . . . I don't want my grandkids going to our local high school. It's not a very good school anymore, unless you wear a tea towel on your head.'

An inquiry was under way, in Canberra, into the so-called 'Children Overboard' affair. During the 2001 election, the front pages were plastered with photographs of the children of boat people, apparently thrown overboard by their cowardly parents in a blackmail bid. The Prime Minister, Immigration Minister and Defence Minister all came out saying the type of people who threw children overboard were not the type we should let into our country.

For some jurors, the unfolding exposure of the 'Children Overboard' story as a fiction was not a cause for surrendering old prejudices and misconceptions, but rather for reaffirming them.

'Children!' the Retired Gent brandished his *Daily Telegraph*, its front page showing children in the water. 'I mean, these people are animals! Children!'

I felt like saying, 'Hang on – the point is that they *didn't* throw the children overboard.' But – a common malaise at the time – I was too timid, too defeated, to open my mouth. The inquiry seemed, here as elsewhere, to have zero political impact. Half the people in the country didn't seem to care if the government lied, and the other half seemed to think the lie was justifiable in order to keep Muslims out.

The jurors were not unintelligent people; we'd seen, and would see, vivid examples of the group's individual and collective ability to sort through complex evidence, despite the handicap of not knowing the first thing about how the criminal trial process worked. Every person in the room would repeat the adage that you can't believe what you read in the papers. But when it came to these boat people stories, they swallowed them hook, line and sinker.

The episode helped convince me that jury duty is a far more authentic expression of democracy than voting is. As jurors, my 11 colleagues exercised their democratic duty with seriousness and rigour; as voters, they treated their duty with prejudice and gullibility. As jurors, 'Antennae we didn't even know we possessed were erect and twitching,' as Trevor Grove writes. As voters, we were sound asleep. In short, everyone took jury duty much more seriously than we took federal politics. And why not? As a juror, you have one-twelfth of the ultimate power; as a voter, you are an ant.

When they set their minds to it, jurors consume media with admirable scepticism. The way jurors read newspapers – when the coverage is of their trial – has been studied in NSW, and the conclusion was that they were resistant to the ill-effects of that publicity.

The NSW survey found that in 38 trials only 4 per cent of jurors said they'd been influenced and 7 per cent thought their fellow jurors were influenced. Jurors often made a decision that ran against the grain of the publicity.

Individual responses from jurors backed up this scepticism of media coverage:

> *There was not very much discussion in the coverage and no 'meat' in it.*
>
> *Some jurors resented the characterisation of them as 'the little old ladies on the jury'.*
>
> *There was some joking discussion when a drawing of the jury appeared in a paper. We tried to pick ourselves out – no one was recognisable – by where we sat each day. We said 'That's me!' and 'That's you!'*
>
> *I don't know how stupid they think jurors are. When something wrong was reported, we didn't read it and go, 'Oh, was I asleep for that?' We knew we had heard everything, so the papers didn't influence us.*
>
> *If you didn't know any better, you would have thought that the reporter was watching another murder trial, not ours.*
>
> *[The media coverage] was the comic relief of the day.*

In general, 98 per cent of respondents said they easily put publicity aside, and 99 per cent said publicity didn't stop them assessing the evidence impartially.

For me, as a journalist, this is sobering news. But any experienced reporter knows that jurors will not let a newspaper report change their perceptions of what they have seen and heard in a trial. Fred Graham, a television legal correspondent in the US, once said:

> *I was assigned by CBS to cover a series of some of the most sensational trials of the century (Watergate, Hinckley, Connelly, DeLorean). It became absolutely clear to me that jurors were absolutely unphased [sic] by all of that broadcasting that my colleagues and I had been doing on television . . . As citizens, [jurors] were given responsibility over the high and the mighty. They were not going to let someone like me tell them what to think because I had been on television two and a half minutes on a few nights when they had sat through six weeks of trial; it was so clear to me that we were not affecting that process.*

Australian judges have gone some way to recognising the independence of jurors. Although sub judice laws still prevent newspapers reporting some material that may influence jurors, as far back as 1982 a High Court judge acknowledged that:

> *. . . the growth both in intensity and range of mass media coverage in modern times carries with it a greater liability to transience in its hold on the public mind. What is news today is no longer news tomorrow.*

In the leading case of *R v Duff*, in 1979, the Federal Court said: 'It is wrong to assume that jurors do not have or will not exercise a critical judgment of what they see, read or hear in the media.'

In September 2004 the Chief Justice of NSW, James Spigelman, rejected the notion that jurors were 'fragile' or easily influenced by media reports. On the other hand, he said courts might have to 'rethink' the challenge of the internet, with the Crown perhaps asking websites to remove references to an accused during a trial. Chief Justice Spigelman said the suggestion that jurors would be influenced by newspaper reports was 'most unlikely to be true'. Recent cases had 'decisively rejected the previous tendency to regard jurors as exceptionally fragile and prone to prejudice'.

But how do judges know this? How, apart from their intuition, can they speak for what goes on in jurors' minds? The essential mystery of the juror was put forward by Justice Gordon Samuels in a 1985 appeal court hearing on a case involving John Fairfax Ltd and the journalist Wendy Bacon:

> *It was suggested . . . that jurors, as ordinary members of the community, have developed defences or analytical filters by which to repel or dilute the remorseless assaults of the media. I have no idea whether this is so or not.*

My experience was that we acted more seriously as jurors than we did as voters. Was it just because the person sitting in the dock seemed so much more real than the future of the country, forcing us to think more carefully about the consequences of our vote? Was it because each of us was one in 12 rather than one in millions? Both of the above, no doubt. But a bigger part of the answer lies in the very special nature of the jury room itself, as John Ralston Saul told me some months after the trial: 'Think about how it is in that room. The single greatest influence on how you act, the greatest pressure on you to be responsible and conscientious, is the presence of those 11 other people.'

Speaking in praise of the jury system, Trevor Grove says that while no two juries are the same, 'for the system to function we have to assume that every jury is the same. Because the jury is not so much a tool, as an idea.' This idea, he argues, makes juries more than the sum of their parts:

> *The jury . . . contained as much intellectual machinery as the Tin Man in* The Wizard of Oz. *But besides being considered responsible enough to vote, drive cars and bear children we also seemed to have common sense, good humour, scepticism and patience. These strike me as far more useful qualities for the task in hand than a wide vocabulary or 'range of idea'. And in my view it was the jury system itself – the fact that we were forced to act together in this rather daunting undertaking – that helped bring these qualities to the fore.*

Exactly! Juries work because newcomers to the court will buy the idea, and listen carefully before rendering a fair verdict. As US Supreme Court Justice Charles Evans Hughes said in 1936, 'Impartiality is not a characteristic of who or what a person is but rather a state of mind.' It was a state of mind we jurors might not have inhabited in our usual roles as citizens, but we adopted it earnestly as jurors. When we stepped into the court, every member of our jury folded our personalities into this single idea of civic-mindedness, for possibly the first time. This is why the jury system is great.

And here's another big difference between the jury room and the outside world: When it came time for us to vote, we would have to be in total agreement. Out in the world, the majority could outvote me. But due to the unique requirement of unanimity in jury verdicts, no general argument could steamroll the others. We wouldn't be voting from self-interest. Greed, apathy, credulity and malice would not enter the jury room as they entered the ballot box. A jury is not, as Lord Devlin described it, 'a little parliament'. It must be better than a parliament. It must take into account everybody's view. It must be democratic.

CHAPTER TEN

THE STAR WITNESS: LES IS MORE

It didn't take us long to work out that the Crown was building its case around two peak witnesses: Spike and Les McAtee. Its strategy was to play us the tapes, fix them in our minds, and take care of the particulars later. In doing so it was sacrificing some continuity and losing the chance to construct a 'story' in our minds, but it was, like a bridge player who leads with trumps, playing a confident hand.

After Spike, the jury was itching to hear from the much-mentioned Les. Every break, some juror would say: 'I wonder if Les's going to come up next.' Whenever a man stepped into the back of the court, jurors would speculate on him being the mysterious Mr McAtee.

The Crown produced three minor witnesses after Spike, giving us time to absorb the tapes we'd already heard. We were told that a witness was 'on his way down by car from Brisbane' and would arrive the next day. We formed a picture of Les on the Pacific Highway, nervously going over his recollections for the thousandth time.

A former manager at Silverwater jail, Cliff Teague, came up and confirmed the times Spike had visited Steve Rusher. A policeman named Wrench came up briefly to say he had supervised the listening devices and phone taps. A Sergeant Baraka gave evidence that he had conducted the tapping of Les McAtee's telephone, recording 254 calls in a one-week period, 26 of which were to and from Steve Rusher.

Finally it was time for Les. He walked through the courtroom with a swaying gait, not a swagger but the kind of walk you'd expect from a tough schoolboy. He kept his face low, his dark-brown hair concealing his expression as he passed us. He wore a dark suit and a white shirt, as if attending a funeral. When he gave his oath and confirmed his name, his voice came out sandpapery, with a strong Australian drawl.

Les's testimony underlined this rough-as-guts first impression. He'd met Rusher when the suave American came into the council library in Surfers Paradise where Les worked as a part-time public information officer. With his little boy SJ in tow, Rusher asked Les for help sending anonymous emails.

Les helped him, although he became suspicious after a couple of weeks. He liked Rusher, but there was something not quite right about the dramatic way Rusher portrayed his situation – something 'beyond the usual American bignoting', Les said. Having helped Rusher set up his mailbox, Les knew the password. One day he read Rusher's emails and saw that a lot of the messages he was sending to the States were in some kind of code, 'as if he had something to hide'.

Rusher cultivated the friendship, dropping in to the library on Les's workdays to chat and send emails. Rusher seemed to feel that Les was in awe of him, and regaled him with stories about Hollywood, dropping names that invariably seemed to impress the Australian. Having secured Les's allegiance, Steve took it a step further. He confided that he'd come to Australia under a false name, and solicited Les's help in obtaining other false documents – council rate notices, parking permits, and so on, establishing his fake identity. One day Les asked Rusher to come clean, and Rusher gave him the whole story about abducting SJ from Los Angeles and coming down under to 'serve documents' on Terri Maxfield. In his usual way, Rusher ranted about lesbians and gay marriage and 'sex perverts', convinced that he had Les on side.

Steve Rusher did not know that before Les had joined the council, he had been a journalist with *The Gold Coast Bulletin* newspaper. From those days, Les had kept a couple of contacts in the Federal Police. He phoned one and asked about this Steve Rusher character. The contact came back with an answer: Rusher was wanted by the FBI.

Les, a widowed father of three struggling to make ends meet, said he'd taken pity on Rusher. But once he knew Steve was wanted by police, Les's concerns turned to little SJ, who now seemed less a partner in Steve's quest than a pawn, or a victim.

One day about three weeks after they'd met, Rusher had dropped in to the library and said: 'Hey man, as a token of my gratitude, can a Yank ask an Aussie over for a barbecue?'

Les accepted the invitation but instead went and dobbed Steve in to the police. Feeling uncomfortable about betraying him, but certain he'd done the right thing, Les believed he had heard the last of Steve Rusher.

But the American called the next day, saying: 'Raincheck on the barbecue, dude.'

Rusher moved to Silverwater, in Sydney, but continued calling Les, insinuating that Terri Maxfield had sexually abused children in the past and Les was Steve's 'last best chance' to 'save SJ'. He was thinking of any way to stay in Australia. He even (Les told the court) proposed that Les find 'some chick' to marry him, to stave off his deportation. 'He told me he'd make it worth my while,' Les said, clearly unimpressed.

But Les kept helping Steve. 'I dunno, I s'pose I felt sorry for the poor bugger.'

He found Terri's ex-husband in Hobart, and Rusher instructed Les to promise the guy money if only he could 'remember' the sexual abuse of any children by Terri. Les did not pass on Rusher's offer. Les then told the court that Rusher had given him a back-up plan. He had given Les a letter, which

Les described as a 'sick' and 'pornographic' account, purportedly by 'some slag in Hobart', of Terri Maxfield's physical and sexual abuse of her young nephew. Les said he had read it once and then, disgusted, thrown it aside. He hadn't been able to find the letter since.

Rusher had shown – in a judge's words – 'genius' in devising the tactic of issuing a subpoena against himself in Sydney, on the matter of kidnapping SJ, so as to get himself moved from Brisbane to Silverwater. He was a clever man, Rusher. But not so good with money. Around this time, he arranged to give Les US$10,000 in cash. He'd also left the registration papers for his car in a place where Les could find them. He wanted Les to sell the car for him, for about $5,000.

Les told the court he'd put the US$10,000 in an envelope in his computer disk box at home, where he'd left it for several weeks. After a phone conversation with Rusher, Les shifted it to the safe in the library. Rusher had told him the money would be used for 'legal fees'.

What Les didn't tell Rusher was that, shortly after he moved it to the library, the money disappeared. Les testified that a former council employee, 'Jodie', was the chief suspect. Eventually, about a fortnight after Rusher moved to Sydney, Les told him about the missing money. Rusher 'was mightily pissed off', Les said, 'but he needed me too much to rock the boat about it'.

Rusher then lost a Family Court hearing, after which Fiona, Terri and SJ went back to Tasmania. Enraged about 'Fiona being in the dyke's bed', Rusher began to talk about having Terri killed. He would spare Fiona, because as SJ's mother 'she still serves a purpose.'

Les said Rusher had given him the phone number of a friend of his named 'Atillio' in Los Angeles. Les was to call Atillio and ask for a 'favour' on Rusher's behalf.

Les said: 'I laughed it all off. The guy lived in a fantasy world, like a movie, and I didn't take it seriously.' After pretending to have tried Atillio unsuccessfully for a few days, Les eventually made the call. Atillio said Rusher still owed people money for past favours, so he might as well forget it.

During this time, Les kept his Federal Police mate apprised of developments. The policeman told him to keep cool and try to assess Rusher's seriousness. For his part, Rusher insinuated that he was having Les followed, to ensure he 'wouldn't do anything, y'know, foolish'. Rusher described Les's dogs and his children, as proof that he was having Les's house watched.

'Yer full of shit,' Les said.

'But how do I know that you have two corgis?' Rusher asked.

'I woulda told you before,' Les said.

Still, they kept talking on the phone almost daily. Then, Rusher told him about meeting Yanni Diamondopolous, another inmate in Silverwater. 'The Good Lord,' he said, 'has come through.'

'Meaning what?' Les asked.

'You work it out,' said Rusher.

'I don't understand, Steve.'

Then, according to Les's testimony (Rusher denied this had taken place), Rusher said he was going to arrange to pay Diamondopoulos's $15,000 bail from Silverwater. Diamondopoulos had agreed to travel down to Hobart, kill Terri and Fiona in 'an apparent druggie burglary gone wrong', and then skip the country and return to Greece or head to America.

To pay the bail, Rusher said he was leaving the $15,000 in Les's name at the front desk at Silverwater. Diamondopoulos's de facto, Christine Farragher, would pick it up and bank it, securing Diamondopoulos's release.

'I'm stoked with how things are going,' Les recalled Rusher saying. 'Man, I just sit here and think positively, y'know, emit good vibes, and then my little guy and me will be together again. Y'know how important family life is, don'cha?'

The focus of Rusher's anger had shifted, after the Family Court hearing, from Terri to Fiona. Les said Rusher had then given him a mobile number for Diamondopoulos, and Les was to send the SMS message: 'Yo dude. If you can't bag the double, just go the mother.'

'Up to then,' Les said, 'I reckoned Steve was a dreamer. With all his positive thoughts, he reckoned he could make something out of nothing. I thought he wasn't the full quid.' But now, with Diamondopoulos about to be set loose, Les dramatically revised his ideas, and figured Rusher might be serious. The day of Diamondopoulos's release from Silverwater, Les saw Detective Peter Wise in Brisbane, who put him in touch with NSW and Federal Police. They had Terri and Fiona moved out of the Maxfield house in Hobart, and tracked down Diamondopoulos and his de facto. It turned out that they were less dangerous than Les had feared and Rusher had hoped – they were doing a runner with Rusher's money. New South Wales Police met Diamondopoulos and Christine Farragher at Sydney Airport, where they were to leave together under false names. Diamondopoulos confirmed that Rusher had supplied the money for his bail, but wouldn't tell them why. (After the trial, I was to find out that Diamondopoulos tried to offer a statement in return for a blind eye to his skipping bail. The police refused, and arrested him.)

Not that Rusher knew this, at first, anyway. We can't say for sure what was in Rusher's mind, because he was to deny that any of this had taken place. But according to Les, when Diamondopoulos had not conducted the hit within a week of his release, Rusher started looking for new back-up plans. He was, Les said, 'completely feral'. Les testified that Rusher had given him the name and number of a local Hobart hitman, one 'P'. Les gave this number to the police and called P, who said he was going on holidays and couldn't do it.

The Federal Police set up the sting. Les said they told him to 'go along with it, and they'll place a tap on the phone'. Thus he became a full member of Operation Wilko. Under police instructions Les told Rusher he had arranged a waste contractor, Spike, to come and see him in Silverwater and arrange the 'job'.

This took us up to Spike's first meeting with Rusher, the tape of which we'd already heard. Les McAtee, so far, had testified under questioning from Mr Crown. He came across as slightly unsavoury, but not dishonest. His story, if true, was at least consistent. But this was only evidence-in-chief. We'd have to wait and see what Rusher's counsel made of him.

In the meantime, we'd hear 15 taped phone calls between Les and Steve. This took the best part of a week (a 'court-time week', that is; it took five days to hear about five hours of recordings, with time added on for foul-ups, technical hitches and dead batteries on our headsets). For me, this was the most gripping time of the trial.

The first tape was of a conversation a few hours after Spike had met Rusher in Silverwater. Rusher called Les at his home near Surfers. They chatted about the music Les was listening to (Midnight Oil's *10,9,8 . . .* album), and moved on to Rusher's Family Court case. He was preparing for his appeal against the earlier ruling.

'You've got to finish the things you started, don't you, Steve?' Les asked.

'Sure thing, man,' Steve said. 'Positive visualisation can work wonders.'

'Speaking of which . . . ?' Les asked nervously.

Rusher talked of meeting the man 'to serve the papers', and how Les was guaranteeing the payment. He concluded: 'As we say in the motion picture business: Action!'

Les asked if it was going to be 'just one or two'.

'In the best of all worlds, two,' Rusher said, but 'one would be nice.'

A short while later, Les started to try to dissuade him but Rusher said he had exhausted every alternative; he complained about his lawyers on the Family Court case, how he kept losing, and how the courts would never be able to help him get what he wanted, which was to stop Fiona and SJ living with Terri Maxfield.

Les complained about Rusher 'talking in riddles'. A terse Rusher replied: 'Hey man, I'll give you the dots, all you gotta do is join them together. And let's roll, we're nearly outta time.'

They progressed to some banal small talk about Les's daughter's birthday, Rusher doing his best to sound interested, Les doing his best to sound normal.

'Anyway,' Les said as they finished up, 'you sound like you're happy enough.'

'I've learned a lot of techniques in my time,' Rusher said. 'I can see what we've gotta do, and now the stars are in alignment.'

The following evening, they had a short discussion about getting the money ready. Rusher, who was evidently hoping to hear from Spike, spoke anxiously about running out of time. He said that if Fiona were to get out of town the next day, she'd 'be gone forever'. Les assured him Spike had said everything was on track.

'Well tell him to get the heck on with it, because they're gonna be out of there first thing in the morning. We need to serve those documents, buddy.'

Les said he was worried about the safety of SJ, being close to Fiona at this moment. Les tried to talk Rusher out of it: 'Mate, I always told you not to do this.'

'I'm at the bottom of the ninth,' Steve replied.

They discussed the Family Court hearing. Chipper now, Rusher boasted about his performance, and about how he'd applied for refugee status to buy more time in Australia, saying the whole thing was 'funny as a barrel full of monkeys'.

Les butted in: 'I have to tell you something.'

'Be very careful what you say,' Rusher replied.

'Just don't do it. Right? Don't do it, Steve.'

Rusher said repeatedly that he had 'no choice' and had explored every other avenue. As both became frustrated with this conversation, it was cut off unexpectedly.

Les called him back again, apologising: 'I was in the middle of giving you a spray and I leant on the button.'

Rusher laughed this off, but Les resumed: 'I still believe you started out with the right motives –'

Rusher cut him off: 'I've still got the right motives, bud.'

Rusher complained that his judge in the Family Court hearing agreed that Terri Maxfield 'would' hurt SJ, but Rusher would have been deported to the US by then so he could do nothing about it.

Les replied that Steve had to 'draw a line'.

'I will never ever ever ever stop,' Steve said. 'I can't stop, man. I have to protect SJ. And if it kills me, it kills me, and it nearly has, right? This is my life. I ain't trying to get heavy or emotional, but I gotta decide where I give up my life, and I have made that decision, okay? I'm dead serious. If I lose everything – you know what I'm saying – it doesn't matter, I'll swallow the shit sandwich, coz I'm doing this for my boy.'

'But the consequences, I mean, what if it does turn to shit? It's not just you, it's me too . . .'

'I've made my bed, bro. If you wanna hop outta it, be my guest.'

Les tried, again, to dissuade Rusher from his course, to which Rusher replied that he was getting anxious about Les's loyalty.

'I'm beginning to wonder, buddy, if you're completely with me on this.'

'Of course I'm not bloody with you! Are you psycho?'

'Well we oughta say goodbye then.'

'Hang on, hang on. I'm not saying that. I mean . . . I mean, what about you told me how Fiona serves a purpose, right? As his mother? What about that?'

'A mother's purpose is to protect her child,' Rusher said.

'Yeah, great. She's done a great job at that, hasn't she.'

'I don't disagree with you, Steve,' Les said. 'I'm with you on all that. But you know, Steve, the punishment's got to fit the crime, and does she really deserve what you've got coming to her?'

'I got no choice,' Steve said.

'Bullshit, Steve, you're a smart bloke, you're the smartest

bloke I know, all the things you've done in life, I reckon you can solve problems a better way than this.'

'You're like a stuck record.' Running out of patience, Rusher told Les to 'just do it' and tell 'them' to get on with it.

Changing the subject, he talked about an inmate in Silverwater who wanted his help. The man was a heroin smuggler.

'A drug dealer, shit, that's nothing, is it, Steve?' said Les. 'Tell him what you're about to become.'

'They see me as their conscience here. I'm the soul of the place.'

'Maybe you should get one of your own.'

'Well, that's my bad luck, I'm the guy who sold his soul to the devil.'

We took a break. Unfortunately, Borderline whipped off his headphones and, as we stood in the jury box, exclaimed: 'This man's going down for a long time!'

Well, the court knew where Borderline stood. His outburst is not unusual in criminal trials. Crown prosecutors told Lorana Bartels that they'd seen jurors stand up in the box and 'indicate their unwillingness to consider the evidence', hand in their verdicts three weeks into a 12-week trial, and give a bunch of flowers to the fiancé of the deceased. Jurors all make up their minds at different stages, some earlier, and more publicly, than others.

We were shuffled downstairs to our room, where we made coffee and tea and stretched our legs. There were various comments about Les's hair and manners, but what stuck in my mind was Rusher's comment: 'I gotta decide where I give up my life, and I have made that decision.' It was almost as if he'd expressed this directly to any juror who was going to convict him. He'd made his decision. He'd take the consequences.

Back in court, we were played the next tape, a call from Rusher to McAtee later that same night.

In a joking mood, Les told Rusher he'd rung Spike and said, 'Go home, boys, Steve's changed his mind.'

Rusher didn't see the humour. 'You can joke about it,' he said, 'but I'm here worrying for my son.'

Rusher talked about some of his favourite movies and books, referring as he often did to 'my pal Harvey Keitel'.

'You live in this fantasy world, Steve,' Les said.

'I used to live in every man's fantasy world,' Rusher said, half-misunderstanding.

They talked about how they'd sleep. Les doubted that he could, but Rusher said he'd sleep very soundly 'knowing that we're going to have all the papers we need served by tomorrow'.

They returned to analysing Rusher's meeting with Spike. Rusher said there was no small talk – 'he's a professional' – and that if the police looked at the visitors' records, 'I'll say I saw someone to serve papers on Ms Maxfield. I said everything's gotta be done legal, and I remember doing it over and over, like, "Keep it legal."'

'Can I ask you a little question?' Les asked.

'Any time, bro,' Rusher said.

'How could he do what he has to do "legally"?'

'It ain't my style to ask people to break any laws.'

'Gee, really?' Les said, then laughed. 'Oh, I get it. We're speaking in codes again.'

'Nothing illegal, Mr Policeman,' Rusher said, laughing along.

Trying to talk him out of it again, Les said people 'become illogical and irrational' when they became obsessed. 'I don't know who pisses me off more, you or me,' he continued. 'You because you think you're righteous, or me because I can't talk you out of it. Like am I dumb or what, because you've made up your mind, haven't you?'

'Yessiree.'

'Come on, Steve, it's not too late to pull them out.'

'No way, man, we're so close I can smell it.'

'Well, I hope you have a shitty night.'

By the time they spoke again the next evening, Rusher had talked again with Spike – the conversation about Fiona and SJ flying to Sydney, and 'Morgo' promising to get the job done by following Fiona up from Hobart.

'I thought you might have some news,' Les said, sounding edgy.

'No, no news. I'm just sitting around planning my court appearance.'

Rusher asked Les if he'd done some research for him on family law issues, and complained again that the judges would 'let this dyke hurt SJ . . . and then it will be too late'. Les urged him to give Terri Maxfield the benefit of the doubt.

'Well, she's guilty,' Rusher said. 'She's a deviant and she's been a deviant before.'

Les assured him that Terri Maxfield would never hurt SJ. 'Sometimes you've just got to leave things to fate.'

'Well, I'm hoping fate will come in and play its role, Les, I promise you that.'

'Well, some things you can't control . . . If it's not going to be Terri it might be someone else down the line. You don't know who Fiona's gunna hook up with some other day.'

'Well, if I can serve these documents, I'll be a happy man, because then she won't be hooking up with anybody. But thus far we're not getting any papers served and we'll have to rectify that, won't we?'

'You're an extremist,' Les said.

'Yeah, dude, I'm Mr All Or Nothing.'

'If you can't get it one way, you'll take it all the other.'

'It's a Californian thing.'

'I thought you Californians were all laidback and that.'

Rusher said that in five years, he would have recovered from this trauma, but in five years 'SJ will have had his entire life fucked up.'

'Jeez, Steve, as a dad, all I can say is there's a point where you just have to let go. Your kids'll do what they want anyway. You can't control everything.'

'But I can control some things,' Steve chuckled.

'Just try what you can do legally, and that's all you can do, you won't be a failure, you'll have done your best for him.'

'Everything I'm doing is legal. Remember that, Lesley.'

Les called later that night. 'So,' he said, 'have you heard anything?'

'Man, can you just call them? Tell them we want some documents served on these people, and they haven't been doing it, and when's it going to happen?'

'How do you know it hasn't?' Les said.

'If it had happened, I wouldn't be ringing you from here, if you know what I mean.'

'Nah, mate, if it had happened, they'd have locked you up in chains, no more phone privileges. You'd be in there for the rest of your life.'

'We may be dealing with idiots here,' Les said. 'I mean, what if Spike and co. screw it up?'

'They're your friends, you tell me.'

'Come on, I didn't know them . . .'

'It's a joke, man, lighten up. Look, that's the risk we take. But if they got the job done three or four days ago, we wouldn't be having this conversation. But that's the way life goes and y'know, if you're given lemons, you make lemonade.'

'I'll have to go away and think about that one.'

'There's a lot more lessons where that came from, my man.'

'So you still want it done, then?'

'More than ever. More than ever, I'm desperate to protect my son. There's something sacred between a father and his boy, as you know, Les.'

Now Les put a question to Rusher. Why did he want to kill Fiona if that left Terri still walking around, when it was Terri he really hated?

'Who said I was gonna leave her out of it?'

'I thought you said if it had to be one, it'd be Fiona.'

'For now, sure. But it's first things first, isn't it?'

'You mean you're going to get her later.'

'I don't know what you mean by "get her". I just have to protect SJ.'

'But SJ won't need protecting from Terri if Fiona's, um, out of the picture.'

'I got principles, man. That's all I'm gonna say. I got principles, and it's the dyke who deserves to pay.'

Two hours after this call, Les called Rusher, who made some derogatory remarks about Chinese and Vietnamese inmates. (A penny dropped in the jury box: this explained why the defence didn't want Asian people sitting up here.)

'Did you get a phone call, Steve?' Les asked.

'No.'

'Shit.'

Rusher, increasingly frantic over not hearing from Spike, resumed his self-pity line, threatening to take 'downers' for his anxiety over SJ. He repeated his urgings for Les to tell them to 'get it rolling'.

Rusher said he had to take another call. This, as it turned out, was the second phone call from Spike, where the undercover policeman complained that Fiona had the Federal Police officers guarding her.

An hour later, Rusher called Les and told him that Fiona was going around 'with two shadows'. Les asked him what he wanted, but Rusher went on about not wanting anything illegal.

Les interrupted him. 'I don't mean to be rude, mate, but does Spike really understand what you're trying to get him to do? If you keep saying "don't do anything illegal", maybe he's . . . he's taking your word for it.'

'Hey, I'm not asking anyone to break the law.'

'No, of course not, Steve!'

'But I think they understand what I need. It's just they fuck around so much.'

'Shouldn't you just lay it out in common English so there's no riddles, no doubts?'

'The walls have ears, man.'

Les tried, for what seemed the hundredth time, to talk Steve out of it. He said people would have sympathised with his original plan because they'd understand a father's wish to keep strong male role models in his son's life. But 'then you had to double it to include Fiona.'

'I had to think of the big picture, you know?' Steve said.

'Yeah, as in, if you knock Terri, Fiona will find someone else, and your problems start all over again.'

'We're not knocking anybody off, Les.'

'Oh well, you know what I mean. Get rid of her, like, you know, move Terri on to greener pastures. There could be another one, is that your excuse now?'

'I gotta take control,' Steve said. 'I've spent all my life being in control of my world. I'm a leader. People look to me to take the hard decisions. That's how I've run my companies, and people understand you've got to do some tough things in life.'

'Maybe it's time you retired to Florida.'

During this period, the trial became tough work. Beforehand, when we'd be sitting in the jury room and the sheriff's officer's phone rang in the corridor, the Retired Gent would say: 'Here we go!' and we'd spring to our feet like Pavlov's dogs, ready for the officer to come and take us to court. But during the week of listening to the gruelling Les–Steve tapes, we spent our breaks lethargically silent in our room, some dreading the summons of the phone.

But more than that, it was the relentless sound of Rusher's voice in our heads when we went home. The JP said he couldn't sleep at night, hearing Rusher going on and on with his desperate persuasions. I was hearing it too – the charm, the American condescension, the bignoting Hollywood talk, the forced conviviality from both sides, for they were both using each other. Sometimes, worst of all, I could feel traces of it seeping into my own conversations with my wife. It was as if I'd been exposed to a virus. I would be sitting at dinner and not hearing a word above the wheedling of Rusher's American accent in my head.

I remember trying to drag myself back to the presumption of innocence – that they were talking about 'legal' document-serving, whatever that may be, and this whole thing about the hit was just Les's imagination, or, perhaps, some kind of plot on Les's part to have Rusher put away because Les had his money and his car. But it was getting harder and harder. In the tapes, Rusher was frantic with anxiety; and whenever he felt Les's loyalty flagging, he pressed him with the story of how SJ was being 'damaged' and Les was the little boy's only hope.

The next call was from Les to Rusher, the following morning. Rusher, in better spirits, talked about his Family Court hearing the previous day. 'Feds are crawling all over me... They're sure, you know, that I might shoot my way out and take my boy and the dykes with me.'

'And that would not be the truth, would it?' Les said.

'I'm a non-violent person. I don't do the shooting!'

Les laughed grimly. 'There's a word for people like you.'

Rusher continued talking about his impatience regarding the 'legal work', and made another joke about having to speak loudly so the police would hear 'the tape recording of this conversation'. Les laughed it off, nervously.

'I'm very happy with the decision I've taken,' Rusher said calmly. 'I'm an executive, I do this every day. I stand by the results, whatever they be, I'm responsible.'

'Is that the truth, though?' Les asked, his voice thickening with the weight of his knowledge. 'Will you stand by the results of this?'

'Sure thing,' Rusher said. 'It's all good.'

Again, I felt I was hearing the direct message to the jurors: 'I stand by the results, whatever they be, I'm responsible.' His suspicions of being tape-recorded sounded almost pathetic, in retrospect. He suspected he was being recorded, yet he just ploughed on, in the belief that he was covering his tracks by saying he was doing nothing 'illegal'. How it must have eaten him up to sit in court and be humiliated like this. I almost felt sorry for the guy.

He called Les briefly that afternoon, and talked about other inmates to whom he was giving money. 'You wouldn't believe what I do here for charity.'

'Well, you have to start charging for your services.'

'Jailhouse lawyer, inc.'

'Specialising in illegal immigrants?'

'All criminal law.'

'Being an illegal immigrant yourself.'

Whenever there was some mention of immigration, and Rusher's status as an illegal, Mr Crown would sneak a look our way. Once, early in the trial, he rolled his eyes at us when it was revealed how Rusher had entered the country, and how he'd applied for refugee status. To my recollection, this was the only 'psychological anchor' Mr Crown used in an otherwise straight-up-and-down presentation of the evidence. Just as I hadn't liked Mr Nisbett's sneaky smiles, I didn't like Mr Crown's obvious appeal to the negative atmosphere around illegal immigrants. Surely he wouldn't have thought we'd judge the evidence on the basis of Rusher's immigration record. Maybe he was hoping we would. Either way, I didn't like it.

The next day, Les called Rusher and remarked, during their obligatory small talk, on how 'positive' he was sounding. Rusher said that that was because he'd read his horoscope.

He read: 'You have a near-perfect set of cosmic opportunities to take advantage of this week. Saturn, Jupiter and the Sun are urging you to stand up and be counted. They suggest a precarious situation urgently needs an assertive contribution from you. If you have faith in your talents you will make an amazing contribution to the drama which needs sorting out. This is not the time to start doubting yourself.'

Mockingly, Les read the stars from his paper: 'Here's what it says: you're on a downhill path and the actions you have chosen to pursue will lead to nothing but negativity.'

'Ha ha.'

Rusher said he'd talked to his solicitor. 'I said to him I thought the feds were taking a lot of interest in me. He said, "That's 'cause they're probably tapping your phones." He said, "They can't use it as evidence but they will react to it."'

(I hope Steve Rusher didn't pay his solicitor for that piece of advice.)

It was hard not to wonder how Rusher was feeling now, to hear himself gloating about outwitting the police. He told Les that if they taped his call to his solicitor, they'd find him saying, 'I've been running a joke with a friend. So the cops are chasing a wild goose if they think we're doing anything illegal.'

Not quite following, Les said: 'Oh, right, who have you been running the joke with?'

'Who indeed?' Rusher laughed.

'Tell me, tell me!'

'You, you asshole!'

The 'joke' turned serious in the same conversation, however, when Rusher told Les that if they didn't come up with the money to pay Spike, 'they'll kill me. It's dead simple . . . It's not an option play, it's a fact, and I accepted that, y'know, that's what happens when you don't pay these guys.'

'Yeah, but that's because you know they can't get to you,' Les said.

'Wanna bet?' Rusher said, adding that 'there are more than a few guys in here who can follow orders.'

Les asked him if he wanted to send any messages to anyone in America. Rusher replied that his ex-wife could send a message to his mother. 'Tell my mother I'm cool . . . But I don't, y'know, I don't have any feelings for my mother. But I guess I oughta tell her I'm cool.'

Family talk brought out Rusher's self-pitying streak. He complained that Fiona 'does not want me to have anything to do with SJ at all. She wants to take SJ away from me,' so Fiona 'has to take the consequences'.

Les asked him if he did this when he lost his business.

'That's business,' Steve replied. 'You don't fuck with my family.'

The next day was the day of Rusher's fourth and final conversation with Spike. This was when Spike huffed about the money not having been transferred from Les; 'Morgo' was ready, but wouldn't act until the money came through. Shortly after Spike left, Rusher called Les McAtee, saying he wanted the money put over now, because 'they've got a once-in-a-lifetime opportunity of serving those papers today.' He told Les that 'they' would call him and, 'You've gotta sell the car, whatever, you can get the money out on your credit card, whatever, I don't care. Get that money over to them . . . It's gotta be, it's like, every minute counts.'

'I'll just say, yes, yes, yes, I'll agree to everything,' Les said.

'Right on.'

Half an hour later, Rusher called Les in a rising panic. He said Les had to sell the car 'now', scrounge all the cash he could, and pay 'them' straightaway, because, 'They can do it now, okay? But maybe not in half an hour.'

'Oh,' Les said, 'it's that urgent?'

'It's that urgent!' Rusher fairly screamed.

Nearly an hour later, Les called him with the bad news. 'They had her lined up for an accident,' he said, 'but because the money wasn't there, she'll live another day . . . He said, "Oh well, you've missed the boat for today. She lives another day."'

'Yeah, you know, this may – this opportunity may not come again,' Rusher said.

'Well, I'll ring immediately and tell them we're getting the money together and it's all go. Then I'll call you back.'

'Right on.'

'Okay.'

When they talked again that night, Rusher's mood ranged from angry and stern, to fearful, to depressed and self-pitying. He said he was 'disappointed about today's events' and 'concerned that we've missed this opportunity and it may not come back again . . . And I still wanna know why nothing – they didn't sort the thing out in Hobart.'

For the first time on the tapes, Rusher reminded Les of his

money that Les had lost, saying that was the reason he was 'desperately short'.

'I got such a need to protect SJ, and you know it's gotta be done. Oh man, why couldn't they do it today? If this was the States – they know how to do it there.'

Les tried to placate him, saying perhaps 'fate' had stepped in.

Rusher begged Les: 'Please don't let me down.'

The last time Steve and Les spoke was at 9.40 the next morning. Rusher told Les a long cryptic story about an inmate being arrested after someone overheard his phone calls. Les joked about Steve's paranoia.

Rusher noted that it was a bad line, because 'Their tape recorder is obviously wired into the wrong thing.'

'What tape?' Les said. 'Oh, very funny, Steve.'

A little while later, Rusher said: 'Listen, I can't tell you how much I appreciate your help and you know I will be back to see you, I promise.'

'Well, listen, I tell you what, I'll do you a deal. Don't bother coming.'

'Hey dude, don't be like that!'

'It's all right, Steve.'

'I want to see Bonnie [Les's youngest daughter].'

'No, she'll be all right.'

'I'll see you soon.'

'Seeya.'

'Thanks for your call.'

'Seeya.'

'Bye.'

The Federal Police must have thought they had enough by now. Agents arrested Rusher later that day and charged him with soliciting to murder Fiona Emery and Terri Maxfield. Rusher and McAtee never talked to each other again, and next saw each other in the District Court in Sydney.

It comes back to me how awkward and circuitous were those conversations between Rusher and Les McAtee. It was a clumsy, complicated dance. They had five or six peripheral topics, like satellites around the main planet. Sometimes they'd touch on the central issue glancingly, at other times full-on, particularly as Rusher's panic grew later in the week. Their conversations held up a mirror to all of us and our ways of communicating with each other: the way we avoid, circle around, dive into, bounce off, and shy away from the things that really concern us.

But it was stressful. Even the hot meals began to look appetising. It's amazing how appetite works: after shifting in our chairs for hours, we were dizzy with starvation. Our Christian Mother brought in extra loads of fruit, which were devoured even by the chocolate zealots.

My birthday came, and I brought in an embarrassingly rich, chocolatey mud cake. Ravenous after another hour in court, the jurors didn't leave a crumb. They did everything but sing me 'Happy Birthday'.

Throughout the tapes, both Mr Crown and Mr Nisbett tended not to look at us. Steve Rusher scribbled notes busily. Les sat in the box, shoulders hunched forward, hands clasped in front of him, eyes darting out from under his fringe. Every now and then, when he heard one of his weak jokes on tape, he'd chuckle.

Soon after the last tape was played, it was Mr Nisbett's turn to have a crack at Les. Everyone knew that this was the key point in the trial. We'd just heard such a mountain of evidence against Steve Rusher, it was going to take some flashy footwork from the defence to reverse the impression we'd got. My mind went to the Old Hand's words on the whiteboard in our room: INNOCENT + EVIDENCE = GUILTY. For myself, I figured that in the Les tapes and the Spike tapes, we had the EVIDENCE. It was now up to Mr Nisbett to rub it out.

Predictably, he went after Les's background. He'd been a police rounds journalist? That would suggest a familiarity with surveillance techniques. He'd quit journalism and worked for the council? And why was that? (Mr Nisbett put ironic quotation marks around a lot of Les's activities.) Did he still work for the council? No, Les said, he'd quit after the stress of the Steve Rusher affair. Now he ran a small computer business. How did he fund this operation? His father had taken out a $20,000 Westpac loan, and Les was paying him off with the business income. How did he live and support his children? He received government benefits. (Mr Nisbett shot one of his looks our way, as if to say: They have a go at our man for being an illegal immigrant, but this witness is a welfare cheat!) So, Les was scamming benefits while using a loan that was nominally in his father's name. (Wonder if the bank would like to know that!)

Mr Nisbett returned to Les's statement that he'd had the cash in his computer disk box for six or seven weeks.

'In your computer disk box?' Les only looked more dodgy as he shrugged this off. 'But,' Nisbett said, 'this is a large amount of money – similar to the amount your father had borrowed for you to start your business – and you left it in your computer disk box?' Again, Les had nothing to say, except that he'd eventually transferred it to his work safe, on Steve Rusher's suggestion.

'Now, about this robbery.' Les suspected that the employee had stolen the money. Les thought she had a boyfriend who was not a very nice guy.

'But,' Nisbett said, 'wasn't the safe locked?'

'No,' Les replied. It was in the office, and nobody ever thought of locking it.

'All right.' Nisbett shuffled papers on his lectern. 'You went to the police to tell them the accused was trying to have someone killed, and yet you never told them about this stolen money?'

'I told them,' Les said.

'But there was no police report?'

'There was no formal report,' Les said; the police had suggested he chase it up if he wanted, but there was little hope of getting the money back.

Nisbett was shooting us so many sidelong glances, his eyes must have been falling off their stalks.

He moved on to Les's relationship with the now-retired Federal Police officer. Les admitted speaking to the man about four times a day during the time of his friendship with Rusher. Yet the officer was not testifying at this trial to back up Les's story. What was going on there?

All Les could offer was that the officer was a personal friend, and didn't know anything first-hand.

A long weekend fell in the middle of Les's testimony. He had to go home to Queensland for the break and, due to difficulty lining up other witnesses, the judge offered us an extra day off. Addressing Storeman Foreman on the Thursday, he said: 'Mr Foreman, you might like to consult with the other jurors about this, but it might be convenient if we take a day off tomorrow . . .'

Storeman Foreman chirped: 'All right!'

And that was it. We had our day off. I was a little cranky at Storeman Foreman when we returned to our jury room. I wanted to get the trial over with and return to normal life. I was feeling the pressure. During the second week of the trial, a weird skin rash had broken out on my hands. My fingertips felt dead, kind of loose, for a day or so, and then began to peel. Before I knew it, my entire hands were peeling off. A doctor told me it was a common reaction to stress. I wanted this trial behind me. But I'd have been in the minority even if Storeman Foreman hadn't jumped in with his answer: everyone except me was happy to have the day off and prolong the trial by a day.

After the long weekend, Nisbett continued grilling Les. We were working our way over the hump where the novelty had worn off and the end was not yet in sight. Mercifully, the sheriff's officers had acceded to our request to take a walk outside during the lunch breaks. We were to shovel down our gruel from 1.00pm until 1.30pm, when an officer would come and ask who wanted to take a walk. Usually about half of us would go, sometimes more. We'd leave by the side door, wander in groups or alone around the local blocks, and be back at the door by 1.50pm. We were luckier than most juries, who are locked up inside, and luckier than the jury in the Chesterman study who referred to an enclosed courtyard in which they could exercise as 'the prison yard'.

I enjoyed these walks, if only for the fresh air. That part of Sydney is an interesting one, because it always seems in transition. When I was younger, the seedy end of Pitt Street was home to second-hand record shops, sex shops, an adult cinema, army-disposals shops, Chinese restaurants, and grimy old pubs. Some of those shops still remained, but a colony of high-rise apartment buildings had mushroomed alongside them. Chinatown and its fringes were being gentrified; the pubs had been done up and a couple of four-star hotels built. Convenience stores replaced dusty coffee shops.

After hours in court, everything had sharpened contours, as if I'd been in a sensory deprivation chamber. Outside Ashwoods, a venerable second-hand record shop and one of the survivors of the area's past, I ran into a friend, David. He told me that he, his wife and their two young sons had nearly been killed the day before when they'd turned up a one-way street and a garbage truck, careering the wrong way, collided with them. Their car was almost a write-off but, David said, if he'd been at that same point one instant later, they'd have been completely wiped out. I was amazed – the very air seemed pregnant with danger and unprecedented scenes – but I didn't have time to sympathise with him fully. I had to get back to court, or else I'd be in big trouble. Scurrying back like a school student or a mental patient, I felt I was becoming institutionalised.

Back in the jury room, there were surprises from day to day. After hearing some derogatory remarks about Asians during the day's evidence, the Stickybeak was scandalised.

'That's a bit racist, isn't it?' said the same woman who'd told us she couldn't understand the 'chingchong' train guard and didn't like the local high school because it favoured 'towel heads'. 'They were pretty awful, those comments.'

People are always more complex than they seem. How could those lawyers possibly guess what we were thinking? We were complete mysteries to ourselves.

I suggested that the racist comments might have explained why the Asian men were challenged at the jury empanelment stage.

'But still,' the Mechanic said, nodding at me and my chrome pate, 'they didn't challenge you, even though Rusher called someone a "bald-headed coot".'

The Retired Gent, who had a shock of white hair and a flowing Santa Claus beard, laughed. 'Don't worry about that, Mal,' he said clasping my shoulder. After sitting next to each other, the Retired Gent and I had grown fairly close, in the jury sense of closeness. He coughed and spluttered throughout the evidence, annoying some of the jurors, but I kept up a friendly face even though I was in the line of fire. Sometimes we'd share our lunchtime walks. He'd tell me about his grandsons. I found him warm-hearted and generous – too nice a guy to really believe his rant about the 'extreme Muslims', but I didn't press him on this. In a jury, you always have to bear in mind that later, down the line, you might need a friend. We were virtually living together. It just didn't seem worth raising the things that divided us.

I'd also taken him under my wing a little when it came to the technology we had to use in court. Repeatedly he'd had problems with his headphones. Whenever he stuck up his hand with a problem, the police had to stop the disc and start it again from the very beginning, which often wasted ten or 15 painful minutes of re-listening. At one point, in the jury room, the Stickybeak joked to him that 'if you have a problem with your headset, don't say anything! We don't want to hear it all again!'

One day in the jury room, I said something about the restrictions on what we could and couldn't say after the trial finished.

Borderline said yes, we had to be careful, because there might be an appeal against what we did. I said no, there could be no appeals against the jury's reasoning or verdict. We were the sole judges of fact, and couldn't be appealed except in extreme circumstances. The judge, on the other hand, determined the law – how to instruct us, how much of the evidence to let us hear – and if Rusher lost the case, he could lodge an appeal against what the judge had done.

The Old Hand asked how I knew so much – had I been reading up?

'I studied law,' I said.

A certain number of jaws hit the table. Right at that moment, a sheriff's officer came in and asked if we wanted to go for a lunch walk. I got up and walked out.

It felt good to get that off my chest. There was so much mystery between ourselves, between us and the court, and of course the ultimate mystery of Steve Rusher, that I felt unburdened by having revealed something. In a way, being on a jury is like walking into a nudist colony every day. You see so much of the private lives of strangers that your own parameters of modesty change, and before long you're walking around in the (metaphorical) buff yourself. It wasn't that my half-completed law degree was such a big secret to keep, but I'd been generally reticent with the other jurors, as I didn't want to be seen as Mr Smarty-Pants Novel-Reading Journo Semi-Lawyer. Or similar.

The Retired Gent joined me on my walk. He asked if I'd finished my degree. I said no, I didn't want to be a lawyer.

'Ever had second thoughts?' he asked.

'No. And if I'd qualified as a lawyer, I'd never have been able to sit on a jury.'

'You should have finished it then. You'd be eating better food.'

Over several days of cross-examination, Mr Nisbett built up a new portrait of Les. According to this portrait, he was a wily, deceitful 'ex-journalist' (wink, wink) who knew how to get someone framed by police. He was a tax evader and a welfare cheat, and his business had been struggling so he needed money. When he'd met Steve Rusher, he found his goldmine. Steve was vulnerable in his desperation to save SJ. Les won Steve's confidence, got hold of his money and his car, and then turned him in to police. After skimming some more money off him – pretending it had been stolen – he sought a more permanent solution, which was to have Steve put away in prison. So scheming Les had outwitted Steve and the police, setting him up by taping these supposedly incriminating phone conversations in which Les, with his experience as a muck-raker and possibly helped by his shadowy police friend, led Steve into some revenge fantasy – pure fantasy – about Fiona and Terri.

After watching Nisbett tear strips off Les, we were let out of court for another day.

The Retired Gent sidled up to me and said: 'I can see why you wouldn't want to be a lawyer.'

We were being asked to judge Les's credibility as a witness, and that would be a matter of subtle shades rather than a big bang. As one jury researcher has written:

> *The unschooled public largely and erroneously believes that convictions are mostly obtained through the use of one form of tangible evidence or another. This naive impression is shaped by watching too many TV shows like* Perry Mason *or* Matlock. *The reality is that in most criminal trials the verdict more often than not hinges on whose witnesses – the state's or defendant's – the jury chooses to believe. It boils down to a matter of credibility. There is no 'smoking gun' scientific evidence that clearly points to the defendant. This puts an extremely heavy burden on the jury.*

Had the tapes not existed and the case been a question of Les's word against Rusher's, then Les's credibility would have been all-important. I can't speak for the other jurors, but it seems, looking back on my own thought processes, that it didn't matter what I thought of Fiona, Terri, Les and Rusher as human beings. What counted was the tapes.

Still, Mr Nisbett put on a good show when he had Les in the box. He followed a barrister's dictum that the better the witness is for you, the longer you keep them up there. In the furnace of cross-examination, Nisbett certainly tried to make Les seem dodgy – the absent policeman friend, the dicky bookkeeping, the 'stolen' money – and Les's demeanour was a mixture of evasive, pugnacious and cool-headed. The annoying thing, from a juror's point of view, was that I didn't feel I was getting the full story. Because jurors grow accustomed (very quickly) to having the keys to other people's lives, we become demanding. I could have speculated on ornate tangents – Was there a homoerotic dimension to the Les–Steve thing? Had Les been disappointed by Steve, after idolising him? And what about the stolen money – what was really going on there? But all I really had to go by was what Les said, and what the Crown and the defence chose to ask him.

This kind of fervid speculation is an occupational hazard of being on a jury, as Graham Burnett found:

> *Now, as I look back, some of the hypotheticals we entertained (however briefly) have about them a feverish and fantastical quality. Such are the perils of the imagination in a trial: the sense of drama goads one to raise the dramatic ante; to conceive of fantastic resolutions worthy of the setting, the cast, the deeds. But not only that. This sort of reasoning – compounding improbabilities, dreaming up still more intricate motivations and counterplots – has, I think, much to do with a shared, deep idea about the nature of truth and the means of reaching it: namely, a sense that getting to the bottom of things should be hard work, should be difficult, should lead through long and knotty webs . . . once let loose in a jury, however, such a worthy veridical work ethic can lead to the collective construction of giant follies.*

Beyond that, there is always the chance of a trial turning into a talent contest between the barristers. Jurors unfamiliar with the legal process will generally fit the trial into some sort of spectacle with which they are more familiar. Commonly, trials are compared with theatre. Your feelings towards the actors/players/barristers become personal and passionate.

The longer Mr Nisbett spent with Les McAtee, the greater the drama. Like theatre audiences, jurors like to see drama. It may not swing the verdict, but it will keep them entertained, and as Jeffrey Abramson tells us, all lawyers 'understand that a trial is like a play: no matter how good the play, it will flop if the audience is not receptive'.

Mr Crown bobbed up and down with objections, evidently trying to protect Les and his case, and also to interrupt Mr Nisbett's flow. Objections may frustrate everyone except the objector, but the defence in the O.J. Simpson case made no fewer than 16,000 objections, and it worked for them. As a defence lawyer played by Robert Duvall in the film *A Civil Action* says:

> *The plaintiff's case depends on momentum. The fewer objections he gets, the better his case will go. So whenever you can, you should object . . . Relevance – objection. Hearsay – objection. Best evidence – objection. If you fall asleep at the counsel table, the first thing you say when you wake up should be 'Objection!'*

Jurors, of course, can get frustrated with too many objections, like the juror in a Californian product liability case who stood up in the jury box and shouted at the defence counsel: 'Why don't you sit down and be quiet? We want to hear what this man has to say!' Michael Chesterman says one juror-respondent to the 2001 survey likened the defence counsel to 'a Jack Russell terrier, and whenever he'd jump up, the juror would make a growling-dog sound'. Nevertheless, most of our jurors were loving how Mr Nisbett got stuck in, Les fought back, and Mr Crown bounced up and down with his objections. Mr Crown and Mr Nisbett were snapping at each other. At last, some needle!

Some lawyers will exploit the drama in conflict to score points with the jury as several lawyers who I interviewed told me:

> *If I'm speaking, and the Crown shuffles his papers noisily or pours a cup of water or distracts the jury in any way, I'll pause and draw attention to that. The jury will judge you on your manners, one way or the other.*

> *At a trial in Mildura in 1982, the prosecutor, Mr Ray, said to the jury: 'If you believe the stories these men have told you, ladies and gentlemen, you must still believe in the Tooth Fairy.' At which the defence counsel, Mr Jones, flipped a two cent coin into Ray's glass.*

Yet there can be as many points to be scored in restraint as in aggression:

> *I did a murder trial, and later read a Church newsletter in which one of the jurors wrote about the trial. She said she'd made her decision not based on the evidence, but because she felt it was so terrible, the way the lawyers tore this man apart on the stand, she had to acquit him.*

> *Sometimes you have to hold yourself back. You want to liven things up, because that'll work to your advantage and if the jury's relaxed with you, you're halfway there, but there's a line you can't cross. I want to make it fun for the jury, or at least interesting, and hopefully they'll reward me by thinking that the guy didn't do it.*

Yet few barristers can be so optimistic as to think their personalities can negate the effect of the evidence. While interviewing jurors for the 2001 NSW survey, Shelley Saltzman heard prosecutors described as 'dreamy' and 'dishy', and heard jurors say they either would or wouldn't like certain lawyers representing them if they were in court. But overall, says Saltzman:

> *I don't know that any juror ever claimed that the barristers' personalities were a deciding factor in their deliberations. The evidence was strong enough to support the verdict and the barristers' quirks, foibles and/or skills were merely fodder for jury gossip or appreciation.*

Which is no solace for the insecure trial lawyer.

Liz Gaynor, now a judge, reveals how as a barrister she asked herself: 'Did I look okay? Were my earrings a bit much? Did I smile too much, or perhaps not enough? . . . Did they like me or the prosecutor best? And the agonised answer is – "Please, please, let it be me".'

A fortnight – feeling like a month – after his first appearance, Les McAtee was finally excused. We'd seen Mr Nisbett at his most penetrative. In hindsight, this was probably the defence's high-water mark. There'd been the sloppy recording of times by Spike, the complicity of Silverwater staff in letting the undercover cop in, and the overall bad odour of Les's story about the missing money. Could there have been a conspiracy between the police and McAtee against Steve Rusher? Mr Nisbett had shredded Les's reputation. Maybe, just maybe, there could have been some doubt mustered about the authenticity of these tapes. Had the trial ended at this point, there's no telling which way the jury would have gone.

Chapter Eleven

Survivor XII: The Jury Room

Although comradeships were established quite quickly, I think we all instinctively understood that it was best not to form into camps: one day we would be locked up together to reach a verdict and would not want to be taking sides for the wrong reasons . . . My parents never tired of saying the war brought out the best in people. Maybe jury service does the same in a lesser way, the sobering ambience of the court turning even men prone to behaving badly into jurors behaving, well . . . well.

– Trevor Grove, *The Juryman's Tale*

Having heard the Crown's strongest evidence – the tapes – and the defence's strongest rebuttal – against Les McAtee's character – it would have been easy to jump to conclusions. But there was still a way to go. We battled to reserve judgment until we'd heard everything. Keep an open mind, keep an open mind.

We conducted hypothetical discussions about credibility, and how we should treat our doubts about a witness's credibility. If Les's story of the lost money was hard to believe, did that mean he was hard to believe as a witness overall? We all conceal things from time to time, and our memory fails us. If my actions today were the subject of a cross-examination in 18 months, I'm sure a half-decent lawyer could make me look as if I'm hiding a skeleton or two. If reconstructed as evidence in a trial, requiring corroboration and alibis and so on, nearly everything we do could later be made to smell very, very fishy.

Defence barristers use in-court techniques to illustrate this problem. Tom Molomby says:

> *In a case depending on identification, say, I ask jurors who was challenged and what were they wearing? What did they look like? Write your answers on a piece of paper, and compare them. I say that you won't all get it wrong but you won't all get it right either. Or, it's a gift during a trial if a noise happens, say a helicopter flying overhead. I'll ask later: 'Who was giving evidence when the helicopter flew over?' If they can't remember, how can a witness claim to remember every little thing?*

My work colleague David put a similar task to his fellow jurors: 'We were talking about remembering things, and there was one juror who couldn't remember the date of his own wedding.'

Cross-examination raises an interesting question about the nature of evidence. Is a witness's testimony a house of cards – where pulling one piece out will bring the whole thing down – or is it composed of more solid material? If Les told one lie, did that mean he would, or could, be lying about everything?

And what about the presumption of innocence? Of course we had to presume Rusher, the accused, was innocent until proven guilty. How did that presumption apply to a witness? Les was not on trial here – though a skilful defence lawyer can always divert the jury so that a hostile witness, rather than the accused, appears to be on trial. But Les's movements were not going to be corroborated or otherwise. He was only a witness. Maybe he stole Steve's money. Maybe he didn't. We'd never know. It was irrelevant, and yet the defence was trying, by inference and insinuation, to make it appear central.

Liars trick people every day. However hard it is to judge a person's credibility in ordinary commercial dealings, the task is infinitely harder in court, where barristers are twisting things this way and that, and the witness is well prepared and polished. Stephen Adler, *The Wall Street Journal*'s legal editor, reported on an experiment showing that good liars have an advantage over honest bumblers. He wrote:

Compared with truth-tellers, liars typically make fewer hand gestures, move their heads less, speak more slowly, and sit more rigidly, but . . . they betray their anxiety by shifting their feet or tapping their fingers. In addition, liars tend to relax their facial muscles and affect pleasant expressions, as if aware that observers will be watching their faces for signs of deceit.

In the New Zealand jury study, jurors made the obvious point that 'frank, forthright and genuine' witnesses who 'gave consistent evidence' were believed more than 'witnesses who contradicted themselves, were defensive or evasive, or became annoyed with cross-examining counsel'. More tellingly, though:

The fact that witnesses contradicted themselves or were proved to be telling lies did not necessarily mean that their evidence as a whole was rejected. In determining whether they should be believed or disbelieved, jurors in the main were prepared to look at all of the surrounding evidence, including any reasons there might be for their lies or contradictions. In some cases, they recognised that a witness was fudging the evidence, either because they were acting in self-preservation or because they were covering for someone else. Because the consequent lies and contradictions were

> *explicable in these terms, they accepted other aspects of the testimony where it was consistent with other surrounding evidence.*

The surveyed juries, in other words, rejected the 'house of cards' notion of a witness's credibility. Moreover, the New Zealand study found that 'credibility did not pose a problem for most jurors' and in nearly every case jurors were sensibly able to see through the smokescreen a lawyer would put up by 'putting the witness on trial'.

A complicating factor for juries on long trials, including ours, is the lack of clarity over whether transcripts of evidence will be supplied. Most of our jury seemed to think we'd get a transcript at the end of the case; and if there were parts of Les's evidence we wanted to go over again, we'd be able to.

But this was never made explicit, and eventually we had to ask the judge for a copy of Les's evidence in cross-examination. (Steve Rusher, who was obviously pinning great hopes on our doubting Les's credibility, seized on this morsel of information about the jury's leanings and gave us a big nodding smile.)

We should have been provided with transcripts as a matter of course. Our judge was typing away in a frenzy, and unless he was sending emails, I'd think he was making notes on the case. If he needed help remembering evidence, why shouldn't we?

New South Wales judges have a discretion to accept or reject a jury's request for a transcript. One juror in the 2001 NSW study said 'he only took sketchy notes during the trial because he expected the transcript to be provided for deliberations. He observed that, had he known that a transcript would not be provided, he would have put more detail in his notes.' Others referred to the inaccuracy of their notes and inconsistencies with the transcripts: 'Even though we all took our own notes throughout the trial, when we compared them they were often completely different accounts of what was on the record.'

One juror took 17 exercise books of notes and wanted to

work through every book during deliberations, recalling Elaine Hudson's character in *Joh's Jury*:

> Juror played by John Howard: *If the court reporter missed a word, he could come to you.*
> Hudson: *Just because I took notes and you didn't.*
> Howard: *I didn't have to. I've got a memory. How many of these bloody things did you fill up all full of gibberish and bullshit? You can't even work out if we're all at the same trial!*

One reason judges don't provide transcripts is that, in the words of a barrister, 'Once they know they've got them, the jurors can fall asleep during the trial and read it all afterwards.'

I thought this was a cop-out and an insult, and typical of a process that pays lip service to the importance of jurors yet treats us like children. In almost every recorded case, jurors take their duty far too seriously to 'fall asleep during the trial' and rely on transcripts later. And a juror who does fall asleep during a trial is not going to be interested enough to pore over transcripts to fill in the gaps. As for the problem of accuracy and provision of the transcripts, that is the court's problem, not the jurors'. If there is a contradiction between a juror's recall and what shows up on the official transcript, then jurors are smart enough to work out the true version. This is what they do anyway, without the assistance of a transcript.

Of our group, about half took notes, in varying detail. I filled about four exercise books. The Stickybeak made conscientious summaries of all witnesses' evidence. Shut The Gate doodled. X-Files scribbled furiously. Our Christian Mother tried to keep up, in her large looping handwriting, but struggled with the sheer volume of evidence. We all did these things in the expectation that a transcript would turn up later on to flesh out our skeletal notes.

(The New Zealand jury project proposed that witness statements and oral evidence be provided to the jury at the end of each day of the trial, noting that this would reduce deliberation time, and reduce the possibility of jurors making decisions based on false recall. The disadvantages, it said, would be that jurors might place too much weight on witnesses' words and not enough on their body language and general demeanour. One way around this, the authors suggested, would be to videotape all oral evidence and give the jury a VCR so they could play back parts of the testimony to refresh their memory. In my view, this would be ideal.)

As the Rusher case ground towards judgment day, while we were mulling over the peripheries – transcripts, the barristers' style, Les's evidence, Terri Maxfield's supposed actions – and eating lunch and bringing in fruit and cakes and taking our lunchtime walks, a magical thing was happening within this jury. We were becoming a deliberative body, identifying our leaders, developing our own ways of listening to minority views, debating issues in a reasonable and courteous manner. To each other, the blurry grey forms we'd been on Day One had sharpened into real characters who played set jury-room roles. Since I'd blurted out that I'd studied law, I was looked upon as a kind of oracle on procedural matters.

The Old Hand said that I should take on a role as 'mentor' to the jury. My fears that I'd be seen as a know-all were unfounded. Jurors who had stated confidently that the barristers earned $5,000 a day now genuinely wanted to know the real story. They were very curious about what the sentence would be if we found Rusher guilty. I didn't know, and the Old Hand added that considerations of the sentence should play no part in our thoughts. This wasn't *12 Angry Men*, where a guilty verdict would mean the electric chair for the accused. We estimated that if Rusher was to go down, he'd go for anything between five and 20 years, and that was where we left it.

The jurors were relentlessly curious about everything in the process, from why the judge wasn't wearing a wig (we all agreed now that he wasn't) to why defence lawyers always seemed more theatrical and manipulative than prosecutors.

While I didn't want to force my views on anyone, I appreciated the jurors' interest in letting me fill in a few gaps which, to be honest, I thought the court should have filled. For instance, nobody knew about the possibility of a hung jury until I raised it. I just said that that was a third option if it came to it. And it seemed wrong to me that a jury shouldn't know about this option. The judge, eventually, only offers two paths: unanimous conviction or unanimous acquittal. Nobody wants a hung jury, but yet again it is contemptuous of jurors to hide the reality.

My colleague David who was on a jury at the same time as I was said:

> *I would have hung the jury. I was that committed to an acquittal, and I didn't believe anyone could have talked me out of it. Besides, we'd spent several weeks in there and I wasn't going to let some idiot waste all that time.*

David stood at a knowledge advantage to other jurors because he'd been a court reporter for some years. Like me, he tried to use that advantage diplomatically:

> *I knew more about it than other jurors, but I had to balance that against the overall aim of trying to get the verdict I believed in. You don't want to be a know-all or a bully. What helped in our group was that there was a bully, and I took up the role as mediator between him and the others. He was an older man, hard of hearing, and he'd made up his mind in the first three days. He spent the rest of the time trying to push other people around.*

As it turned out, David was lucky – the bully also believed in an acquittal, and the unanimous verdict was smoothly achieved.

How does the transformation from 12 strangers into one deliberative group occur? Juror Trevor Grove thinks something akin to the Stockholm Syndrome, where hostages develop a kinship with their captors, occurs in juries: '. . . one could feel something growing between jurors, barristers, witnesses and judge which if not exactly a bond was certainly a sense of being all in this thing together.' As a result 'one could sense a determination on the jury's behalf that this trial should come out well in the eyes of everyone in court.'

It was the same with us. The Old Hand and the Stickybeak would often bring our discussions back to our overriding responsibility to 'make sure everyone hasn't been wasting their time'.

It's not only on legal points that jurors turn from a 12-person rabble into a deliberative body. It can be anything, as the leading American jury experts Valerie Hans and Neil Vidmar write:

> *Even before an actual jury retires to the privacy of the jury room, forces unconnected with the evidence presented at the trial are at work that will affect the goings-on of deliberation. Over the course of the trial, the jury undergoes a metamorphosis from a collection of twelve individuals into an enclosed group. Alliances between members develop during recesses, over lunches, while car-pooling, and even as a result of the location of the jurors' assigned seats. The social forces that promote this transformation are especially strong during an extended trial. However, during the presentation of evidence, jurors are forbidden to discuss the one thing that is on everybody's mind: the case itself. So jurors explore similarities and differences among themselves by discussing 'safe' topics like food, politics, current events, or sports. Views on these subjects provide clues to the jurors about the perspectives of their fellow jury members on the forbidden topic, the trial.*

Juries find all sorts of ways of bonding. Barrister Phillip Boulten recalls one:

> *I had a nine-month drug trial. The accused was on bail, and he wanted to go to the races on the weekend. The judge asked the jurors, and it turned out that some of them liked to go to the races too. It was improper for the accused and the jurors both to be at the races at the same time, so every Friday we had this routine where the judge asked jurors if they were planning to go to the races on Saturday. If not, the accused could go. It ended with an acquittal. Afterwards, the jury had a party in the top of a pub. They invited the police, and barristers, and eventually the accused was downstairs and he was invited up as well. Then he went to dinner, and shouted the jurors a huge Chinese meal. Two of them weren't invited to the party. They were the only ones. It turned out that the jurors had fought a lot, but in the end they were able to come to agreement on the charges.*

Sometimes dominant characters take over juries, not during the actual deliberations but during this alliance-building period while the evidence is heard. In the 1974 trial of John Mitchell and Maurice Stans, two alleged conspirators in the Watergate cover-up, one of the jurors was Andrew Choa, a highly informed, college-educated bank vice president. Choa had apparently lied during the voir dire, concealing a friendship with an assistant US attorney. The prosecutors were very happy that he came on.

Once on the jury, Choa emerged as the dominant personality. He took jurors to see a movie in his bank's private auditorium and arranged for them to see the St Patrick's Day Parade from a branch office. Choa was then able to call upon the ties he had forged with fellow jurors to influence the deliberations. Eventually, he converted the initial majority for conviction into a unanimous verdict of not guilty.

We had to listen to several more witnesses before the Crown closed its case: the courier who had collected the bail money for Yanni Diamondopoulos; the Queensland police officer first alerted by Les McAtee; and the federal policeman, Inspector Jim Fraser, who ran the phone-tapping operation. Most fascinating in all this was the videotape of Fraser's interview with Steve Rusher on the day of the arrest.

This was our first chance to connect the voice we'd heard on all those tapes with the man sitting across the courtroom. In the tape, Rusher wore a scarlet knit shirt and kept his arms folded defensively across his chest. Fraser gave him the boilerplate assurances about rights and freely given information and so on, and then got into the meat.

Rusher was calm and controlled. In his choice of what questions to answer and what not to answer, he showed a crystalline recollection of all the conversations we'd heard on tape. When he knew he might be incriminating himself, he gave a brusque 'No comment'. When the question was on some ancillary issue, he was expansive, even charming.

He had total mastery of himself. After Fraser read the charge, Rusher asked for a definition of 'solicit'. He asked if he'd be allowed to pursue his Family Court hearings without interference. He gave them his birth date, said he'd been 'living with' SJ until he went into immigration detention in Brisbane, described his daily routine at Silverwater, laughingly asking them back if they 'want the short answer or the long answer?' He said he'd received 'one or two' visitors, but didn't care to say who they were.

When they asked about his relationship with Fiona and hers with Maxfield, Rusher was charm incarnate: 'Hey man, I got nothing against her [Terri]. She ain't my kinda gal, but you guys would appreciate that . . .'

Did he dislike Fiona?

'No way, she's the mother of my boy. I don't dislike her at all . . . I got nothing against her – she and me, you know, together we gotta look after our son the best we can.'

Fraser asked if Rusher knew what would happen to SJ if Fiona and Terri died.

'Beats me,' Rusher said.

When they said they had recordings of his phone calls with Les McAtee, Rusher pulled in his horns: 'Cool, man, I hear what you're saying but I ain't saying it happened.'

Had he met Diamondopoulos?

'I meet a lotta people,' he said. 'But I ain't so good on names.'

Fraser asked him how long he'd known Les McAtee, but pronounced it 'Macarty'.

Rusher replied: 'I ain't never met anyone called Macarty.'

Fraser looked at his notes. Rusher thrust his chin.

'We just asked you about your phone calls with Les McAtee,' Fraser said. 'Now you're saying you don't know him?'

'Hey man, you said Macarty. I don't know anyone of that name. They may not even exist. But are you asking me about McAtee? That's a different matter.'

The longer it went on, the more his pedantry came out. He corrected Fraser when he called Fiona 'Mrs' Emery, saying she'd be 'Ms'. Before long he was fanatically pedantic. Correcting Fraser seemed to be the one outlet for the stress he was otherwise hiding.

When Fraser asked if he'd come to Australia on a false passport, Rusher said it wasn't a 'false passport', but 'a passport that had a visa that was cancelled'.

When Fraser asked if he was SJ's natural father, he said with sarcastic literalness: 'To the best of my knowledge.'

He asked for a break so he could make a phone call regarding his Family Court proceedings. When the tape resumed, Fraser asked him to affirm that the break had taken place and that he'd been given a glass of water. Rusher refused to affirm this. The detective looked at him.

Rusher pointed to the polystyrene cup of water on the table.

'I wasn't given a glass. I was given a cup.'

At the end of the interview, almost as an afterthought, Fraser asked him if he had intended the murder of anyone.

'No comment,' Rusher's hauteur oozed through.

That was the end of the interview, or almost. A policewoman came in to ask Rusher if he'd been beaten up or offered any 'inducements' to give the information he'd been giving. Rusher said yes, he had been given inducements. This set in train a long series of conversations outside the room between the police officers. Through the camera's eye, we watched Rusher sit on his own. He read a form and sipped his water and sat with his arms folded. It was a moment of eerie intimacy.

Finally the policewoman came back and asked him to explain these 'inducements'. It turned out that Rusher was just being a pain. The police hadn't offered him any inducements for the information he'd given in the interview. Rather, he said, an unnamed person had told him when he was leaving Silverwater that if he cooperated with the police then he might not have to come back.

We were getting a clearer and clearer picture of Steve Rusher.

On cross-examination, Mr Nisbett gave Inspector Fraser a hard time about the setting up of the phone taps. Nisbett couldn't work out why, given the possibility that a contract killer might be on the loose, they'd taken almost a month to get organised. Fraser answered that resources didn't permit quicker movement. Nisbett kept shooting us his now-expected sidelong looks: There are stories within stories here, and the cops are hiding something from you.

He was good at creating suspicion around the witnesses, Nisbett, but unfortunately for him he had scarce foundation on which to base it. He was just sowing suspicion for its own sake.

His grilling of Fraser did lead to a more fruitful line. Fraser produced phone records, in various forms, of calls coming in and going out of Les's line. One of these records was called a 'web trace', supplied to the police by Optus. Nisbett called for an adjournment to study this web trace. When the court resumed, he figured he'd hit paydirt: the web trace did not record five calls from Rusher in Silverwater to Les. Fraser had no ready answer for this.

The suggestion was clear: perhaps these calls hadn't taken place! Did the hint of a police conspiracy against Steve Rusher have some weight? Could it be that none of the calls had taken place?

The Crown team made some calls that afternoon, and the next day produced a new witness, Jessica Orrell from Optus. Orrell, a middle-aged technician-manager, gave a ready explanation for the calls not being recorded on the web trace. In short, the web trace was neither failsafe nor comprehensive. For example, Orrell said, if a call was made from a Telstra network and switched onto an Optus network, or vice versa, then the web trace would not pick it up. And so on. There were plenty of ways in which the web trace could miss a call.

'Including,' Mr Nisbett asked, 'the possibility that the call wasn't made?'

Ms Orrell could only agree.

The Crown finished its case in a rush of witnesses. Christine Farragher, the de facto of Diamondopoulos, came in. Well dressed and plummy-accented, Farragher, a secretary, impressed my fellow jurors, particularly the Retired Gent.

Others have noted the tendency among 'mature jurors' to value looks. As one juror-correspondent says:

> *One thing that struck me when we first began talking was how much store the older members of the jury put in appearance: we'd all seen the accused in court, and a couple of (older, male) members of the jury commented on the fact that he was so neat and clean, he presented very well, how could he possibly be capable of the crimes of which he'd been accused? There wasn't much comeback to that until the same jury members saw photos of the accused when he'd first been arrested – unshaven, long-haired, singlet-wearing, tattooed, desperate-looking,*

> etc. It struck me at the time, how much we rely on superficial appearances. Look neat and clean and you'll be accepted as a Good Citizen. A case for, appear in court as you appear in life?

Christine Farragher told how she'd met Diamondopoulos (in Athens, in 1998, while she'd been travelling); how they'd discussed marriage when they came to Australia together (but Christine, who was 'not so sure', 'played for time'); how Diamondopoulos's tourist visa had expired and they hadn't had the money to pay for a spouse de facto visa application; how he'd been arrested after apparently robbing an elderly man in Hornsby, and was thrown into Silverwater; and how he met Steve Rusher, who gave him advice on visa applications. At that time, Diamondopoulos had told Rusher that Christine was pregnant (she wasn't, but it didn't surprise her that Diamondopoulos would play for sympathy). Diamondopoulos then told Christine that Steve was offering to pay his bail. Christine said she hadn't liked the sound of Rusher, and wasn't keen on doing any kind of deal with him. But on her boyfriend's insistence, she'd played along. She collected the $15,000, and banked it in an account to secure Diamondopoulos's release, and bought air tickets to America. Now, 18 months later, she was no longer with Diamondopoulos, who in turn had been deported on his release from jail.

Mr Nisbett used Christine to retouch his portrait of Steve Rusher as a naive man who trusted people too much. She and Diamondopoulos had taken his money and tried to run off. Naughty Christine, abusing a benevolent man like Steve in this way.

For the Crown, the importance of Christine's evidence was in her corroboration of the Diamondopoulos money story. Rusher was insisting that he'd paid the bail for purely altruistic reasons, to help out a friend whose girlfriend was pregnant. But, the Crown was saying, if Rusher was paying the money innocently, why did he have to cover up his link with it? Why not just write them a cheque? Surely that would have been smarter. As a bail bond, in 30 days, the money would revert to whoever wrote the cheque. So why did he leave it at the desk in Les McAtee's name, for Christine Farragher to bank? It was a convoluted way of transferring some money to other people, and it heightened his chances of losing it.

The Crown's last witnesses were Detective Wise and a Silverwater guard named Tony Reginald (who confirmed that Rusher had made phone calls from his office). This was a tedious process where the witnesses were just corroborating minor facts – obviously for the Crown to safeguard itself, in case it won, against an appeal.

But our biggest test, as jurors, was still to come.

The Guessing Game

The participants in the trial must all have been dying to gauge our reactions. Detective Inspector Fraser said later that guessing juries:

> *. . . is a game we all play. We can only go on body language, which isn't much, but we try to work out which way they're leaning . . . The way they look at the accused and the witnesses tells you a lot . . . I'd love to be a fly on the wall of the jury room, but ultimately it's one of those things where you've just got to have faith.*

Mr Crown later said he'd more or less given up on guessing juries: 'There are the nodders, but you never know why they're nodding . . . There are jurors who start to fall asleep during a trial, and that might mean they've made up their minds – but you don't know which way.'

Says barrister Malcolm Ramage, more simply: 'We fantasise about what goes on in the jury room.'

Just as we jurors are voyeurs into the lives of the participants, they are trying to spy on our inner selves. Our mute anonymity seems to give them licence to scrutinise us in a way that, one juror says, 'Should any of them try it on the [train] they would get thumped.'

In response, we give them little to go on. Jurors almost never exercise their right to ask questions of witnesses, so the only data the players can collect is what we betray with our gestures, our demeanour and our questions to the judge.

Sometimes barristers are confident. 'When you speak,' says one, 'within a couple of seconds you can pick up so much from jurors about their receptivity to you.'

Barrister Phillip Boulten says that despite the paucity of information, guessing juries is a game played keenly:

> *All the time you're assessing what might be the dynamic in the jury room. You use that information and add it to snippets you pick up during the trial, to build some sort of picture of who's in which camp. Body language is the most frequent indicator. There is a juror who exclaims 'Bullshit!' when a witness says something, and a juror who smiles and winks at the accused. Some jurors refuse to look at you. They send messages to the judge, and you try to guess from that information which way they're going. When the jury comes into court, you assume that the people who sit next to each other there are also the ones sitting next to each other in the jury room. You can also tell things from the looks they shoot each other in the jury box in court. For example, if a foreman asks a very obvious question and the judge answers it and says, 'Does that answer it for you?', everyone in the jury looks at the person who had the question. So that's how we know.*

Among some advocates, there's a great science to guessing the jury. Sonya Hamlin advises lawyers to: Watch jurors as they wait

(Who paces? Who jokes? Who's alone? Who's preoccupied?); notice their posture (shifting, distribution of weight, slouching, upright, restless); notice how they file in and sit down (anxious, checks out room, fidgets, grips arms of chair, jiggles foot, crosses leg, primps with clothes or hair); notice what they carry in (book, expensive/cheap bag, newspaper); notice unusual physical characteristics (handicap, tall, short, extremes of weight or attractiveness); notice clothing (casual v formal, trendy v not, showy v subdued, matching v unmatching); notice how women hold their purses; notice what colours they wear ('Reds, yellows, oranges, greens show positive feelings, outgoing people, youthful, vigorous approaches to life'; 'Green shows growth and expansion, while blue indicates a cool, trustworthy, more cerebral personality. A blue suit on a man means that it is his best dress-up outfit and he takes the trial seriously'); notice how they listen to other people's answers (nervous, judgmental, indifferent, concerned); watch their eyes (contact etc.); notice who seems responsive to you.

As jurors, our natural instinct was to disguise our thoughts. At one point midway through the Rusher trial, the jury wanted a transcript of Mr Nisbett's opening submission. I had my doubts – I was pretty sure that a barrister's submission was not evidence – but I'd already put my foot in it, trying to downplay the weight people put on counsel's words by likening them to estate agents, so I figured I'd just let the judge deal with it and keep my big trap shut.

Storeman Foreman was writing the request to the judge on a piece of paper when someone said: 'Hold on, don't you think this will show them what we're thinking?'

Others agreed. So, to disguise our intentions, Storeman Foreman said: 'How about I ask for copies of both their opening statements?'

It was a clever suggestion, as far as disguising our thoughts was concerned. But it came to nothing. The judge told us submissions were not evidence, they wouldn't have been recorded in a transcript, so we should just concentrate on what the witnesses were saying.

I can't help wondering how barristers get by without slitting their wrists or turning to religion. All their preparation, all their time, their very livelihood, is poured down this mystical black hole of the jury box. They can only do their best, but in the end they know nothing. As Victorian Justice Richard McGarvie once said, 'The law has always been thought of as a chancy business. Even in the newspaper, the law list appears flanked by the weather and the shipping.'

Every so often, barristers will hear feedback from jurors after a trial.

> *A few years ago I had a seven-week trial that resulted in a hung jury. A week later, I was at a public function at which my presence had been advertised. I saw someone come into the room who had been on that hung jury. I remember jurors' faces for a few weeks after a long trial like that. She came straight to me. I said: 'Have we met before?' She said: 'Too right we have', and proceeded to tell me about what had gone on. What she said was very disturbing. There was one man on the jury who had always sat apart from the others. He took the view that women shouldn't be on juries, and he didn't talk to the women at all. There were ten people on this jury. Two had been excused. Three of the four women in the group were on our side. Overall it was 5-5. This man so objected to women speaking that the only way they could voice their deliberations was to give them to a man who would repeat them for the group. We had picked this man as a ratbag, a convicter. We'd picked another man as a Henry Fonda character, he looked intelligent, thoughtful, seemed to care. It was just his expression. But you get to a point in any trial where if someone is going to be against you, they will shut you out. But this particular woman, we had*

> *no idea that she was very strongly on our side. Jurors don't show you much if they don't want to. She saw through the prejudicial stuff. And partly thanks to her, we got through to half of them.*
>
> *In my first case, as a junior, a babysitter was accused of killing a baby. The whole case rested on medical evidence about the effect of shaking on the baby's brain and so on. The jury acquitted her. Later, I ran into the foreman. I expected him to say something about how complex the medical evidence was, but instead he said: 'We didn't know anything about that evidence. We just thought the babysitter had suffered enough already.' I learned then that no matter how carefully you go through evidence for them, the jurors will come up with their own reasons for their decision. In that same case, one juror tried to convince the others that the mother asking the babysitter not to throw the baby in the air was a 'lawful command'. This is crap. The juror was just making up his own law to impose his views. But he failed.*
>
> *I cross-examined a policeman in a murder trial. I thought I'd done pretty well. Had I convinced the jury, though, that he was a liar? One of my colleagues was talking to a sheriff's officer, and asked him that question. The officer said yes, he thought he was a liar. Was it because of my skilful cross-examination? No. The officer said: 'You only have to look at his face to know he's a liar.'*

The most experienced barristers will hold back from forming strong opinions about the way the jury is going. As we'd shown, juries like to put on a mask. Tom Molomby opines:

> *You can't read your own personality into the jurors. It's what they think, not what you'd think in their shoes, that*

matters . . . I never reach a firm conclusion about what the jury is thinking, so I won't plan a strategy based on that. We've all had warm, open juries who convict and cold, alienated juries who acquit. It's a fascinating guessing game, but one that can only leave you feeling insecure.

CHAPTER TWELVE

'LADIES AND GENTLEMEN . . . I CALL STEVEN RUSHER'

Like Marlow in *Heart of Darkness*, we had been travelling up a long river in search of Mr Kurtz. Our Kurtz sat opposite us in the courtroom, five or six paces away, yet he remained as elusive as Marlow's quarry in the African jungle. We held a composite portrait – from the barristers' submissions, from Spike's tapes, from Les McAtee, from the arrest videotape, from all the witness statements – yet the man himself seemed tantalisingly out of reach.

From a juror's point of view, the centre of gravity in the courtroom lies heavily in the person of the accused. Similarly, to the accused it is we jurors who are the mystery, and our faces, our unknown personalities, our prejudices and influences are both crucial and unreachable. Essentially, the criminal trial is a mute dialogue between the accused and us. The judge, the barristers and solicitors, the witnesses, all the participants who make so much noise, dissolve into the background of this two-sided puzzle.

Steve Rusher had been examining us with decreasing subtlety as the trial wore on. When there was something to laugh at, like Mr Nisbett he would join us in the joke, making eye contact wherever he could. Under his glossy dark blond mane, his eyes had the habit of following you around. In the jury room one day,

Storeman Foreman said Rusher had been 'staring at me all the time. I s'pose he reckons I'm the one who has all the say. Silly bugger. I just look straight back at him and give him a smile.'

Other jurors said they couldn't look at him. One, the JP, said after the trial that he was unable to sleep at night for fear that Rusher might be lining up a hitman to knock him off.

'When I'm walking home from the station, I never look behind me,' he said. 'I don't know who might be following. My street's full of crims. You never know if he's been talking to one of them.'

Far-fetched as it sounds, JP's fear is commonly shared by jurors in murder trials. The authors of the New Zealand jury project wrote:

> *Jurors in four cases spoke of feeling intimidated and scared after the case, and one commented that although the court attendant had warned them after the trial of the accused's violent nature, no assistance was offered in getting home.*

In an American trial of Mexican drug-charge defendants, a juror wrote that another juror 'thought that perhaps the reason so many of us were suffering various kinds of stress symptoms was "brujeria", or witchcraft, which might be coming from Mexico.'

In Australia, one of the jurors on Ivan Milat's 1998 trial received a threatening telephone call, and in the case of *R v Richards and Bijkerk* in 1999, the jury was given an envelope containing allegations against one of the accused that had not been raised in court. An Australian juror who contacted me after her trial said it wasn't only the accused who struck fear into jurors:

> *During the last two weeks of the trial, jury members including myself were stalked and intimidated by family members of the accused. They knew where we were*

leaving the building and they would follow us. We informed the judge and he took precautionary measures for our safety.

This may suggest that the jurors had ceased to presume the accused innocent. But it is more complicated than that. The surroundings of the court and the exceptional strangeness of jury service imbue a sense of fear that you cannot understand until you have been a juror. You, as much as the accused, are on show in a matter of awesome importance. It's not something you face every day. Inside this pressure cooker, fear of the accused or his family and friends is a natural response, even if you don't think he's guilty of the crime.

Another fearful jury took steps against what they saw as intimidation by the accused:

We started off sitting in the same seats in the jury box every day, but the accused was staring at the woman in the front left corner, closest to him. After a while, she said she was getting the creeps from the way he was looking at her. So we decided to rotate through that seat.

I can't say I was afraid of Steve Rusher. He seemed too alone in the world to pose a threat. It wasn't as if he had a posse of shadowy friends coming to court to intimidate us. It wasn't as if *anyone* had come to court on Rusher's behalf. But, as a journalist, I've had the odd death threat and I've developed a gut feeling for which are serious (almost none) and which are just hot air (almost all). My life experience, in this regard, would not be typical for a juror. Most jurors, I imagine, are already softened up by the intimidation and novelty of the criminal trial, and the distance from this general fear into a specific sense of peril is not a great one.

We really wanted Steve Rusher to come to the witness box. In most trials, it is natural for jurors to want to hear the accused's side of the story from the horse's mouth, not just from a patchwork of testimony and counsel's sales pitch. As a juror, you are probably the only person in the courtroom who has no personal agenda – you just want to find the truth. And who better than the accused to satisfy that desire?

'Again and again I found myself sitting in court looking across at Milcray,' juror Graham Burnett says of the accused in his trial.

> *Only he knew what had happened . . . the truth was therefore in the room with us, in our midst, in a physical form, almost tangible, but totally illegible . . . Who was he? That was the inescapable question . . . Infuriatingly, we could only learn this if he chose to testify.*

The juror just wants to sit face to face with the accused and hear his or her story. If the accused does take the stand, the middlemen and their rules are swept away. All that remains is the accused, and the jury.

If you were looking upon a trial as entertainment, the non-appearance of the accused would be *Hamlet* without Hamlet, *Seinfeld* without Seinfeld. If you are looking upon a trial as a truth-seeking exercise, where can truth really lie except in the head of the accused?

'This was good news,' Johnathan Carter says when the accused takes the stand.

> *I think we all need to hear what he has to say because the situation up to this point could go either way and in some ways he has come across as a manipulator . . . but there are a lot of imperfect people in the world; that did not mean he was a murderer.*

This was how we felt about Rusher. We'd heard the evidence against him, but we were open-minded enough to want his side of the story. (This curiosity is backed up by research, says

Abramson, which 'shows that jurors find it far easier to convict persons they have not personally encountered'.)

Yet most defence lawyers will not call the accused to the stand. Some will go to great lengths, such as the accused man in a 2005 trial in the Downing Centre who came to court with a pear in each pocket and hurled them, with a volley of abuse, at the jurors. If his intention was to have the trial aborted, he failed; the judge reprimanded him but retained the jury. Most defendants will opt out. Barrister Ian Barker feels that it's a risk either way:

If a case is going well, it is usually safer not to risk calling the accused. If it is going badly, it may be that only the accused can save the day. There are many examples of cases lost because of the accused's own evidence.

Barker, who prosecuted Lindy Chamberlain, says that her first trial, at which she took to the stand, was a 'good example' of an accused person being her own worst enemy.

There are often good tactical reasons for not calling the accused, as some trial lawyers point out:

For me and for anybody I know, you don't call your guy unless you have to. He might have a hot temper, and the Crown will wind him up. He might be guilty, and not smart enough to protect himself. In those cases, you definitely don't call him up . . . There's so much courtroom drama on TV these days, jurors will understand why you've chosen not to call your guy.

The decision to call or not call the accused is totally jury-dependent. What is the jury thinking? What will they think of him? That's all that matters.

> *Normally, the defence is at its strongest at the end of the Crown case. A defendant's evidence isn't going to do a lot for you. You've been exposing cracks and creating doubts about the Crown case all week. Why on earth would you put your person in the box to have the same done to him? You can undo all your good work. On the other hand, if your case isn't looking good after the Crown case, then your client probably won't be able to turn it around. So I generally leave him out of it. But it's the client's choice. If he doesn't come up, he may seem to be hiding something. But then again, he might come up and bury himself.*

In most cases, the only courtroom input from the accused is to hope for the best and give off an innocent vibe. One criminal lawyer says, 'I tell the client to keep an eye on the jury and try to look likeable, because they're sussing him out.' But, he adds, sometimes this can rebound, as the client 'will also want to suss them out. I've had male clients say that a female juror wants to fuck him – after they've been looking at the jury for long enough, they can get these ridiculous delusions.'

Aware of how potently a silent defendant can influence a jury, lawyers will use every trick to help that impression be a positive one.

> *If he has family or friends who are there, I always get the solicitor to talk to them and show the jury that we have support in court. If there's a kid, we bring the kid in on at least one occasion, especially if the accused is the mother. A man had his wife and four daughters behind him in one trial, and somehow we got into the evidence that he was the breadwinner for that family. There will be at least a few people on the jury who will be looking to acquit him after hearing something like that. Sometimes those things are more important than the evidence.*

> *It can even work with judges. We took the prisoner in with us to the Court of Criminal Appeal, and one of the judges smiled at him. He was 18 and looked 14 . . . I knew that that judge had a son the same age, and figured he'd be less likely to lengthen the sentence if he saw the prisoner himself.*

Is there more to gain or lose by the accused taking the stand? Steve Rusher and his legal team must have been debating this at some length. Did he think that his tendency to weep and wipe his nose with a handkerchief every time SJ's name came up was making a good impression on the jurors, or a bad one? Did he hear how his voice on the tapes changed from self-assured to shrill? Did he hear himself as we'd heard him – and if so, how would this influence his decision to take the stand or not?

I can't say what was in Rusher's mind when he decided to give evidence. Perhaps it was simply, as he later told me, that 'I've done jury service as well, and I know that when jurors walk into a courtroom they immediately assume that if this guy has been arrested then he must be guilty.'

I disagree. Most jurors are responsible enough to presume innocence, even if it runs contrary to their instincts. But, in the mind of the accused, things can get distorted. Being under armed guard isn't great for your image.

(The bad odour around the accused has, at times, led to humorous court exchanges, such as this one from a 1980 case where the defence lawyer said to the jury: 'You may be misled by the arrangement of the court into thinking that the accused are [sic] guilty. It has been said that if the Archbishop of Canterbury were sitting in the dock that he would look like a criminal. Now my client doesn't look like a criminal . . .' At this point the prosecutor butted in: 'Nor does he look like the Archbishop of Canterbury.')

The accused's so-called right to remain silent has evolved from the earliest days of our trial system. It wasn't always the case that the accused could keep quiet. Indeed, the fundamental safeguard for the accused 'was not the right to remain silent but rather the opportunity to speak'. But in his 1637 heresy case, John Lilburne refused to answer questions on oath, and the House of Lords upheld Lilburne's conduct, saying it was 'contrary to the laws of nature and the kingdom for any man to be his own accuser'. Over time, this was mistakenly thought of as a 'right' to silence. That's not correct. It's not a legal 'right'. But the accused is under no compulsion to give evidence, and if he makes that choice, the jury is not to draw any adverse inferences from that silence.

But do they? Wouldn't any ordinary juror see something suspicious in a defendant's silence? The 2001 NSW jury study found that:

> *Two jurors admitted that they thought it odd that the accused did not testify in his defence. They said the jury discussed it and pronounced it 'weird'. However, both jurors were certain that this was only one element among many that proved to them that the accused was guilty. One of these jurors stated that eleven jurors took to task a fellow juror who openly declared that his conclusion that the accused was guilty was based solely on the fact that the accused did not give evidence.*

Misguided, yes, but quite instinctive. If a defendant fails to defend himself, it's only natural for jurors to suspect him more. Yet the courts cling to the fiction that the jury will not draw any adverse inferences from silence.

One judge seems to be more clued in when he says that:

> *. . . the reality mocks the rule. Judges solemnly tell juries not to draw adverse inferences from a defendant's silence, knowing that they will. Juries draw such inferences notwithstanding instructions to the contrary because to do so is plainly common sense.*

His solution seems a good one to me:

> *In the first place juries should be told that they cannot draw any adverse inferences unless it would be reasonable to expect the defendant to deny, explain or answer the question, answer or evidence. And they should be told about any possible innocent explanation for the silence. But they must be told that, in the end, it is for them to decide whether, having regard to any possible explanation, they think it reasonable to draw an adverse inference from the silence.*

In other words, jurors can draw adverse inferences from silence (as they undoubtedly do), as long as there's a reason to do so. But also, if they choose to draw those inferences, they're not a 'knockout blow'. As with everything else, those inferences must be weighed up against everything else.

From a juror's point of view, this judge's suggestion seems not so much a radical plan as a recognition of what already happens.

The Crown case was closed after nearly a month, and after a short adjournment Mr Nisbett got up and made a solemn little speech. He told us that there was no compulsion on Steve Rusher to take the stand, and he did so knowing that he'd be cross-examined. It was a risky move, Nisbett implied. But Steve Rusher wanted to assure us, personally, of his innocence. He was prepared to take the risk because he thought we would believe his version of events.

'Ladies and gentlemen of the jury,' Nisbett said as if he were introducing the Prime Minister, 'I call Steven Rusher.'

(The gravitas of Mr Nisbett's address was slightly diminished by a minor slip-up. Having been a cheeky, even impish figure in cross-examination, he now addressed us with great solemnity. Yet he hadn't got his wig on quite straight. As he addressed us in the severest terms about Rusher, Nisbett's side curly bits were all skewy, around his forehead. On the other side, the curly bits disappeared around behind his ear. It was surprising – in all other ways, he'd been smooth and professional. Despite myself, I couldn't help staring at it. It was like a headmaster dressing you down, but all you can look at is his slipped toupee.)

Rusher was let out of his box. He strode across the court in front of us, confidently. He didn't look our way. Inevitably, when you've formed such a comprehensive picture of a person on limited evidence, you're going to be surprised when you see and hear him up close, in the flesh. Rusher was bigger than I'd expected. He was tall, with a bullocky strength in his chest that gathered up into his neck. His head was large and his thick hair even glossier than from afar, and his eyes had a penetrating, almost mesmeric blueness. He gave an impression of self-belief, assurance, and charisma. He couldn't help fancying himself. I wondered if what we saw was Steve Rusher trying to hide his self-regard, or Steve Rusher pushing himself to the front, in the belief that he could positively visualise his way to an acquittal. I suspect the latter. When he started answering the pro forma questions about his details and background, he spoke with a half-smile, almost a cocky smirk. His voice was deep and relaxed. One thing caught our eye: his left hand, which he waved about to illustrate a point, was quite badly burnt. The fingers were waxy-webbed. This was to give rise to furious speculation in the jury room: Accident? Self-immolation? Tortured by thugs in the movie industry, or in jail?

In any case, Rusher didn't mind showing his disfigured hand. He waved it about like an amputated stump in a compo case. He half-turned in our direction while answering questions, as if to take us into his confidence. He didn't quite look at us, though, adhering to advocacy teacher Sonya Hamlin's caution: 'The witness should look at the lawyer, because that's what most people expect . . . If you ask the witness a question and he turns to the jury to answer, it looks like a performance.'

He gave his version of the full story. Most of the early

chapters were consistent with what we'd already heard, although he was somewhat patronising about Fiona's status when she met him. She'd been 'laying about' at the time, whereas he was 'just your average millionaire'.

After their relationship broke down, Rusher portrayed himself as a victim in the battle over SJ. Fiona had capriciously refused to let him see his son, communicating through her lawyers and taking harsh measures to keep him away. He said a court order had entitled him to access to SJ, and it was to defy that order that Fiona hatched the plan to move to Australia – again, Rusher implied, to keep him away from 'my little guy'. Yes, he admitted kidnapping SJ to come to Australia illegally, but he said 'no father wouldn't at least think of doing the same.' He'd met Les McAtee and asked him in good faith to help conceal the source of his emails, because he was on the run. He intended to serve documents on Terri Maxfield for use in the Family Court hearings.

He hadn't known that Les was the one who turned him in. He'd planned, once he'd 'served the papers' on Terri, to turn himself in. But he didn't want to be deported while Fiona and SJ moved down to Tasmania to live with Maxfield. So he served the subpoena on himself for the kidnapping matter, and also applied for refugee status.

We were played an audiotape of Rusher's appearance at the Refugee Review Tribunal. It was another enlightening source on his state of mind. He said he'd been on suicide watch in jail, and was taking Valium at night. This tape was meant to show that he was suffering an unbalanced mental state. It didn't, really. He spoke a little slower than usual, but this was Steve Rusher at his sharpest. He argued – absurdly but eloquently – that he faced persecution by being in the USA because SJ was going to be harmed by Maxfield in Australia. It was a long bow, and the RRT recognised it as such. It was another of those incidents where I couldn't help admiring Rusher's wiliness and imagination, and felt grudging pity for his failure.

He said he'd given Les the money, and Les had 'lost it'. He'd given Diamondopoulos money for his bail because 'I gave help to people who asked me for it.' He was a pro bono jailhouse lawyer and philanthropist. In the end, he said, he'd been a bad judge of people, but that was all. People had stolen money from him and abused his naive trust. He'd been deeply depressed. He was vulnerable and suggestible. Every now and then he'd half-turn to us in the jury, and stress his point with his burnt hand.

He said he had 'good reason' to believe that living in a 'lesbian household' would harm SJ, and this may have affected his judgment. Had Rusher planned to have Fiona or Terri murdered?

'No way, sir.'

Were the tapes, then, fabrications?

'I assume so, sir.'

Back in the jury room, some were looking forward to Mr Crown's cross-examination. In response to their view that Mr Nisbett had a lot more personality and verve than Mr Crown, I'd explained that a prosecutor's job differs from a defender's, and gives him less latitude to play up. But all the same, up to this point Mr Crown had been calmly, even dozily, presenting his witnesses while Mr Nisbett had hit all the confrontational high notes. Now it would be Mr Crown's chance to show what he was made of – unless he'd grown overconfident.

Our brains were being slowly baked by a month in the jury room. The Old Hand, the Stickybeak and Shut The Gate had a spirited, good-natured argument about what we'd had for lunch the previous day – canneloni, lasagne or chicken? The meals were not, needless to say, the most memorable part of the experience. Jurors discussed parking fines, speeding fines and personal appearances before magistrates – our brushes with the justice system that seemed so piffling now. We talked about movies and TV shows we'd seen lately. The JP said he'd won first prize in a bingo competition. The younger generation – the clique of Shut The Gate, Friday Night and Storeman Foreman – began to poke fun at JP's stutter more and more brazenly. The Old Hand shot them a warning look. It wouldn't be long now, she was saying. Let's just get out of this without hurting anyone's feelings.

Borderline, who'd seemingly given up on trying to chat up Friday Night, turned his attentions to me. He'd been impressed by the fact that I'd done half a law degree – though I couldn't tell if he was more impressed that I'd started it, or that I'd dropped out. He murmured bitterly about how the judge was 'dining out on lobster and a bottle of Verdelho' every lunch and that we should 'go in there and turn him upside down, mate, the revolution won't be televised!' As a kind of compliment, he confided to me that he thought *Daily Telegraph* readers were much dumber than *Sydney Morning Herald* readers. Now that Friday Night was hanging out with the more normal young guys, Borderline started to entertain me with his plans for seducing her. One Friday afternoon, I asked Borderline what he was planning for the weekend, and he said with a mischief he'd gathered, like lint, the longer the trial wore on: 'I think I'll take out a certain young lady with an expensive bottle of red – a quick blow to the head – the expensive ones don't break so easily – my head that is – and let her have her wicked way with me. Pity she's wearing that bloody potato sack today.' She'd turned up in a loose beige linen dress, slinging her Friday night clobber along in her carry-bag.

(We were all lucky that Borderline was, as he would confess, 'more fart than shit' on the question of seduction. Had he so much as touched Friday Night, we could have been discharged, like a District Court jury in a 2004 trial which was aborted after a male juror groped a woman.)

More than ever, now that we were nearly home, jurors opened up about themselves. Borderline told exaggerated stories about how he'd been 'shipwrecked' once off the coast of Queensland. Shut The Gate said that down at the leagues club he knew a lot of professional footballers who were on steroids and ecstasy. Friday Night, who seemed most bored by proceedings and most willing to get away early, suddenly revealed that she was adopted, but she'd never sought out her natural mother because she hated her.

'I laugh just like my [adoptive] parents, even though I'm not theirs. I've even got red hair like my [adoptive] mum. My real parents could be dead for all I care.'

The jury room had become our second home. At the start of another day, Borderline said: 'Welcome to the Heartbreak Hotel. You can check out, but you can never leave.'

With the end in sight, we appreciated each other's company more. The Old Hand said the trial had taught her the names of all the train stations between her home and the city, which she'd never known. For others, like JP and possibly Borderline, this group of 12 had become their primary social circle. JP kept trying to get the Old Hand to join him at 'the club' for dinner, and the Old Hand kept trying to hint that she was married. Borderline issued several invitations 'to get together and get snot-blind once this is over', though his invitation seemed directed exclusively to Friday Night. Since she'd confessed to being adopted, Borderline had renewed his forays in her direction, saying softly: 'I think I might be adopted, too. But if I'm not, I wish I was.'

It was easy to get sidetracked and lose focus on the real reason we were here. And our most serious task was still in front of us. We had to make a decision about this man in the witness box.

We didn't say much about Rusher during the days of his cross-examination, other than a few physical observations. He wore the same navy blue suit every day, and the same tie. He alternated between a white and a blue shirt. (It's interesting that the accused should dress in his best, notes Trevor Grove, to impress a jury 'whose male members are generally the worst-dressed people in the courtroom'.) The Retired Gent noticed that Steve wore thick green prison socks unchanged for three days. Rusher nicked himself shaving, and sported a cut on his chin. The women jurors gossiped about whether he had to sleep in his cell during the trial, or if he was out on bail.

Mr Crown kept Rusher in the box for three solid days. It seemed a lot longer. From Mr Crown's point of view, it soon turned into an occasion where the better the witness is for your side, the longer you keep him in front of the jury.

Mr Crown went back to the weakest point in the defence, or the strongest point in the prosecution: the tapes. Rusher had said the conversations were fabricated. He didn't know how, but said the inaccurate timings on Spike's records and the absence of a web trace record of some of his calls to Les strongly suggested that these conversations had never taken place.

The prosecution team had been doing some analysis on Rusher's speech patterns. He often used the expressions 'Man', 'Dude', 'Buddy', and so on. He also repeated the word 'like' in the middle of sentences, stuttering slightly, as if to marshal his thoughts.

Rusher accepted that this might be so.

'Hey man, that's for you guys to judge, but like, I accept this might be the way I speak,' Rusher said. 'There you are, I'm doing it now.'

This was quite funny. I laughed, looking down into my lap. When I looked up at the courtroom, Mr Nisbett was laughing along with me.

Mr Crown showed where these expressions and tics had surfaced consistently throughout the taped conversations. He asked Rusher how he could possibly argue that this wasn't him speaking.

Rusher admitted it was his voice, but said there must have been samples stitched together and reconstituted into incriminating conversations.

Rather than challenge him yet, Mr Crown went through the transcripts, piece by piece, asking Rusher to explain why he'd said what was on these tapes.

Rusher was up to the task. He said that some conversations – the harmless ones, about music or movies or TV shows – were authentic, but others were not. This went on for hour after hour – Mr Crown pointing to an incriminating portion of the transcript, and Rusher replying that this was one of the bits that had been spliced in.

Softly, Mr Crown said: 'Do you mean to tell the jury that some devious person has cobbled together parts of your conversation from other tapes, and then reconstructed them into the tapes we've heard?'

'Yes sir, that's what I'm saying.'

'And who would this devious person be?'

'I gotta theory – and it's only a theory – that it was Les McAtee.'

'Oh, and how did Les McAtee do this?'

Rusher can't have heard the first rule of politics: When you're in a hole, stop digging. He started to improvise, saying that Les had framed him by building a 'voice bank' of his speech from other taped conversations, and then created these new conversations which we'd heard.

Mr Crown made merry with this. Was Les some kind of evil genius with the expertise and equipment to splice together all these conversations and recreate all these incriminating tapes without a hint of discontinuous background noise, without a bump or a jump or a blip?

'I can't say how the guy did it,' Rusher said. 'All I'm saying is, like, it's my theory. I mighta said these things, but I did not say them the way they come out on these tapes.'

He was sliding deeper and deeper, like a man wriggling in quicksand. I can't speak for the rest of the jury, though I know there was one member – Borderline – who couldn't keep his emotions to himself. We'd have barely pushed ourselves to our feet to take a break, and would still be near Rusher, who was only a few feet away, when Borderline would blurt 'How stupid was he?' or 'Doesn't look good for Mr Rusher!'

At one point, in open court, when Rusher went into yet another elaborate explanation of how he might have said such-and-such words in a different context but not in the context we'd heard, he finished by saying: 'Does that make sense?'

Borderline, who could contain himself no longer, shouted: 'No!'

He might have made up his mind, but Borderline had no close friends on the jury and zero influence. Most of the others just wanted him to keep his opinions to himself. He was, nevertheless, capable of coming up with a good line. After Rusher had been giving evidence about his home in Hollywood, the Retired Gent, who seemed obsessed with the glamour of Hollywood and couldn't shake off the idea that Steve Rusher was some great mogul, asked: 'I wonder what's become of the Hollywood home now.'

'I know!' Borderline piped up. 'Mr Nisbett owns it!'

The longer Mr Crown's cross-examination of Rusher dragged on, the deeper Mr Nisbett sank into his seat. He gave up looking at us. He shook his head. I may have been wrong, but I caught the vibe that Nisbett and Rusher had had a falling-out. Maybe Nisbett had counselled him against testifying. It wouldn't surprise me if they had disagreed – Rusher was more lawyer than the lawyers, clearly a strong-willed defendant. (After the trial I was told that they had fallen out even sooner. So pessimistic was he about winning, Rusher had started preparing his appeal early in the trial. Understandably, Nisbett took offence. But Rusher said that the lawyers cost so much, he may as well knock over two birds with one stone.)

Nisbett's dismay was visible. He'd built the best case he could by querying police methods, insinuating corruption, attacking Les, and so on – building a case on doubt, and hoping the jury would find these doubts reason enough to acquit – and here was Steve in the stand, constructing a whole new defence: that Les McAtee was an evil genius who fabricated the tapes. What this did was give Mr Crown the opportunity to bring our attention back to what Nisbett wanted us to forget: the tapes, the tapes, the tapes.

Lawyers don't generally like telling anecdotes about their failures, but Malcolm Ramage tells a couple that reflect squarely on the risks in calling – and not calling – the accused to give evidence: 'I had a case where the accused, while he was in the box, kept jerking his head towards the jury while he was answering questions. It didn't look good, very jerky and nervous. I was sure the jury didn't like it. When I asked him what he was doing, it turned out that a paralegal had told him to look at the jury while answering.'

But in another case, the jury did draw adverse inferences from the accused's non-appearance: 'I did an assault case, in which the jury convicted. A juror came to the sentencing and heard what a good character the man he'd convicted was. Later, the juror came up to me and said, "I'd give him a job, he seems a nice cut of fellow." So why had they convicted him? The juror said: "Because you didn't call any witnesses."'

At times Steve Rusher's evidence was tedious, particularly when the exchanges repeated themselves over and over. There was a moment when a deep, slow breathing filled the courtroom. I looked around. Was the judge asleep? The court reporter? No, it was one of the guards, catching up on some kip.

Perhaps fearing the onset of slumber in the jury box, mild-mannered Mr Crown showed some fire. His exchanges with Rusher grew testy. He was running out of patience with Rusher's incessant hair-splitting. Clearly Mr Crown wanted to give us the impression that Rusher had come up into the stand because he'd thought he could bamboozle us dimwitted jurors. Mr Crown's spin was that this was an arrogant man hoist on his own petard.

After mining the tapes for all they were worth, Mr Crown progressed to the discussion of money with Spike. If Spike was just a guy Rusher was commissioning to 'serve legal documents' on Terri Maxfield, why was Rusher offering him $30,000?

'To protect SJ,' Rusher drew himself up, 'no expense would be, like, too much.'

'But,' Mr Crown countered, 'you said you'd already hired a private investigator in Hobart to "serve documents" on Terri Maxfield. Where's the record of this?'

Rusher said that it had come out of a fund of money he'd left with his solicitor. He hadn't been sent an account.

Mr Crown doubted this, which led to some digging from the defence and the production, the next day, of an account from a private investigator. He'd trawled the gay bars of Hobart for about 15 hours, at $40 an hour. There was evidence of this, at least. But it backfired on Rusher, because Mr Crown came back at him with: 'You paid a private investigator around $500 to serve documents on Terri Maxfield. He failed to do that. So now you're saying you would give an unknown waste contractor $30,000 to go down there and do exactly the same thing over again?'

'I did it because SJ was worth it,' Rusher snapped. 'I'd spend $40,000, or like, anything, for my little guy.'

With this, the ever-present handkerchief was in his hand, wiping his nose and eyes.

I'd noticed during Mr Nisbett's cross-examinations of Crown witnesses that he'd save the direct question – 'Did you shoot Montgomery Burns?' – until the very end. It must be in the barrister's handbook that you build up your argument against a witness, undermine their credibility, slowly, steadily, and then at the end, to pull all the threads together and re-focus the jury, ask quite simply whether he dunnit.

So we knew Mr Crown had reached the end of his long, long cross-examination when he asked Rusher:

'Did you solicit to murder Terri Maxfield?'

'No, sir.'

'Did you solicit to murder Fiona Emery?'

'No way, sir!'

I looked at Rusher. You had to admire his cool. He must have been rehearsing this in front of the prison cell mirror for months. When the moment for the big performance came, he didn't miss a beat.

CHAPTER THIRTEEN

SUMMING UP
OR
HOW JURORS ARE SOLD A BILL OF GOODS BY MEN IN GOWNS

If you say he is guilty when he is innocent there's a killer on the loose – and if you say he is innocent when he is guilty there's a killer on the loose.
— Trevor Grove, *The Juryman's Tale*

When he was a Supreme Court judge, Sir John Barry was presiding over a case in which the last witness left the stand at 3.45pm. He asked the jury if they'd like to hear the closing address from the prosecuting barrister, Don Campbell, immediately or in the morning.

The foreman stood up and said: 'If he hadn't been repeating himself over and over again, this whole case would have been over now.'

Nevertheless, the jury agreed to hear him straightaway. Campbell opened up by saying: 'It's very hard for us barristers down here to know what's going on in your minds.' To which the foreman interjected: 'If you knew what's going on in my mind, you'd shut up now.'

At the end of a long trial, it's hard indeed for a barrister to know if he's about to make his most crucial contribution, or wasting his time. Jury surveys indicate that most jurors have made up their minds about their verdicts before they retire to deliberate. But a responsible lawyer must assume that every case is winnable and every case is losable, right up to the last breath.

Mr Crown got up first, and guided us on a painstaking tour of the principal evidence. Mostly he concerned himself with the tapes. He'd made several dozen notes about the tapes which, he said, proved that Rusher had solicited Spike to kill, or order the killings of, Terri and Fiona.

'Solicit,' Mr Crown said, 'means simply to ask, or try to persuade.'

So if we thought Rusher had commissioned the murders but later changed his mind, that would not save him. Once he'd asked Spike to do the job, the crime was committed.

Mr Crown appealed for us to use our brains, not our hearts. Even if Terri Maxfield were a 'sexual deviant', or even if Rusher believed she was, this did not excuse the crime. The point was Rusher's intent, and the tapes 'make it crystal clear what Spike and the accused were talking about'.

Mr Crown informed us that we had to decide unanimously. He believed, trying to sound more like a commentator than an advocate, that the Crown had a very strong case against Steve Rusher.

After a break, Mr Crown tried to anticipate what Mr Nisbett would come up with. He would say the tapes were faked and Crown witnesses were lying.

'Well,' Mr Crown said, 'it's clear that one side or the other is lying.'

He predicted that Mr Nisbett would say Les McAtee had manipulated Rusher and cajoled him into saying things he didn't mean – but, Mr Crown said, we'd seen what a 'cunning and resourceful man' Rusher was, and we could never believe he could be manipulated by Les.

Mr Crown expected the defence to target Les's mysterious police friend, and ask us to wonder why he hadn't given evidence. What was this relationship? Mr Crown's rebuttal was that whatever the unnamed policeman could have said had already been corroborated by the police witnesses Wise and Fraser.

He said it was irrelevant whether or not Les had stolen the money from the library safe. He didn't believe Les had, but this still had no effect on whether Rusher commissioned the killings. He said the defence strategy had been to stir us up on speculations about Les, and Terri Maxfield's sex life, and the police paperwork – 'to get you lost in the detail, peripheral issues that can be seductive in a trial of this length' – but we should stand back from those details and just ask ourselves whether Rusher had committed the crimes.

Mr Crown concluded that it was 'ridiculous' to accept that Rusher was talking about 'serving legal documents'. If it was legitimate legal business, why did he not want Spike's phone number? Why did he refer constantly to his worries about being bugged? Why would it cost him $30,000? Why talk about 'causing pain', 'making it look like an accident', or 'poisoning'? Why would he tell Les they would 'kill me' if they weren't paid? Why didn't he contradict Spike when Spike mentioned 'knocking them'? Why the conversation about Fiona 'living another day'?

There was more, but we could see that Mr Crown thought his case was pretty rock-solid. When he'd finished, we were let out for a break. Borderline said: 'Jeez, I wonder what Mr Nisbett can say to that?'

We went back into the court, and Mr Nisbett stood. He leaned on his lectern and smiled at us. His first words were: 'I imagine you're sitting there thinking, what can I possibly say to that?'

We smiled as one. He smiled back.

Mr Nisbett's closing address was strongest when he did the boilerplate stuff on reasonable doubt, the burden of proof being on the Crown, and the presumption of innocence. When you thought about it, a conviction is difficult to attain. 'The highest amount of suspicion,' he said, 'is not proof beyond reasonable doubt.'

He played a nice card in flattering our intelligence if we acquitted Rusher.

'The accused does not have to win a popularity contest. You don't have to like him. The strength of our jury system would be proved by acquitting a man you don't like, basing your acquittal on the evidence.'

It sounded good. We'd look like real smart cookies if we acquitted him, even though we might not like him. (I'm not sure if Steve Rusher would have conceded the point about his likeability so readily. Indeed, he looked horrified when Nisbett said, 'You don't have to like him.' Steve Rusher probably thought we loved him.)

Mr Nisbett's homilies about the jury system were also impressive. Our role in deliberation would be 'a cooperative effort . . . You bring to this court a sense of community values . . . Juries, through their sense of justice, remain a check on lawyers who would propose that judges sitting alone should be the sole judges of fact.'

This stuff made me warm and fuzzy. I imagine it was a speech Mr Nisbett plied in all his closing addresses. It did give me pause to think. (Though a retired English barrister, Alan Jones, once wrote in his book *Jury Service: A Practical Guide* that any barrister who makes much of principles instead of the facts of the case is doing so because he can't think of anything else to say, 'in other words he thinks the defence case is hopeless.')

Mr Nisbett rebuked Mr Crown for anticipating his arguments. Like a high-school debater, Mr Nisbett scored a kind of hollow point by saying: 'If he has such a strong case, he'd just state it and not worry so much about me.'

But then, when he moved on to the specifics of this trial, his resounding endorsement of the jury system faded into the background. He was obviously having trouble knitting together the line he'd pursued through cross-examination – negative, yes, but playing up doubts over Crown witnesses – with Rusher's eleventh-hour story about the tapes being fabricated. Mr Nisbett said 'there is always context' for what's said on the tapes, and 'the content doesn't prove that they must be genuine'. But it was a bit lame. To ask us to leap from a lingering suspicion that Les had a few skeletons in the closet, and may have stolen Rusher's money, to having reason to believe he could fabricate the tapes, was a very big ask. A big ask indeed.

Flattening down his white collar tabs and taking a breath, Mr Nisbett continued. He said that if we were to believe the authenticity of the tapes, we had to be satisfied that (a) it was Rusher's voice, (b) it was an accurate portrayal of actual conversations, and (c) we understood the meaning of what we heard. He pointed to the web trace, which did not record some of the transcribed conversations; and to the fact that seven conversations of less than two minutes' duration between Steve and Les hadn't been transcribed at all. He reminded us that the Les tapes were only an 'aid to understanding'. Steve Rusher wasn't accused of soliciting Les to kill anyone. The proof, if we were to find it, had to be in the Spike conversations.

Mr Nisbett described Rusher as a 'naive man' who was 'accomplished in some areas but stupid in others'. (Rusher sat up straighter, looking affronted by what his barrister was saying.) Mr Nisbett said Rusher had been a poor judge of Les's character, failing to detect the 'ex-journalist's' greed and deceit. Les was a tax dodger, a benefits cheat, and his story about the 'pornographic' letter was a lie. (There was no 'presumption of innocence' for Les, by the way.) The Diamondopoulos story, Mr Nisbett said, was all nonsense, as was the tale about the other 'hitman' who'd gone on holidays. Whatever else we may think of Steve Rusher, we had to agree that he was overwhelmingly concerned for his son's welfare.

In conclusion, Mr Nisbett said, we had to ask ourselves if the conversations on tape occurred, and if so, did they show that murder was Rusher's intent? If the answer to either 'could or might be' was in the negative, then we had to acquit.

Alan Dershowitz, the Harvard law professor who advised the

O.J. Simpson defence team among others, recommends in his book *Letters to a Young Lawyer* the 'Aha!' theory of persuasion. Don't, he says, tell the jury what to think. Let them feel as though they're discovering the truth themselves.

The 'Aha!' theory, says Dershowitz, originates in a story about his Uncle Abe. Every single day, Uncle Abe goes to the same restaurant and orders the same chicken soup. Then, one day, he's sitting with the chicken soup in front of him, uneaten. The waiter comes up and asks him why.

'Too hot, Abe?'

Abe shakes his head.

'Too cold, Abe?'

Abe shakes his head again.

'Well,' says the waiter, 'I'll sit down and try it myself.'

The waiter pulls the plate of soup across. Then he discovers: there's no spoon on the table. The waiter looks at Uncle Abe and says: 'Aha!'

Mr Crown didn't need to be that subtle. He figured he could layer on the evidence so thickly that any potential acquitters among us would have no room to move. But I thought Mr Nisbett, who had a tougher job, ran the 'Aha!' theory pretty well. He flattered us into thinking that if we were really responsible jurors, who took the presumption of innocence seriously, and put our emotions aside, and applied ourselves like intelligent individuals, we might discover an acquittal on our own.

Most good barristers will refrain from belting you over the head or begging you to see things their way.

> *When you've summed up on a case that is heavily against you, you can hope for a miracle in the jury room but you can't plan on it. If you run up a lot of rubbish arguments and insult their intelligence, just on the off-chance that you might hit a button with one of them – juries are going to see through those sorts of tactics.*

A skilful barrister will also consider all the tools at his disposal: visual aids, emotive appeals, any connection he thinks he has made with jurors during the trial. Most of all, he will avoid legalistic language, the type of convolutions that lead John Travolta, in *A Civil Action*, to complain to the judge that a ruling 'sounds like English translated into Japanese and back into English again!'

> *You've got to speak the jurors' language. You have to communicate with them but your word has to be valued as well, so you can't be too informal. You should be authoritative but understandable. I don't try to sound affectedly ocker or plebeian. It's important to pitch your language a little above, but not too much above, what they hear on radio.*

> *I use movie and song references to connect with younger jurors. I had a client called Brian and did my whole closing address on the theme of* Life of Brian.

Jurors complained in the New Zealand study about barristers speaking in 'complex sentence structures (double negatives, overuse of the passive voice, verbs converted into nouns, a succession of "loose" sentences)'.

In *Joh's Jury*, the narrator sums up the difference between a diligent but dull prosecutor and a more playful, evocative defender:

> Narrator: *Mr Cowdery's summing up went on for two more days. He took us through the evidence in such detail it was like starting the trial all over again. Mr Greenwood had a more colourful approach . . .*
> Greenwood: *After years and years of allegations that that man there is a crook, all they can come up with is this. Goldilocks could knock it over!*

I realise, when I come to the point where the judge summed up the evidence for us, how little I have said about him.

Since the controversy over whether or not he was wearing a wig, and whether we could ask him to turn his microphone away from his laptop, there had been little to say about the judge. He was reassuringly meticulous, polite, and boring – just the way a criminal court judge should be. When I make criticisms about the lack of help and respect juries get from courts, I make no criticism of this particular judge. He was as good as a judge could be. Which confirms my belief that the kinds of reforms that are needed depend not on individual judges, but on systemic change.

While we took a break before the judge's summing-up, the Retired Gent said: 'It'll be interesting to see if he gives us a hint on which way to go.'

It would have been interesting indeed – especially to the defence. The judge is not allowed to hint to juries 'which way to go', and if he does, a conviction will surely be appealed. The jury is to make a finding on fact, and the judge is to direct on the law. The majority of appeals against criminal convictions are based on either the judge's rulings on admissibility or his directions at the end of the trial. So he has to be very careful.

The Retired Gent was not alone in looking to the judge for a hint. The New Zealand jury study found that 30 per cent of 312 jurors thought the judge had conveyed an opinion in his summing-up.

In *Joh's Jury*, one of the two holdout jurors (played by Elaine Hudson), misunderstanding the jury's role, says she wants guidance from the judge:

> Penny Cook: *You can't ask the judge what he thinks of the evidence.*
> Hudson: *Why not? That's what he's there for!*
> Cook: *Yes, but he can only tell us how to look at the evidence.*

John Howard: *You want to ask him if he thinks Job's guilty.*
Hudson: *Not exactly.*
Howard: *Yes exactly. That's what you want to ask him.*

The jury is the finder of fact not only because that is its historic role, but for the very good reason that the judge might be prejudiced. There have been some celebrated and humorous instances of blatant judge bias.

In a case in September 1979, the Victorian Justice O'Bryan summed up an attractive female defendant for the jury: 'If she is guilty, so be it. If not, she is entitled to go home to her children, free, and without a stain on her character.' Unsurprisingly, she was acquitted.

Once, in the Kimberley Court of Petty Sessions, three Aborigines stood up and pleaded not guilty. The chairman of the court roared: 'What do you mean, not guilty? If you were not guilty, you wouldn't be here!'

But juries can resist biased judges. A celebrated recent case of flawed directions was when in 1993 a South Australian Supreme Court judge, Derek Bollen, implicitly condoned a husband's 'rougher than usual handling' of his wife in summing up on a rape case. The public outcry over Bollen's attitude consumed the nation, rightly enough. But it was widely assumed that Bollen's words had influenced the jury to acquit. What was less widely publicised was that the jury foreman said it was 'absolute rubbish' to say Bollen's attitude had swayed them. They acquitted on the evidence, and in any case, by the end of the trial were too tired to take in much of what Bollen was saying.

Two respondents in the 2001 NSW study volunteered the information that their judge favoured a certain verdict. One said that the judge provided 'a clear pointer regarding the legal issues ... It was very good and made it pretty clear what the judge thought the right decision was.' The other said: 'I thought the judge's summing up hinted at guilt . . . I think that he may have overstepped the mark. A couple of other jurors talked about it and they also thought that he was hinting at guilt.'

Australian law allows for a couple of interesting exceptions to this rule. It used to be that judges could direct an acquittal if they considered a conviction would be 'unsafe or unsatisfactory'. But a 1990 High Court judgment, narrowing that discretion slightly, said a judge could only direct the jury to acquit if 'there is a defect in the evidence such that, taken at its highest, it will not sustain a verdict of guilty'. In other words, if the Crown persists with a particularly unsupported line, a trial judge can tell the jury they should ignore nonsensical evidence.

On the other side, judges can also direct a conviction in extreme cases. In the case of *Yager v R*, a drug dealer admitted importing the drug, and the trial judge told the jury that there was no real factual question left, so the appropriate verdict was guilty. The High Court agreed, though one, Justice Harry Gibbs, said the judge could tell the jury that 'if they do their duty they will return a verdict of guilty', but 'he cannot dictate the verdict they are to return.' Dissenting on his own, Justice Lionel Murphy said the direction was tantamount to a directed conviction – not just a suggestion, but a direction – and violated the accused's constitutional right to a jury trial for a federal offence.

It is understandable that some jurors look to the judge for help. If the judge is perceived as a fair, honest judicial officer, he or she can become the one true friend the jurors have in the courtroom. This relationship used to be a lot cosier than it is now. For the first few hundred years of the jury system, judges and juries collaborated on verdicts. Judges advised juries on assessing evidence, and asked them for their reasons as they went along. In the 1697 case *Ash v Ash*, Lord Chief Justice Holt set the jury straight when they were about to make an excessive damages award – £2,000 to a youth who had been falsely imprisoned for a couple of hours – saying the jury 'are to try cases with the assistance of the judges, and ought to give reasons when required, that, if they go upon any mistake, they may be set right'.

But when counsel began to play an increasingly important part in the trial, the casual intimacy of judge and jury was broken. Juries ceded to the judge their power to rule on law, and the judge took up a role as impartial referee. Nowadays the relationship is akin, in one juror's words, to the judge acting:

> *. . . like the host at some awkward office social event, once explaining to us, while we were waiting for a witness, who was portrayed in a courtroom painting. The atmosphere made it clear to us that we must not talk in the courtroom except to respond in chorus to the judge's daily 'Good morning, ladies and gentlemen.'*

Over a couple of hours, our judge summed up the evidence we'd heard over the previous four weeks. He defined 'soliciting' as 'a communication asking for the murder . . . with the object of persuading Spike to arrange the murders of either Fiona Emery and/or Terri Maxfield'; and reiterated that we must give the benefit of any reasonable doubt to the accused.

But what did he mean by 'reasonable doubt'? Judges must dance coyly around this question, for it is something – the key thing – that we jurors must decide. It is the crux of the whole case. But, as with so many shortcomings in the criminal trial, the jury is never actually told that the judge can't define it. So we went back into our jury room unsure if the judge had forgotten to tell us, or wasn't meant to tell us, what 'reasonable doubt' means. Aware that any question we might have for the judge would necessitate rustling up all the participants in the trial, we were unwilling to cause inconvenience with what we feared might be a dumb question.

In the 2001 NSW jury survey, this problem was found to be endemic. One juror said: 'We wanted a definition of reasonable doubt because the jurors didn't understand its limits, but the guidance from the judge wasn't really of any use.' Another jury used a dictionary after the judge refused to define 'reasonable doubt' when they asked him.

The New Zealand report found jurors assigned percentages for 'reasonable certainty' ranging from 95 to 50 per cent: 'Our study elicited responses that also revealed a wide range of interpretations . . . As one of these jurors commented, "It was never proved to me 100 per cent and I still think about it."'

The American juror Graham Burnett defined 'reasonable doubt' as 'doubt motivated by "reasons"'. That sounds fair enough. So for us, the question wasn't, 'Is there any possibility the Rusher tapes could have been fabricated?', but 'Are there any reasons to believe the tapes might have been fabricated?' Applying this definition, jurors can avoid the daft speculations someone will propose as a 'doubt', such as that which provokes this exchange in *12 Angry Men*:

> Henry Fonda: *Supposing we're wrong.*
> Jack Warden: *Supposing we're wrong. Supposing this whole building will fall down on my head. You can suppose anything.*

Controversies over juries defining 'reasonable doubt' have provided rich fodder for cinema. From *Joh's Jury*:

> Malcolm Kennard: *It's not beyond reasonable doubt.*
> Elaine Hudson ('Val'): *Yes, reasonable doubt. Do we all agree about reasonable doubt? I mean, I have reasonable doubt, but does anyone else here have the same reason as mine?*
> Noah Taylor: *I've got a few doubts about you, Val.*

The judge gave us a lot of help in his summing-up which I couldn't help thinking we should have been given, in writing, earlier in the case. It was wrong for the court to assume, for instance, that the jurors all knew they had to make a unanimous verdict; that the onus of proof was on the Crown; that we didn't have to be 'satisfied that the accused is innocent in order to acquit him'; that witnesses need not be taken as either wholly reliable or wholly unreliable (thus demolishing the 'house of cards' theory of credibility); and that we could take a line of reasoning that had not been offered by either counsel.

These are standard directions, but crucial. Many jurors have complained that they are not given these directions until the end of the case, and not given them in writing. Doing it afterwards, said an American judge, was like 'telling jurors to watch a baseball game and decide who won without telling them what the rules are until the end of the game'.

Some respondents to the 1994 NSW jury survey 'commented that they found the judicial directions confusing and, thus, of little (if any) assistance in reaching a verdict'. But overall, 68 per cent said the judge's directions were clear and 81 per cent said they were helpful. Only 14 per cent rated them 'confusing', and 63 per cent said the summing-up didn't influence their verdict. Where it did influence their verdict, there was no pattern of bias towards convictions or acquittals.

Judges use a 'bench book' for guidance on how to give directions, but the bench book allows for wide discretion. Judges interpret the bench book inconsistently, as the 1994 NSW jury study found: 90 per cent of jurors were told they could ask questions, 80 per cent that they could take notes, 75 per cent that they could examine exhibits, and 65 per cent that they could ask for transcripts. When juror-respondents to the New Zealand study complained about directions, it was for:

> *. . . legalistic language, insufficient explanation of the rationale . . . lengthiness and repetition, complex sentence structures, and directions insufficiently explaining the charges in lay terms . . . The judicial bench book was largely written by judges for judges . . . It is in*

> *some cases confusing or unhelpful when judges do use standard directions from the bench book, particularly where the jury does not understand that the direction is standard . . .*

In that survey, there was overwhelming juror support for written directions. Written directions on law would help understanding, reduce deliberation time, cut down on later disputes over what the judge said, and increase juror satisfaction.

In complex trials, jurors are often blamed for being unable to understand legal directions. My response, as a juror, is that if you've ever heard a judge give directions, you'd stop blaming jurors.

As one juror told me:

> *Court procedure was a complete, total mystery to me. I was astonished when I saw people genuflect in front of the judge. I had no idea you were meant to do that. (I still think it's absurd.) I was so naive I actually halted proceedings on day one to ask the judge if members of the jury were allowed to ask questions of the witnesses directly. You can imagine how well that went down! But in the end the judge was very good to us, even going so far as to express his appreciation, via the ushers, of the clarity of the notes we'd sent him asking him to explain various points of law we weren't familiar with. But I couldn't help thinking, all along, that we really shouldn't have needed to send the notes. The points of law should have been crystal clear, and they weren't. I was also astonished to discover that, even though we were furnished with notebooks every day, they were taken away from us each night and we were never allowed to take them out of the court. I could have wept! I meant to rely on them for my final judgment, and instead had to memorise them as best I could. When I'd finished my stint*

> *and started talking to my friend who also found himself on a jury, we both agreed that an all-purpose introduction to the jury system/court procedure should be available to all new jurors. But neither of us came up with one, and it has never eventuated.*

Is this just a procedural quibble? Not if you take into account the finding from the 1994 NSW survey that:

> *... over 50 per cent of the jurors surveyed understood legal terms and complex facts most of the time, but fewer than 20 per cent understood them thoroughly; and 43 per cent of jurors who only understood legal terms some of the time were involved in juries which convicted.*

The jury is about to undertake its real job – to render its verdict – and the courts, which most of the time assume that jurors are very dimwitted, now suddenly assume that we're sharp enough to take in a complex, legalistic explanation of the law aurally, without any written aids or reminders.

When consulted, jurors cry out for written directions. The New Zealand study proposed:

> *The judge should provide the jury with not only an outline of the elements of the offence but also a flowchart with a sequential list of questions derived from the elements of the offence and applying those elements to the facts in the case, which the jury can use as an aid to decision-making.*

The very good reason for this, the New Zealand project found, was that:

> *... trial by jury evolved when the principal method of communication was the spoken word [and] literacy rates*

> *were low . . . Today the visual media are ascendant . . .*
> *The oral skills of previous generations remain largely with*
> *those generations. The exception is the courtroom [where]*
> *jurors sit for days listening to people talk. It is on their*
> *collective recollection of that talk . . . that they base their*
> *verdict.*

The importance of getting this stage of the trial right doesn't need emphasis. If we convicted Steve Rusher when he was innocent, we'd be committing a terrible error. If we acquitted him when he was guilty, we may be committing an error and putting Fiona, Terri and even Les at great risk.

After the judge summed up the evidence, he sent us out briefly while his performance was reviewed by the barristers. If a defendant is allowed to make a correction to the judge's summing-up before the jury, then he has fewer options for appealing against it afterwards. Mr Nisbett must have had a quibble, because the judge called us back in and said we had to make a negative finding about the authenticity of the tapes 'if we had reason' to believe they were faked. Which seemed obvious to me, but as always, Steve Rusher had to get the last word in.

The Learned Friends

Throughout the Rusher trial, the two barristers were sometimes testy with each other, but unfailingly courteous towards the judge — in front of us jurors, anyway. I have no idea how far their courtesy lasted during private legal argument. But it was wise for them to stay onside with the judge in front of the jury. We liked and respected the judge, and any rudeness from either barrister would have been marked against him.

But that's not always the case. One NSW defence barrister told me that he would vary his behaviour vis-a-vis the judge in accord with how popular he thought the judge was with the jury: 'If it's a fair judge, I'll be very polite, but if it's a tyrannical judge, and I sense that the jury doesn't like him, I won't suck up to him. Instead, I might take steps to show up his bias to the jury.'

Not everyone can hold back. Bill Hosking, a leading QC who was to become a judge himself, once had a lively exchange with Justice Adrian Roden, a known martinet. Asked by the judge how he was going to explain why his client's gun was loaded, Hosking said: 'I don't fucking know, Your Honour.' Roden spluttered and threatened to have Hosking disciplined unless he answered the question politely. How would he explain why his client's gun was loaded? Hosking replied: '"I don't fucking know". This was answer number 46 in my client's record of interview, Your Honour.'

Scandalising an unpopular judge can make for great theatre in front of a jury. But defence barrister Murugan Thangaraj says it's more about evening up the field: 'Sometimes, on the defence, you get the idea that the space in the courtroom is divided into this judge-Crown-jury triangle, where they're thinking between them that they've got the case sorted out. We and the accused are on the outside.'

Thangaraj recalls:

> *In one case, the judge promised to give one hour to each case in our summing-up. After I'd summed up, he changed his mind. Maybe he thought things were slipping away for the Crown. So he devoted a whole day and a half in his summing up to the Crown's side . . . I requested the judge to direct the jury on a certain point. He didn't. Then the jury came back with a question on that exact point. I was pleased when they eventually acquitted. I felt vindicated against the judge . . . There is the off-chance that the jury will acquit a guy because they hate the judge.*

As a juror, all I can say is that juries generally respect any counsel who's giving their client a good chance. If they want to fight the judge, then that can make it more interesting for us. But the one piece of advice I'd give from the jury box is that wasting time is the quickest route to unpopularity.

Hence, in a Victorian Supreme Court case, Chief Justice Young said: 'How long will your case take, Mr Balfe? It's only a short point, is it not?'

To which Balfe QC replied: 'It is a short point, Your Honour, but it may take some time to get to it.'

Chapter Fourteen

ONE ANGRY MAN: HOW JURIES DELIBERATE

*J*urors *are notified by mail to come down to a place to decide on the guilt or innocence of a man they have never heard of before. Jurors have nothing to gain or lose by our verdict. This is one of the reasons we are strong.*
– Juror played by George Voskovec in *12 Angry Men*

Most readers by now will assume that we found Steve Rusher guilty and sent him to jail. An easy decision; the judge would later call the Crown case 'overwhelming'. And so it seems to me in hindsight: the tapes were so convincing that there was no possible interpretation of them other than that Steve Rusher was trying to have Fiona (definitely) and Terri (if at all possible) murdered.

But hindsight, and a mood of composure, are two gifts that are beyond the juror's grasp. When, at around 3.20pm on the fifth Thursday of the trial, the judge sent us out to deliberate, I was fizzing with doubt, anxiety and an almost desperate disorientation about what would happen next. I hardly slept that night, and for many nights after. The rash on my hands bloomed; I was impossible to live with. I still tingle with sweat when I think of the sheer gravity of what we had to do. And all this for a comparatively easy verdict.

Technically, I must pull the curtain here on our jury room. The NSW Jury Act forbids me to disclose any 'comments, votes or opinions' during the course of our deliberations. Even though I have transformed the accused, Mr J, into Steve Rusher and disguised virtually all the identifying facts and names, this book of course grew out of my experience as a jury member in a real criminal case. For me to invent a deliberation sequence would have little purpose, as it would be pure fiction.

I can say, as it's on the public record, that we retired four weeks after the trial commenced. The judge told us we could stay until we reached a verdict that night, but Shut The Gate had an appointment so we broke after about 45 minutes and went back into the court to say we'd go home and re-convene the next day. We asked for a transcript of Les McAtee's cross-examination. Steve Rusher gave us a big nod and grin.

We were a good jury. We didn't try to contact Steve with an ouija board, like an English jury in 1994. We didn't squabble, or pair off and canoodle like one 1996 jury. We didn't, like a 1993 jury, send a note to the judge asking: 'Is it a question of whether we have to decide whether the person is guilty or not guilty?'

We deliberated for another three hours the next morning, a normal period for a trial of this length. Outside, the lawyers and Rusher would have had differing views on whether a long deliberation was good or bad for them. One barrister thinks that 'as a defence lawyer, if it's been a hard trial, the longer they're out, the better a pass-mark you give yourself'. But various studies have found that the longer the jury deliberates, the more likely a conviction. (Contrary to popular belief, hung juries tend to come to their non-decisions quite quickly. Most hung juries are split 6–6 or 7–5, and the jurors realise early that there's no hope of unanimity.)

We sent a note through the sheriff's officer that we were ready. Fifteen minutes later, we filed into the court. For no special reason, we scrambled up our usual seating arrangement. I moved to the middle of the front row. My heart pounded.

The judge's associate asked Storeman Foreman if we'd reached a verdict, and he said yes. She read out the first charge – the Fiona Emery one – and Storeman Foreman said: 'Guilty.'

She read out the Terri Maxfield charge, and Storeman Foreman, adding a flourish of his own, replied:

'We find the defendant guilty.'

Mr Nisbett threw up his hands and shook his head, violating what John Grisham calls the 'art form' of receiving a verdict: 'One cannot flinch or twitch. One cannot look around for either solace or jubilation. One cannot grab one's client to celebrate or to comfort. One must sit perfectly still, frown hard at a legal pad upon which one is writing, and act as though one knew precisely what the verdict would be.'

Steve Rusher performed better. He gave the slightest of rapid blinks, but otherwise nothing.

The judge thanked us, and we left. We were taken to our room, and told we could contact a counselling service if we encountered problems afterwards, which, we were told, were common after a long trial like this.

We took a vote on whether to stay for lunch, and came to a split verdict. Six jurors liked the court food so much they decided to stay. Last time I saw Borderline and Friday Night, they were sitting at the table chatting merrily, waiting for lunch. Maybe persistence was going to pay off.

I'd have liked to write about our deliberations, because it would have provided one of the rare public records of a harmonious jury working through the evidence in a responsible, courteous manner. I could have described how everyone pitched in, and how different people came to their verdicts in different ways. I could have detailed how, for all his eccentricities, Borderline came up with sober and eye-opening observations; how the Retired Gent contributed his experience; how the Stickybeak was a beacon of commonsense; how X-Files used his thick notebooks to enlighten us all; how the Old Hand played her role of Minister for the Defence. These people all rose to their best during this most difficult period. I'm proud to say that for all our foreignness to each other, we departed with our mutual respect not only intact but enhanced. At the entrance to Museum Station, the Old Hand said to me: 'With all your expertise, do you think we went about this the right way?'

I said: 'I don't have any expertise at all. I'm just another juror. I thought the Crown proved its case, and so did everyone else, and that's all that matters.'

I could also tell you how these deliberations weren't as straightforward as you might suspect. Convicting an accused person is an awesome responsibility. None of us took it lightly. But the most reasoned and persuasive arguments won the day.

Yet I can't tell you, because the law prevents me. I expect this kind of censorship now. Jurors' rights are curtailed, violated and insulted throughout the trial process. It's only natural that after all this our freedom of speech should also be taken away.

I can see the reasons for this secrecy, though I disagree with the blanket prohibition. The safety of the verdict, particularly a conviction, must be protected. Steve Rusher is an intelligent and, above all, crafty man. He could pore over my account of the deliberations and concoct some ground for appeal. He's probably even doing it now. Getting out of jail is, unsurprisingly, a big preoccupation with many convicted criminals, and Rusher is no exception. But I hope he's intelligent enough to see that he got a fair jury.

Because Australian jurors are barred from giving public accounts of deliberations, the work of letting the public know what happens at the end of a criminal trial is left to the fictionalists and to those in countries such as the USA where the ban does not exist. As conflict is the lifeblood of drama, they tend to portray deliberations that turn nasty. Harmonious juries, such as the one I sat in, go unrepresented in the popular culture. Here is another argument against the blanket ban on juror revelations: the only stories that escape the jury room tend to be the disaster stories. By throwing a cloak over all the jurors who can bring good news about their experience, the ban skews our impression of how juries work. It gives juries a bad name.

I'll outline three well-known case studies of dramatic deliberations that inform – and misinform – the popular imagination about juries. The first, *12 Angry Men*, is a stage-and-screen fictionalisation of American writer Reginald Rose's real-life experience on a jury. The second, *Joh's Jury*, is a dramatised television documentary based on Queensland Premier Joh Bjelke-Petersen's perjury trial. The third, *Trial by Jury*, is a memoir by an American juror, Graham Burnett. Two of the three, it will be noted, are American stories. No wonder Australian judges feel impelled to warn jurors to forget everything they've seen about juries on television, or read in books. Due in part to the Australian ban on jurors talking, most Australians would feel more at home in an American court than in one of our own.

12 Angry Men

The movie starts with the judge summing up a case on whether a young Hispanic man has murdered his father. The (nameless) jurors retire to their room and make small talk. Martin Balsam plays the foreman. Like all juries, they have been given no indication on how to structure their deliberations, when to take votes, and so on. So Balsam calls for a vote straight-up, and he arranges pieces of paper and pens for secret written ballots. Dispute emerges immediately.

> Ed Begley: *What's that for?*
> Balsam: *I thought we might want to vote by ballot.*
> Begley: *Great idea – maybe we can get him elected Senator.*

And a short while later:

> Balsam: *Okay, gentlemen, if I can have your attention. You fellas can handle this thing any way that you want to. I'm not going to make any rules. We can discuss it first and then vote on it. That's one way. Or we can vote on it right now.*
> E.G. Marshall: *I think it's customary to take a preliminary vote.*
> Jack Warden: *Yeah, let's vote and maybe we can all get out of here.*

Their complacency dissolves when Henry Fonda writes 'Not guilty'. Playing devil's advocate, he sways the other jurors one by one, achieving the apparently impossible end of a unanimous acquittal.

> Jack Warden: *I'm getting a little tired of this yackety-yacking back and forth. It's getting us nowhere. So I guess I'll have to break it up. I change my vote to not guilty.*
> Lee J. Cobb: *What?*
> Warden: *You heard me, I've had enough.*
> Cobb: *What do you mean, you've had enough? That's no answer.*
> Warden: *Hey listen, you just take care of yourself, huh?*
> George Voskovec (to Warden): *He's right, that's not an answer. What kind of a man are you? You have sat here and voted guilty with everyone else because there are some baseball tickets burning a hole in your pocket, and now you have changed your vote because you say you are sick of all the talking here.*
> Warden: *Listen, buddy . . .*
> Voskovec: *Who tells you you have a right to play like this with a man's life? Don't you care?*
> Warden: *Wait a minute. You can't talk like that to me!*
> Voskovec: *I can talk like that to you. If you want to vote not guilty, then do it because you are convinced the*

> *man's not guilty, not because you've had enough. Or if you think he is guilty, then vote that way. Or don't you have the guts to do what you think is right?*

While some, like Warden, come across because they are tired of arguing, others are swayed by Fonda's keen forensic work. He breaks the odd law – by producing a knife he has bought, identical to the murder weapon, and by revealing that he has visited the crime scene – but it's all good cinema.

What would happen if we in the Rusher trial followed Henry Fonda's lead and did our own investigating? It's unusual for that to happen, but one correspondent from another jury told me that in her trial 'two very dubious things happened.'

> *Both were totally forbidden by law, yet I am firmly convinced that both helped us reach a just decision.*
> *1) A very intelligent young male jury member thought to go to the Fairfax archives one morning before jury duty and look up on microfiche the newspapers on the dates our man had been arrested. From the files he read and related to us in the jury room we learned the background of the accused, and the fact that he was a convicted rapist.*
> *2) A mysterious witness was called who was not identified to us. Over the course of his testimony we gathered that he had been the accused's parole officer, but this was of course strictly inadmissible. Then the judge himself referred to the man as such one day, and I froze on the jury bench, convinced that the trial would be aborted because of such a crass admission. But no one seemed to take any notice, and the trial proceeded.*

From the second point, we note the unspeakable truth about the exclusionary rules of evidence: jurors will speculate on what's been left out. But the first point is more interesting. That naughty 'young male jury member', like Henry Fonda, went out and got his own information. Barrister Tom Molomby says this is becoming more prevalent:

> *It can become a nightmare when jurors start doing their own research. The internet has made it easier for them to find out if an accused has previous convictions. I have had a trial where the sheriff's officer detected a juror bringing swathes of research into the jury room. The judge discharged that jury.*

In a 2005 speech, NSW Supreme Court Justice Virginia Bell noted that a website called CrimeNet 'raised acutely' the danger of jurors accessing the internet when it started in 2000. But CrimeNet later became a subscriber-only service and subscribers had to promise not to use it while on a jury. She said that Crown prosecutors could also search the internet for prejudicial material and have it removed during the trial; courts, too, should remove earlier judgments on active matters from their websites.

More notoriously, a 2002 rape conviction of two Sydney brothers, Bilal and Mohammed Skaf, was quashed in 2004 after it emerged that two jurors had visited the crime scene to conduct a 'lighting experiment'. The 64-year-old jury foreman went to Gosling Park, Greenacre, with another juror to 'clarify something for my own mind'. The alleged rape victim had said she could identify her assailants in the park. The two jurors went there at night and stood in various places asking 'Can you see me?' They reported back to their fellow jurors, and returned guilty verdicts the next morning.

At a barbecue more than a year later, the jury foreman told a solicitor friend what he'd done. The solicitor reported the conversation and the matter went back to court. The Court of Appeal said the main problem with the jurors' action was that it 'introduced evidence that could not be tested by the Skafs' lawyers'. The court also encouraged jurors to 'dob in' others who had disobeyed directions.

The curious jurors were loudly condemned. Only the head of the NSW Law Society's criminal law committee, Pauline Wright, showed any public sympathy for the jurors, saying: 'They've obviously acted in what they thought was for the best.'

We might wonder how the 'lighting experiment' affected the jury's deliberations. Perhaps it didn't at all. But the appeals court was not interested. The NSW Solicitor-General, Michael Sexton SC, appeared in the appeal. He says: 'The court might have been able to make a decision based on the available material, but generally if there has been any irregularity at all they'll simply abort the trial.'

In another case, *R v K*, jurors surfed the internet to find information about the accused, and their guilty verdict was quashed. In the appeal, the Crown argued that the information gleaned from the net probably hadn't influenced the jurors. But Justice James Wood said that this question could not be investigated because of 'the long-established rule that the court will not hear evidence of the deliberation of the jury'. Michael Sexton, who represented the State in this matter, says, 'Courts are reluctant to have jurors cross-examined. Jurors have enough to deal with, so getting affidavits from them should be enough.'

In a 2004 trial, one juror researched the accused man, Attilla Fayka, on the internet and another visited the alleged crime scene and discussed the case with his or her spouse. The judge, Graham Armitage, aborted the trial after the foreman reported the jurors' behaviour. *The Sydney Morning Herald* reported that one of the errant jurors 'reacted sharply' and 'threatened' the foreman after his action. Police investigated, and the NSW Government stated it would come down hard, introducing amendments to the Jury Act that would make unauthorised juror inquiries punishable by up to two years' jail. This would follow section 69A of the Queensland Jury Act, which forbids jurors from inquiring about the accused and punishes them if they do; Justice Wood in NSW described this as a 'very sensible' law. Responding to the Skaf and K trials, the NSW Parliament amended Section 68C of the Jury Act, introducing a maximum two-year jail term for improper juror inquiries.

Yet in a sense, jurors bringing their own information and skills is what the jury system is all about. Common citizens, not experts, 'own' justice. In our jury, for instance, when Mr Nisbett questioned a phone record that showed Les McAtee on the line to Silverwater once for up to a minute even though he said the phone wasn't answered, several of us knew that a PABX system would switch a call through to another line, registering the call, yet it might remain unanswered. Our knowledge was superior to that of the judge or the lawyers, who seemed befuddled by the technology.

Juries do all sorts of weird things to test what's been said in court. In one trial, where the question was how long bite marks would last in human flesh, one juror bit another to find out. In Johnathan Carter's trial, the jurors put one of their number into an esky that had served as the victim's coffin, to test the defendant's assertion that her legs had to be broken so that she'd fit. One juror from the 2001 NSW survey said: 'We re-enacted the shooting by aiming the gun at one of the jurors, and I wish there'd been a bullet in the gun.'

That study noted the growing curiosity, among jurors, to seek out unauthorised information. It found jurors visiting the crime scene, doing their own handwriting analysis, visiting rifle ranges to get information on guns, and reporting their findings back to the jury. In five trials, jurors found out that the accused had previous convictions for a similar offence. In one, the information influenced jurors and caused a compromise verdict; 'In another . . . the jury did not believe the informal source who provided the information, and put it out of their minds . . . They were genuinely shocked and surprised to discover after the trial that it was true.'

Jurors from another trial 'expressed concern that other jurors had discovered the relevant information about the accused from a site on the internet':

One of the interviewees, having been told about this during deliberations, claimed to have taken steps to ensure that an undecided juror, not yet apprised of the information, should be shielded from it until after a verdict was reached. These steps included threatening to write to the judge if a promise to conceal the information from the undecided juror was not forthcoming. The promise was, it seems, given and adhered to. The undecided juror's decision in favour of conviction, reached without knowledge of the information, paved the way for a unanimous verdict of guilty. This was, as we see it, a case where a difficult situation arising from the unexpected acquisition of this prejudicial information was handled as well as might be hoped for.

A judge told the NSW researchers that it would be futile to think jurors could be stopped from finding out such information:

I remember in a trial I did [as a barrister], the judge told them that they mustn't go and look things up on the internet, and I thought that's the first thing they'll do tonight . . . Just drawing that to the jury's attention was sure to make them go home and have a look at it . . . It's like telling someone not to think about something. The harder you try not to think about it, the more you think about it.

But by and large, judges have faith in the responsibility of jurors not to think of themselves as investigators, Henry Fonda-style:

We've all had maverick jurors and maverick juries, but they are very much the exception. I think that the average person called for jury duty is a decent, upright, responsible person who, given proper direction and

> *encouragement, will do what is required and do it faithfully.*

One area for unauthorised research would be to find out what would be the consequences of a conviction. As I've said, we didn't know what jail term Steve Rusher would get if we convicted him. It didn't play on our minds. But defence lawyers will sometimes try to let jurors know:

> *The jury might reconsider a decision to convict if they knew how heavy the sentence was. Or, a witness might be an informant who's doing this to get his sentence reduced. I like to let the jury know that. There have been times when I've let slip the likely sentence for the accused if they convict him. The judge hammers me for it and tells the jury to disregard it.*

But many jurors think it important that they know the likely penalty. My colleague David, a former court reporter, told his fellow jurors what sentence their accused would probably receive, 'because I thought this was important'. In Graham Burnett's jury trial, the jurors stumbled upon a written set of sentencing guidelines while waiting in a spare courtroom. He believed it mattered that they knew they'd be putting a man away for life.

Other jurors have been even more active. In a Los Angeles theft trial in 1996, the jury convicted a man for stealing three guitars from a shop. They later found out that because of the 'three strikes' law, he was facing 25 years in prison. Outraged that a man could be put away for 25 years for three small thefts, the jury petitioned the sentencing judge, George Wu, who took their arguments into account and reduced the sentence:

> *I've never had a jury express itself as adamantly as in this particular situation . . . Their view, while not controlling,*

is a factor I think I can consider. I don't mind the jurors commenting. I view jurors as part of the community at large.

Australian jurors don't decide sentences, but this may change. In February 2005, the NSW Chief Justice, James Spigelman, suggested that juries might be able, in private, to consult with judges on sentencing.

The reaction was almost stereotypically predictable: representatives of the 'community', in the form of spokespeople for victims of crime and their families, came out saying judges needed 'a reality check' and juries must be involved. They assumed that juries would levy heavier sentences than judges.

Both the head public defender, Peter Zahra, and the head prosecutor, Nicholas Cowdery, opposed the idea, Zahra because the secrecy of such hearings was 'contrary to sound traditions of criminal justice as administered in the open public courts of a democratic society', Cowdery because 'it might create more uncertainty and anxiety than it resolves.' The head of the NSW Law Society's criminal law committee, Pauline Wright, was more frank, saying jury involvement could lead to 'mob sentencing':

The fact that the jury might have some input into the sentencing process might be acting on their mind when they're determining guilt and I think that's a very bad thing, because what might happen is that they start thinking 'I'm not really convinced this person is guilty but I'm pretty convinced, but what the heck I'll convict him and I'll have an input into sentencing'.

The NSW Attorney-General, Bob Debus, said: 'The Government's approach will be to advance with abundant caution and only after extensive consultation with the legal and broader community.'

The broader community? I can see how that would involve victims of crime lobbyists and other interest groups, but what about the most interested party of all? What about juries themselves, who are, after all, symbolically and actually the 'broader community'? Our political process does not allow for juries to be heard – we are victims of our own anonymity, too well protected for our own good.

On closer examination, what appeared to be a move to invest jurors with greater trust was not quite what it seemed. Justice Spigelman wanted to prise open the jury room door and uncover juries' mistakes. Here's what he said:

> *What I am proposing is an in-camera consultation process, protected by secrecy provisions, by which the trial judge discusses relevant issues with the jury after evidence and submissions on sentence and prior to determining sentence . . . It is quite likely that, if there has been some fundamental defect, the trial judge will discover it during the course of consulting with the jury about sentence. I do not think that that is a bad thing.*

'Recent experience in this state,' he said, had shown that 'the jury decision-making process can go wrong.'

So, pity the poor juror in all this. On the one side you have lawyers worrying that you will institute 'mob sentencing'. On the other, you have judges pulling a reverse Trojan Horse – inviting you into the sentencing process so that they can find out where you've 'gone wrong'.

When capital punishment is a consequence, the deliberations are even more combustible. Charles Dickens pointed out on a visit to New York in 1842 that when there was an execution, 'the law requires that there be present at this dismal spectacle the judge, the jury and citizens to the amount of 25.' The jurors had to face the consequences of their decision in the most brutal way.

In *12 Angry Men*, knowing that the defendant faces the death penalty adds a volatile chemical to the jury-room mix.

> Fonda: *It's not easy to raise my hand and send a boy to die without talking about it first.*
> Jack Warden: *Who says it's easy?*
> Fonda: *No one.*
> Warden: *Just because I voted fast? I honestly think the guy's guilty. Couldn't change my mind if we talked a hundred years.*

Warden, who has baseball tickets, is constantly trying to get the decision over and done with, but the old man, Joseph Sweeney, pulls him up:

> Warden: *We could be here all night.*
> Sweeney: *It's only one night. The boy may die.*
> Warden: *Why don't we just set up house here then?*

Finally, the spectre of the death penalty reveals the true motive behind Lee J. Cobb's eagerness to convict:

> Cobb: *You all know he's guilty and you're letting him slip through our fingers.*
> Fonda: *Slip through our fingers? Are you his executioner?*
> Cobb: *I'm one of them.*
> Fonda: *Perhaps you'd like to pull the switch.*
> Cobb: *For this kid, you bet I would.*
> Fonda: *I feel sorry for you. What it must feel like, to want to pull the switch. Ever since you walked into this room you've acted like a self-appointed public avenger. You want to see this boy die because you personally want it, not because of the facts. You're a sadist.*
> Cobb (lunges at Fonda): *I'll kill him, I'll kill him!* (Others restrain him.)
> Fonda: *You don't really mean you'll kill me, do you?*

As a model for deliberations, *12 Angry Men* is a wonderful fairy tale about the victory of reason. In real life, however, it's almost unheard of for 11 jurors to change their minds during deliberations. To the contrary: researchers have found that most jurors form fixed views while hearing the evidence and come into the deliberation room with their minds made up.

The Chicago Jury Project discovered that in 90 per cent of deliberations, the majority view at the first vote turned into a unanimous verdict.

In the New Zealand study half of all jurors knew their verdict before deliberations started. Up to 67 per cent of jurors didn't change their minds during deliberations, 23 per cent were genuinely persuaded by others, 7 per cent went along with the majority against their wishes, and 3 per cent shifted their verdict 'in such a way that it was unclear whether they understood what was happening'.

Research shows 'time and again that the best predictor of a jury's final decision is the distribution of opinion at the start of the deliberations,' say the American jury experts Valerie Hans and Neil Vidmar. Rather than defections coming from the larger clique (as in *12 Angry Men*), they say:

> . . . *jurors are much more likely to defect from a smaller faction. . . It is only when a minority juror has initial support, in the form of other jurors with similar views, that the probability that a juror will sway the majority or hang the jury improves.*

But if they swing, which way will they go – towards acquittal or conviction? Hans and Vidmar observed a 'leniency bias': minorities arguing for acquittal are more likely to sway the majority than vice versa. 'Apparently, it is easier to raise a reasonable doubt than to squelch reasonable doubts.' In this, at least, *12 Angry Men* is closer to reality.

The good news from the New Zealand project is that while it's hard to change minds during deliberations:

> *If jurors are persuaded during the course of deliberation, there is greater assurance of a correct result; mock jury studies have indicated that changes in view are likely to be genuine changes, rather than cases of jurors simply going along with the majority.*

The deliberations in *12 Angry Men* turn nasty, with Ed Begley insulting everyone in the room and Lee J. Cobb threatening to kill Henry Fonda. Fortunately for us in real life, nasty deliberations are rare.

The 2001 NSW study found that in 61 per cent of trials, the verdict came quite easily. Responses included:

> *Our jury was fantastic, stable, sane, considerate and democratic. We stuck to the judge's points and methodically went through the evidence together.*

> *We disagreed about the issue of proof beyond a reasonable doubt. [Nine voted for acquittal.] We had a 'think tank' and the next day there were only two guilty-jurors left. We talked it over again, then left the two jurors alone to talk it over and they decided to agree to the not guilty verdict.*

In 22 per cent of the trials surveyed in NSW, unanimity was reached with greater difficulty. The responses make for more dramatic, if less representative, reading:

> *The jurors yelled at and bullied me. I capitulated.*

> *I was the last juror to come to a decision and I was screamed at and abused and put under enormous pressure to agree to the guilty verdict . . . I'll be really honest with you. I'm quite clear in the decision that I made and I know why I made it and on what points I made it. But I did feel that there was a tremendous amount of pressure*

> *. . . I decided that I had to take my decision to the grave and be answerable to God . . . I'm certain that if I had decided that [the accused] was not guilty . . . I would have stuck by that decision and brought in a hung jury rather than be untrue to myself.*

> *It was a very difficult jury. [One juror] was completely irrational . . . very emotional, out of control, acted like a spoilt child . . . [Another] juror had strange religious leanings, kept touting 'an eye for an eye' and had moral reservations about being on a jury.*

An important point must be made about these more difficult verdicts. Yes, jury-room stress created unpleasant behaviour. But in each case, the professional assessors – the judge and both counsel – said they believed these juries had got the verdict right.

Now we can turn to a celebrated real case where a jury was derailed.

JOH'S JURY

Based on interviews with jurors in the Sir Joh Bjelke-Petersen perjury trial, *Joh's Jury* was a teledrama made for the ABC in the early 1990s. It's told through the eyes of one young juror played by Simon Bossell. At jury selection, the lawyers for Sir Joh surprise everyone by allowing a scruffy type, Luke Shaw (Malcolm Kennard), to pass through unchallenged. The next day, Kennard/Shaw turns up clean-shaven, in a suit, and claims the foremanship of the jury. Most of the film is about the deliberations, into which the jurors enter as cluelessly as any garden-variety jury. Kennard tries to hijack the process from the very start:

> Kennard: *Does anyone want to take a vote?*
> Penny Cook: *What, already?*

ONE ANGRY MAN

> Norman Yemm: *Let's not worry about that until we have to.*
> Kennard: *It just seems fairly cut and dried to a lot of people I've spoken to.*
> John Howard: *Whoa, just slow down, we only just got here. You can't walk in after the trial and take a vote. You've got to think about it.*
> Kennard: *It's actually a traditional procedure.*
> John Jarratt: *Where'd you get that from?*
> Noah Taylor: *Does anyone want to take a vote on whether we take a vote?*

A little later, the confusion on how to get started spreads:

> Taylor: *How are we going to start this process?*
> Jarratt: *We have to set an agenda.*
> Betty Lucas: *What do you mean, an agenda?*
> Howard: *Why don't we get a whiteboard?*

There are no guidelines for jury deliberations. You go into the room and do your best. Shaw/Kennard, who is a member of Bjelke-Petersen's National Party and a liaison between the party and the 'Friends of Joh' support group, uses the confusion to take control, but the others soon oppose him.

> Kennard: *How about a secret ballot?*
> Taylor: *How about you take a flying leap out the window?*

At a preliminary vote, the jurors are dispersed between guilties and undecideds. After considering the evidence for two days, however, the battle lines are drawn. Ten vote guilty, and two – Kennard and the prim middle-aged woman, Val, played by Elaine Hudson – hold out. Kennard is usurped as foreman after he misrepresents the jury to the judge, but Hudson steps into the breach, making everyone sit at the table and take turns to speak.

> Howard: *So what about me, Val? You didn't ask me.*
> Hudson: *You weren't sitting at the table.*
> Howard: *I'm part of the jury, aren't I?*
> Hudson: *If you want your say, you'll have to sit at the table.*
> (Howard, standing, gives his reasons for a guilty verdict.)
> Hudson: *It doesn't count if you don't sit at the table.*

Accounts of nasty deliberations create a powerful if misleading impression of juries. In the early 1990s, a juror wrote to the NSW Institute of Criminology saying she'd been called a 'pinko leso' by other jurors, one of whom had threatened to put her on a 'hit list'. She said the majority caved in when their leader, a bank manager, decided he had to go and play golf. Another juror wrote to the institute saying she 'was pushed up against the wall, had my papers snatched out of my hands, had books thrown at me' in the jury room. Terrified, she said she cried every morning over breakfast before returning to the jury. The trauma caused her, after the trial, to 'sell our family home and move away'. Assessing these and other dysfunctional juries, Mark Findlay found the main reasons for jury failure to be a wide age range, an overbearing foreman, impatience, factionalism, and an unwillingness to bond.

In *Joh's Jury*, the deliberations turn dramatically nasty as it becomes clear that Kennard and Hudson are going to hold out. Dishonestly, Hudson retreats behind process and definitions, pretending to be the most conscientious reader of the black-letter law.

> Bossell (voice-over): *She looked up so many words, we started to wonder if she knew the meaning of anything at all. This was the third night in a row we'd been locked up until 10.00pm, and everyone was totally exhausted. Except for Brad [Noah Taylor], who was at a loose end now the batteries on his Gameboy had expired and the bailiff*

> *wouldn't get him any more . . . Hedley [John Howard] was ready to jump out the window. Except it was locked.*

Kennard is more ingenuous than his accomplice Hudson. While she plays the coward's role of hiding behind the law, Kennard continues to argue Joh's innocence.

> Kennard: *He was an old man, he hadn't been premier for over 12 months, and I think he'd lost a lot of his mental powers after he resigned. That happens to a lot of people after they retire.*
> Noah Taylor: *So what's your excuse?*

Abuse, both verbal and physical, eventually breaks out. Taylor explodes: 'When this is over, they're going to build a monument to you. The Big Arsehole, Queensland's latest tourist attraction.'

But it's all for naught. After nearly four days' deliberations, the narrator records:

> *We had lost our way. We were no longer a jury trying to reach agreement on a matter of perjury. The deliberations had descended into a brawl over an old man's memory and the meaning of words . . . We needed a miracle.*

They don't get it. Kennard and Hudson hang the jury, and the State decides not to proceed with a retrial. Effectively, the Joh supporters notch up a not-guilty verdict.

A hung jury – the inability to reach a verdict – is every juror's nightmare. If your jury hangs, you feel you have wasted the court's time, wasted money, wasted your own time – and passed the buck to another jury if the Crown seeks a new trial.

'There is quite possibly no more demoralising experience for jurors than the inability to reach a verdict, particularly after a lengthy and tiring trial,' say Hans and Vidmar. 'Often, anger is expressed at the end of the deliberation at the "holdouts" who are preventing the jury from delivering a unanimous verdict.'

When juries come back into court to say they can't reach a verdict, judges issue what is known in Australia as the *Black* direction, named after the High Court case which authorised a judge to tell jurors that if there is a small minority holding out, they should go back and talk it over and think very carefully about changing their vote. *Black* is meant to safeguard jurors against the ratbag lone holdout. In *Joh's Jury*, the judge issues the *Black* direction but it does no good:

> Bossell: *He said this to you, and you're not doing a damn thing about it.*
> Hudson: *Let's take another vote.*
> Kennard: *No, I think we should forget it.*
> Bossell: *What is it I'm missing, Luke? What are you seeing that we can't?*
> Hudson: *Isn't it awful? There's only two honest people out of the 12 of us.*
> Bossell (voice-over): *I came onto this jury believing I was representing all the people of this State. All my family and friends. All the people. And they would want me to look at the evidence and keep an open mind. For them. Because I was picked. Because that was what justice is supposed to be about. But I don't believe that. I feel like I've let everyone down. Something's gone wrong, and we haven't been able to do anything about it.*

The Chesterman study found that while some jurors were 'refocused' by the *Black* direction, others either ignored it (as in *Bjelke-Petersen*) or misunderstood it. Some felt that:

> ... *being sent back to the jury room to deliberate further gave their fellow jurors added licence to badger or harass them ... Several of these jurors expressed ongoing regret that they hadn't hung the jury, one even going so far as to*

> *write to the accused's barrister to apologise and another talking about ongoing stress that was only relieved when the Court of Appeal overturned the conviction and ordered a retrial.*

A notable hung jury in NSW came in May 2000, when the jury deadlocked after trying two Vietnamese men, Phuong Ngo and Tu Quang Dao, for the 1994 murder of the State MP John Newman. After five days' deliberation, some were in tears when their foreman told Justice James Wood that they couldn't reach a verdict. Giving them the *Black* direction, Wood directed them to work at it over the weekend. The prosecutor, Mark Tedeschi, suggested the jurors give their reasons to the court, but the judge declined to set this precedent.

The deadlock lasted through the weekend, and it turned out to be 10–1 for a conviction, one juror having dropped out. Tedeschi lobbied the State Government to move to majority verdicts, as is already the case in some jurisdictions here and overseas.

At time of writing, the NSW Law Reform Commission is considering a change to 11–1 or 10–2 verdicts, following a 2004 speech by the Court of Appeal's Justice John Dunford supporting majority verdicts 'after a specified period of deliberation':

> *The object of the 10-2 or 11-1 majority is to avoid new trials in cases where the jury is hamstrung by a perverse, disinterested [sic] or unreasonable, or simply incompetent juror, where the result of the new trial is going to be that of the overwhelming majority in the original trial.*

How did he know, never having been in a jury room, that this was often or ever the case? In 18 years on the bench, Justice Dunford said he'd heard a thing or two: 'Bear in mind that a judge often knows the voting figures in the hung jury situation because it is at times included in the note he or she receives from the jury.'

The NSW Director of Public Prosecutions, Nicholas Cowdery, supports majority decisions (having been, among other experiences, stung by being the leading prosecution counsel in the Joh trial). So does the NSW Solicitor-General, Michael Sexton, who says '10–2 verdicts are probably sufficient.'

'Majority verdict is my hobby horse,' says Cowdery.

> *One juror who won't play the game properly can disrupt the entire process by being irrational, pig-headed, and a disruptive individual. Under the system of unanimous verdicts, that person can do something that requires the whole process to go on again. I have letters from jurors – three or four a year – expressing tremendous frustration at not being able to do their job because of one irrational juror. When they're moved enough to write to my office, it suggests that this is something of great importance. Also, [discarding the unanimity requirement] narrows down the possibility of corruption. If you have a lot of money, you may be able to corrupt one juror, and possibly two jurors, but it's hard to see anyone being able to corrupt more than two. The views of the holdout person should always be taken into account, and the rest of the jury should consider them. But the odds of a holdout juror being a hero are pretty slim compared to the odds of the holdout being an obstructive ratbag.*

In Scotland, he says, 'They have 15-person juries and decisions by bare majority. I don't see Scottish society falling apart as a result.'

Cowdery has strong support from NSW prosecutors. Lorana Bartels, then a research solicitor with the Office of the Director of Public Prosecutions, found in a 2001 survey that 85 per cent of Crown prosecutors thought majority verdicts should be available. They were evenly split on whether jurors should be given this option straightaway, or only after they've been deliberating for some hours; and most did not believe the vote should be made publicly known. They did not believe majority verdicts would affect the number of convictions.

The NSW opposition sponsored majority-verdicts bills in 1998 and 2000, but they failed to pass through the NSW Parliament. Abolishing the unanimity requirement would seem an easy way to solve the problem of one ratbag juror. Allowing a 10–2 majority would have got a conviction in the Joh trial. But in rejecting the bill, the NSW Government cited 1997 research by the NSW Bureau of Crime Statistics and Research which found that when juries hung, the vote was most often 6-6, 7–5 or 8–4.

There was no generally recurring pattern of one or two minority jurors holding out against the rest . . . It concluded that because hung juries were relatively rare (less than 10 per cent of jury trials) and because a high proportion of cases with hung juries (in recent years in New South Wales, about 43 per cent) were not in fact retried, the actual saving of criminal court time which might be achieved from introducing majority verdicts in New South Wales might be as little as 1.7%.

There are better reasons than cost–benefit to justify retaining the unanimous verdict. Hans Zeisel, who conducted the 1955 Chicago Jury Project, the biggest juror research study ever commissioned, wrote:

Despite the jury's deep roots in the Constitution and in the consciousness of the people, it remains an embattled institution. Any systematic clipping of the jury's wings is dangerous; curtailments that reduce the jury's

> *performance swell the ranks of its critics, and thus start a vicious circle.*

That vicious circle has been witnessed in the United Kingdom, where the unanimity requirement was dropped for 10–2 majorities in 1967, since when jury trials have been steadily eliminated in favour of judge-only trials. Removing unanimity there was the thin edge of a wedge that continues to drive into the jury system.

Majority verdicts seem intuitively right, because our other democratic institutions work on majority will. Panels of judges, committees, parliaments, councils, company boards don't need unanimous verdicts. Why should the jury remain the odd institution out?

Australian legal systems inherited the unanimous verdict from a tradition dating to 1367, when an English court allowed a 1–11 hung jury because the lone holdout said he would rather go to prison than vote to convict the accused.

The philosophic underpinnings of unanimity go back to Aristotle's *Politics*:

> *For each individual among the many has a share of virtue and prudence and when they meet together, they become in a manner one man . . . Some understand one part, and some another and among them they understand the whole.*

The medieval Church valued unanimity as 'the infallible sign of God's voice', and in the 14th century English parliaments needed a unanimous vote to bind individuals – which, Abramson writes:

> *. . . may have reflected an argument that individuals could be bound legally only by their own consent and not by what the majority decided. As one medieval scholar put it, 'The word consent . . . carried with it the idea of concordia or unanimity' . . . The medieval mind was also*

> *more likely than our own to believe that reason could tolerate only one, correct, answer to what happened; there was no room for reasonable jurors to disagree.*

In the 1993 Australian High Court case of *R v Cheatle*, the principle of unanimity was endorsed for federal jury trials. The court said that when the Australian colonies agreed in 1900 to form a federation, jury unanimity was 'a basic principle of the administration of criminal justice'. Unanimity ensured a genuine consensus, reducing the danger of hasty verdicts and reflecting the fundamental rule that guilt must be proved beyond reasonable doubt.

But do we have to hang on to unanimity just because this is the way it's always been done? Preserving tradition for tradition's own sake is a suspect argument.

The best argument for unanimity is that it forces majority jurors to persuade, rather than bully, the minority. As Abramson writes:

> *It is illuminating that the jury did not develop into just another example of the politics of bargaining. The unanimous verdict rule gives concrete expression to a different set of democratic aspirations – keyed to deliberation rather than voting and to consensus rather than division. Voters pull a curtain and vote in private; jurors meet face-to-face and debate their differences. Numbers are decisive in elections, making problematic the effective representation of small or marginal groups; on the jury, the practice of unanimity represents an ideal where individual views cannot simply be ignored or outvoted. At its best, unanimity disempowers narrow and prejudiced arguments that appeal to some groups but not others. It favours general arguments persuasive to people drawn from different walks of life.*

Cowdery talks about the majority 'taking into account' the views of a holdout juror. But in the 1972 US Supreme Court case of *Johnson v Louisiana*, Justice William Douglas pointed out the difference between 'courtesy dialogue' or 'polite and academic conversation' which the majority may offer minorities in a majority-vote group, and the real argument needed to convince all jurors in unanimity: 'Proof beyond reasonable doubt was met only when deliberation, in this stronger form, harmonised the views of all jurors.'

Because of the unanimity requirement, jurors must persuade, not outvote, each other. Yes, this can lead to ugly and emotional deliberations. 'The unanimous verdict rule makes the deliberations all the more intense,' Abramson says, 'because the alternative of outshouting or outvoting opponents does not exist.'

In arguing against the unanimity rule after the Phuong Ngo trial, Mark Tedeschi relied on the New Zealand jury project. But he did so somewhat selectively. Read closely, the New Zealand study is wary of majority verdicts:

> *It is sometimes argued that attrition – the wearing down of minority jurors by gradual exhaustion – operates in jury deliberation. Although the research shows that considerable pressure is brought to bear on minority jurors, it is not clear that they are forced into verdicts by this pressure. If attrition, rather than reason, does push minority jurors towards verdicts, the effect of introducing majority verdicts may not be to do away with attrition but rather to reduce the amount of it required to produce a verdict.*

Tedeschi cited the alarming increase in New Zealand hung juries, from 3.52 per cent of trials in 1993 to 11.36 per cent in 1999. This is indeed alarming, until we read that of those that were re-tried, 85 per cent hung again or were discharged. In other words, a tiny few – about 1 per cent – of trials seemed to have been 'obstructed' by rogue jurors.

Moreover, jurors who vote in majority verdicts are less certain that they've done the right thing. In 1983, research was conducted on jury deliberations in Massachusetts, where different charges require unanimity, 10–2 or 8–4 majorities. Unanimous verdicts took longer to come, but the level of juror certainty and satisfaction was much greater where unanimity was required:

> *. . . jurors returning non-unanimous verdicts felt far less certain of their conclusions . . . The holdouts left the trial feeling that the majority did not even listen to them seriously . . . The style of deliberation under non-unanimous verdict instructions was likely to be more combative than under unanimous rules, with larger factions in majority rule juries adopting a more forceful, bullying, persuasive style because their members realise that it is not necessary to respond to all opposition arguments when their goal is to achieve a faction size of only eight or ten members.*

If one person stands against the other 11, does that mean he or she is a ratbag? Patently not. In the *Black* case, Justice William Deane came out in strong support of the rights of an individual juror:

> *A juror who conscientiously holds out against a majority and thereby prevents unanimity has not failed properly to 'do what [he or she was] chosen to do'. To the contrary, he or she has done no more than discharge his or her duty to both the accused and society. Any suggestion that a minority juror should democratically submit to the view of the majority is antithetical to the jury process under the common law of this country.*

In 1962 in the case of *Huffman v Huffman*, the US Supreme Court said:

> *A mistrial from a hung jury is a safeguard to liberty; in many areas it is the sole means by which one or a few may stand out against an overwhelming contemporary public sentiment. Nothing should interfere with its exercise.*

Chicago Jury Project author Hans Zeisel called the hung jury 'a treasured, paradoxical phenomenon'.

There's no easy answer. Perhaps we should unearth a practice from 17th-century America, where hung juries could consult outsiders to help them reach a decision.

When holdout jurors have been bullied or ignored, the worst miscarriages of justice have occurred. In a New York murder trial in 1994, at the sentencing stage one female juror held out against the death penalty. The jury was, effectively, hung. But when they went back into the court, the foreman told the judge they had voted unanimously for the death penalty. This miscarriage only came to light some months later, when the woman told a journalist her story. Fortunately, the prisoner had not been executed.

As a juror, one's opinion on majority verdicts revolves around one's own experience. My colleague David said he favoured 11–1 majorities, because 'I'd put in six weeks of my life and I wasn't going to let that be thrown away by some idiot in the jury room.' Yet on the other hand, if he were to be the lone holdout, David would favour the unanimity requirement, because 'I knew we weren't going to walk out of there with a conviction. Even if everyone else went against me, I was going to vote for an acquittal.'

This is a prime reason why the decision on majority verdicts should not be made on anecdotal evidence. The question is, would the idea of deliberative democracy that underpins our jury system be weakened by the change? I believe it would, but I'm open to argument.

The lesson from *Job's Jury* is not about majority verdicts. Individual stories tell us little. For every Luke Shaw villain, there is a Henry Fonda hero. As the narrator says at the end, the jurors felt 'used' not because Luke Shaw was a ratbag, but because they weren't informed of their rights. They didn't know they could tell the judge that Shaw was misrepresenting them as foreman. They didn't know they could make a complaint about Shaw's bias. And the system failed them, by allowing Shaw to get onto the jury in the first place.

Then again, there's always the direct approach. Ian Barker QC recalls a 1997 Alice Springs case when he saw one juror 'punch another jury member [through the jury room door]', then 'dragged him back' into the jury room. A unanimous verdict came shortly afterwards.

TRIAL BY JURY

In February 2000, a historian at Yale University, Graham Burnett, sat as foreman on a jury in New York City. The defendant, Monte Milcray, was charged with the murder of Randolph Cuffee, a transvestite. Burnett's 2001 book, *Trial by Jury*, gives the kind of real-life insight into jury deliberations that is not allowed in Australia or the United Kingdom.

At the end of the evidence, Burnett does not know which way he'll vote: 'I distinctly remember thinking at the moment we crossed the court room to begin deliberating, how strange it was to have heard so much and yet not to have formulated a firm opinion.'

When they start each day's deliberations, Burnett gets his jury to share a prayer and a couple of silent minutes to gather their thoughts. He tries to instil a regime whereby jurors will take turns to speak, and listen politely to each other, but one juror criticises his 'bureaucratic' style and deliberations soon degenerate into a rabble of conflicting views spinning off at tangents.

> *We ran the gamut of group dynamics: a clutch of strangers yelled, cursed, rolled on the floor, vomited, whispered, embraced, sobbed, and invoked both God and*

> *necromancy. There were moments when the scene could have passed for a graduate seminar in political theory, others that might have been a jujitsu class. A few came straight out of bedlam. Before it was over, we had spent three nights and four days continuously attended by armed guards (who extended their affable surveillance into all lavatories); we had been shuttled to outlying hotels, into rooms with disconnected phones and sinks in which we washed our clothes; we had watched one juror pulled from our midst and rushed to the hospital (a physical collapse, caused by some combination of missing medication and the crucible of deliberations), another make a somewhat half-hearted attempt to escape (he was apprehended), and a third insist on her right to contact her own lawyer to extricate her from the whole affair (she was threatened with contempt).*

In part, he blames this confusion on the absence of guidance from the judge: 'He gave us almost no direction at all as to how we were to conduct ourselves in the jury room.'

The *Milcray* jury is sequestered for four days. The jury starts with a 'poll-driven' approach, taking votes and letting the factions use the evidence to support their positions; but, when that proves fruitless, turns to an 'evidence-driven' approach, going through the evidence piece by piece.

Jurors complain about judges not giving them a framework for deliberations. By leaving the deliberation model up to the jury – or, more likely, to its dominant member or members – judges are saying that one model is pretty much as good as another.

Experience shows that this is wrong. A poll-driven approach can be quicker, and is usually agreed on for more clear-cut decisions. But, as in *12 Angry Men* and *Joh's Jury*, early polling can result in disastrous divisions, causing jurors to dig in and defend their positions rather than consider the evidence. Evidence-driven decisions take longer, according to American research, but leave the jurors with greater certainty that they've done the right thing. The New Zealand jury project found that:

> . . . *evidence-driven juries spend more time talking about the important issues in the case, and bring out more facts, than poll-driven juries, and a poll-driven process is more likely to lead to entrenched positions. Judicial direction suggesting that juries might start their deliberation by discussion, and not take a vote too soon, could therefore be helpful.*

Polling is often taken as a substitute for argument. You take a poll and gang up on the holdouts. On the other hand, an evidence-driven jury is more likely to reach the ideal stated by American jury researcher Phoebe Ellsworth:

> *A jury decision . . . is more than an average of the verdict preferences of six or twelve citizens who represent a variety of experiences. Ideally, the knowledge, perspectives, and memories of the individual members are compared and combined, and individual errors and biases are discovered and discarded, so that the final verdict is forged on the shared understanding of the case. This understanding is more complete and more accurate than any of the separate versions that contributed to it, or indeed, than their average.*

As a solution to the great unnecessary question facing juries – What do we do now? – the New Zealand project suggests that 'the foreperson should be provided with some simple written guidelines on techniques for effective small group decision-making – how to structure discussions, how to deal with dominant jurors, how to resolve disagreements, etc.'

In Graham Burnett's New York jury, however, proper structure wasn't the only problem. The jury agreed that Milcray had killed Cuffee. He'd been lured to Cuffee's apartment thinking Cuffee was a woman. After discovering he was a man, Milcray killed him. For its verdict, the jury was given four options: first-degree murder, second-degree murder, manslaughter, and acquittal based on self-defence.

For most of the four days, they're split fairly evenly among the four alternatives. Manslaughter – where the victim's death is both unlawful and unintended – is commonly the hardest concept for juries to understand, and in this jury, Burnett recalls, a manslaughter verdict is proposed as a compromise where the extreme factions – the murder-one group and the self-defence group – can come together.

Burnett opposes this: 'The problem with a compromise is that it would be a violation of our duty as jurors, which is to apply the law ... We aren't allowed to fudge the law because we'd like to see Milcray get punished.'

Compromise, a necessity in most of life's negotiations, is an instinctive but destructive way out for many juries.

Two compromise verdicts in the 1980s did much to undermine confidence in the jury system. In the 1985 Maher–Donnelly 'bottom of the harbour' tax-evasion trial, and in the trial of Builders' Labourers Federation leader Norm Gallagher, jurors thrashed out deals where they'd convict on some counts in exchange for acquittals on others.

The Age asked:

> *What sort of justice is this where verdicts are negotiated between jurors so they can escape from the jury room? ... How many unanimous verdicts in our courts are likewise attained, their unanimity coerced from jurors by the oppression of confinement to the jury room?*

Though the rules on jury secrecy have tightened, studies show that the compromise verdict remains common. The 2001 NSW study found that 17 per cent of verdicts were compromises. Responses from jurors included:

> *The jury was very unusual in its make-up. There were several difficult jurors. There was a juror who seemed to favour a not guilty verdict . . . She was a very forceful woman . . . By day five or six of deliberations, most of the jurors agreed (of guilt on lesser charge) but a couple of jurors were weakly inclined to go along with the antagonistic juror. It looked possible that the jury would be hung and I was personally disturbed about that because it was evident to me that the evidence certainly warranted a finding of guilt on that charge. I intervened and declared . . . that if we couldn't agree on a finding of guilty, we should tell the judge and there would be a retrial . . . She then became a very strong advocate for the [lesser verdict] . . . The remaining jurors were swayed by her advocacy.*
>
> *A lot of jurors didn't want to hang the jury because of the stigma of doing that . . . and because of the cost to the taxpayer . . . I think that we all accepted the lesser of two evils in agreeing to [the lesser verdict]. It was better than nothing.*

And another jury 'traded up' on one charge and 'traded down' on another. But it must be noted that the 'professional assessors' considered these verdicts safe.

Burnett's fellow jurors want to compromise because they're not satisfied with any of the options the law offers them. The majority that forms around Burnett considers that Milcray did not murder Cuffee. Nor did he commit manslaughter. But he didn't commit the act in self-defence either. The jurors are faced with a choice the court has not offered. Their agreed belief on what Milcray did – that he killed Cuffee accidentally, but neither recklessly nor in self-defence – finds no place in the actual charges. He's not guilty of murder or manslaughter; yet the jurors feel bad about letting him walk free.

The jurors, then, are confronted with the oldest problem: justice or law?

One juror, Adelle, asks: 'What is my real responsibility? The law? Or the just thing? . . . Doesn't the whole authority of the law rest on its claim to be our system of justice? So if the law isn't just, how can it have any force?'

As a result of this dilemma, the jury moves towards 'jury equity', or 'jury nullification', probably the single most controversial issue in the history of the jury system.

Nullification means that the jury takes the law into its own hands. It will deny the force of the evidence, and render a verdict it considers 'just'.

Graham Burnett's fellow jurors eventually acquit Monte Milcray. But to convey their dissatisfaction with the legal options offered, they add to their 'Not guilty' the words: 'We the jury wish it to be known to the open court that we feel most strongly that the strict application of the law to the facts established by the evidence in this case does not lead to a truly just verdict.'

Verdicts in Australia are rarely given under such protest – but that could simply be because juries don't know their rights. The jury in the first Lionel Murphy trial in 1985 asked if they could send a qualification of their verdict to the judge, but were told they could not.

In the Scottish system, jurors can couch an acquittal as either 'Not guilty' or 'Not proven'. Other alternative verdicts, such as 'Justified violation' and 'Blameless violation', could convey the jury's feelings about a case much more accurately than a black-and-white guilty/not-guilty verdict. Juries could then use, in battered-wife cases for instance, a 'Justified' or 'Blameless violation' verdict to say that they agree the case is proven, but they want to either acquit without condoning the wife's actions or convict her without condoning the husband's violence.

I believe, at a deep level, Steve Rusher was forging a quasi-nullification defence in his trial. The defence's reliance on how much he cared for SJ, and how much he wanted to protect the boy from living with same-sex parents, seemed to be saying to us: Whatever this man has done, he did it for a just cause. How can you too abandon this defenceless boy to a perverse way of life?

At a deep level – though this was never put in words by the defence – we were being asked to block our ears to the incriminating tapes, and instead think of the father defending his little son.

Nullification, in various forms, has a distinguished history in our legal system. The 1670 case of Penn and Mead was the landmark, in which jurors refused to convict the Quaker preachers because the ideal of free speech overrode an unjust law banning it. In Australia, the 1855 trial of the Eureka Stockade rebels is our most famous jury nullification case. The jurors acquitted the rebels because they sympathised with their protest against the oppressive regime of licensing gold exploration. (The judge, unable to punish the jury, sentenced two spectators to a week in prison for contempt of court for cheering when the jury delivered its verdict.)

In America, the most famous episode of jury nullification was in the 1850s, when jurors refused to enforce the Fugitive Slave Act, which would convict defendants who had harboured runaway slaves.

This notion was embedded deep in the American consciousness, ever since juries had boycotted unjust British laws before the revolution. Future president John Adams wrote in his diary in 1771:

> *It is not only his right, but his Duty, in that Case to find the Verdict according to his own best Understanding, Judgment, and Conscience, tho in Direct opposition to the Direction of the Court . . . The English Law obliges no Man . . . to pin his faith on the sleve of any mere Man.*

In 1794 an American judge, John Jay, instructed a jury: 'You have . . . a right to take upon yourselves to . . . determine the law as well as the fact.' The idea of juries making and interpreting laws only faded in the late 19th century, mainly because the legislature became the appropriate law-making forum.

But nullification – essentially a return to the earlier way, where juries made law – still receives support from the most reputable sources. Professor Jeffrey Abramson writes:

> *I would hope that in 1850 I would have made a stand as a juror against enforcing provisions of the Fugitive Slave Law . . . [As] high a value as uniform application of the law is, it is not the highest value of our legal system. Not even 'the law is the law' states the highest ethical obligation for judge or jury. The highest obligation is to render just verdicts, and jury nullification speaks to that duty, in all its glory and all its dangers . . . For anyone who takes seriously the jury as a bridge between community values and the law, jury nullification is a strong plank. In essence, nullification empowers jurors to appeal to fundamental principles of justice over and above the written law.*

A majority of Americans surveyed in 1998 said they would vote according to their beliefs, 'regardless of a judge's instructions on the law of a case'. This pugnacious view was also dominant during the Chicago Jury Project period, in the 1950s, when jurors were found to be 'at modest war' with laws considered 'too severe'. Judges thought that half the verdicts where they disagreed with jury decisions could be explained as juries rebelling against the law rather than misreading the facts.

The issue for courts is whether or not to tell jurors of this option. A Canadian study found that 93 per cent of jurors would have liked to have been informed of the option to nullify an unjust law, and the constitutions of Maryland and Indiana enshrine jury nullification as a right.

It has been argued that juries should be informed of the nullification option – as something they may do if they cannot reconcile the law with the facts – but it's also argued that giving juries licence to nullify is a gateway to anarchy.

In America, the Fully Informed Jury Association (FIJA) was founded in the summer of 1989 to lobby for laws protecting the right of nullification.

> *The FIJA membership cuts across political lines, drawing together National Rifle Association members, antilogging environmentalists, advocates for the legalization of marijuana, tax protesters and bikers opposed to mandatory helmet laws. These persons, despite ideological differences, are all involved in disobeying some law. They turn to nullification as a way of authorizing the jury to determine whether the disobeyed laws ought to be enforced.*

One reason Abramson says the nullification choice should be brought into the open is that juries do it anyway. When Jack 'Doctor Death' Kevorkian was tried for assisting patients to commit suicide, a jury acquitted him even though he admitted he'd done it. When Washington mayor Marion Barry was hit with an overwhelming case of cocaine possession and use, the jury acquitted him. In the most famous case of all, a Los Angeles jury acquitted O.J. Simpson of murder for deep politico-racial reasons, even though the jurors themselves admitted that the evidence for the murder charge was indubitable. And in England, in 1985 a jury refused to convict a civil servant under official secrets legislation for revealing aspects of the *General Belgrano* sinking during the Falklands war. A 1996 jury acquitted Michael Randle and Patrick Pottle of organising the 1966 prison escape of MI6 traitor George Blake, even though Randle and Pottle had confessed doing it in a book.

Abramson says nullification happens every day, whether courts want to admit it or not. He writes of a 14th-century trial where a man killed another man he found having sex with his wife. The jury didn't want to convict him of murder, so they conveniently twisted the facts to support a self-defence acquittal.

> *The remarkable aspect of this story . . . is how familiar the fourteenth-century jury seems to us. Either openly displayed or hidden, nullification remains a timeless strategy for jurors seeking to bring law into line with their conscience. This reconciliation is what the jury system is about, for better or worse.*

The option to nullify should, in my view, be offered to jurors, but only under the strictest conditions. I don't think it would lead to jury anarchy. The reason is that there is nullification and there is nullification. Legitimate nullification is where juries acquit because they disagree with a law. The Kevorkian jury nullified legitimately, because they thought the law was wrong in banning a doctor from assisting critically ill patients to commit suicide. The Fugitive Slave Act nullifiers were protesting against an unjust law. So, in their way, are those who nullify charges against marijuana growers, bikies who ride without helmets, unauthorised gun owners, and a host of others.

On the other hand, the acquittal of the Eureka Stockade rebels, the *Belgrano* civil servant, O.J., Marion Barry, and anti-abortion protesters who broke into medical clinics are all examples of illegitimate nullification. The O.J. jury didn't disagree with the law punishing murder. The English jury didn't disagree with the law safeguarding official secrets. The jury encouraged to acquit anti-abortion protesters was not being asked to disagree with the law of trespass. In each of those cases, nullification or quasi-nullification happened because the juries sympathised with the defendant's cause. I don't think judges should tell juries they may acquit if they sympathise with a cause. But they should tell juries they would be supported by a long and honourable tradition if they overruled an unjust law;

that is, a law that would be unjust regardless of who is today's defendant.

So Steve Rusher was barking up the wrong tree. Even if any of us sympathised with his cause, we could not legitimately acquit him. None of us thought the law against soliciting murder was a bad law. We all had different ideas about Rusher's motives. The Retired Gent found Terri Maxfield 'repulsive' and gay marriage 'disgusting'. The Stickybeak said, 'It's such a shame for that little boy to grow up without a father.' Shut the Gate said, 'Lesos should be shot.' At the other end of the spectrum, some of us, including me, had no problem at all with gay marriage, and felt that SJ might well be better off being brought up by two loving mothers than by a biological mother and father who were at war. But whatever our opinions on SJ's welfare or his father's intentions, we all voted to convict him. The law, in this case, was the law. No matter how sincere or selfless your motives, you can't just go around having people killed.

Chapter Fifteen

TWELVE ANGRY SUGGESTIONS

Those of us who appear in criminal trials are always impressed by the jury's care, attention and sense of responsibility, and by verdicts which show, when there are a number of charges to consider, an astute awareness of the strength of the evidence on various complicated counts.
– John Mortimer QC

I support the jury system, even though I didn't when I turned up grudgingly at the Downing Centre that winter day. I'm one of those who emerge from the jury experience with the zeal of the late convert. Yet in this book I have related many horror stories about juries. That's as it should be. If the only thing the jury system has going for it is a taboo on enlightened criticism, then it hasn't got much going for it at all.

In my introduction I mentioned the sad fate of the important jury research surveys conducted here and overseas. Their recommendations have been too sensible for headline-hugging governments.

When juries get it wrong, the jury system is blamed. The framework of public debate is always adversarial. This hurts juries, because they have no-one to stand up for them. When a radio shock jock attacks a jury, who's going to reply? The actual jurors aren't allowed. When an Attorney-General or a political party sees mileage in chopping juries down at the knees, who is going to defend them? Jurors are by definition anonymous, therefore unable to organise. There will never be a jurors' union. Therefore, juries will never have a representative voice, and therefore their future is in peril.

As a juror, I want to propose a number of ways to improve the system. Juries will always be assailed by opportunists; this is their fate. The best way of deflecting those assaults is to enact a few changes that will assist juries in making their verdicts. None of my suggestions is particularly groundbreaking, but I think they would cumulatively help jurors get it right more often.

1. Jury Selection

Criticism: Juries are not representative of the community.
Response: Juries are more representative than we'd think, but the extremes – the underclass and the privileged elites – are unrepresented.
Suggestion: Limit the number of people who can get out of jury duty, such as schoolteachers, ministers of religion, public servants and politicians. Make it harder to get out of jury duty. Allow jurors to specify a period in advance over a 12-month period when they'll be able to serve. Allow people with minor offences on their record to be eligible (enabling more Aboriginal jurors). And widen the pool from the electoral roll to include driver's licences and other records, so that Australia's two million adult non-voters can't shirk jury duty.

2. Peremptory Challenge

Criticism: The peremptory challenge, as it currently exists, is a worthless and discriminatory practice and an insult to jurors.
Response: The challenge is, as Nicholas Cowdery puts it, 'a

safety-valve for the accused so he can think he's getting a fair trial'.

Suggestion: Abolish it and widen the scope of challenges for cause, so that barristers can replace a juror for authentic, thoroughly examined reasons rather than on appearance.

3. A Settling-In-Period

Criticism: The first day of a trial, jurors are most unsettled and least able to absorb information.
Response: The opening statements by judge, Crown and defence are crucial to the trial.
Suggestion: Allow jurors a half-hour after empanelment to make phone calls, organise childcare and transport and so on, and get to know each other over a cup of tea before they hear the opening submissions.

4. Foreman

Criticism: The foreman is selected randomly, before the jurors get to know each other, and is often the pushiest on the panel. This can cause problems in deliberations.
Response: A jury needs a spokesman.
Suggestion: During evidence, it doesn't matter who the spokesman is. You don't need a foreman at all until you start deliberations. Jurors should be instructed to elect their foreman at the end of evidence, when they know each other better and have identified their natural leaders.

5. Standard Written Guidelines

Criticism: Jurors don't understand the law they are to apply, nor the cases that are made. They are not aware of their rights.
Response: Written guidelines might bias jurors one way or the other.

Suggestion: The judge's opening statement should contain a written formulation of the law in the indictment. In our case, this would have been a definition of 'solicit'. Also, jurors should be given a standardised information sheet outlining the need for a unanimous verdict, the idea of 'beyond reasonable doubt', the burden of proof being on the Crown, the difference between evidence and barristers' submissions, their right to ask questions, and so on. If counsel agree, they can supply a written outline of their case. Tom Molomby says long trials ask such an 'enormous amount' of ordinary people that 'more could be done to point out the difficulties in advance'. He suggests a 'road map for jurors'.

6. FOOD

Criticism: The food's lousy.
Suggestion: Well-fed jurors are competent jurors. Give them a meal allowance and let them go outside for their own food.

7. WINDOWS

Criticism: As one judge has noted, jury rooms are comparable to the Black Hole of Calcutta.
Suggestion: Jurors are not rats. They should be accommodated in rooms with natural light, adequate air and privacy for toilet visits. They shouldn't be having to make the best of a bad lot. As American juror Mary Timothy wrote in her 1974 book *Jury Woman*:

> *From our unique perspective, we [are] aware that the rights of all jurors can be reduced to a single simple right and need – the right to insist on an atmosphere in which a person can make a reasoned judgment.*

8. Money

Criticism: See food. It's not only jurors who whinge about the payment. A NSW judge told the Findlay 1994 study: 'The money paid to jurors is quite inadequate, particularly in lengthy trials.'
Suggestion: Raising the jury allowance in line with average earnings, regardless of the length of the trial, would be more equitable. It would also make jurors less likely to evade duty.

9. Transcripts

Criticism: Juries cannot remember all evidence presented throughout a long trial. This is not their fault, as Michael Sexton says:

> *Advocacy has changed over time. Instead of focusing on one or two issues, lawyers are throwing every possible theory up, both in the hope that some of it sticks and to open up possible avenues for appeal. This makes things harder for juries.*

Response: Transcripts would encourage jurors to ignore the presentation of evidence in court, and read it in the transcripts afterwards.
Suggestion: Jurors should be informed in advance whether transcripts will be available or not. They should be available wherever possible. A juror who sleeps in court won't be bothered to wait and read transcripts anyway. Best of all, provide video records of witness testimony, so jurors can go over it during deliberations. This suggestion has the support of NSW Supreme Court Justice Virginia Bell, who said in her 2005 speech to fellow judges: 'Perhaps it is time for the jury to be supplied with the transcript as a matter of course.'

10. Written Summing-Up

Criticism: Juries are confused by oral summing-up.
Suggestion: Judges and lawyers have been allowed to get away with mealy-mouthed ramblings and deliberate or inept prolixity for too long. Make judges accountable by having to put their directions in simple written English. Give counsel the option to do likewise. And treat the jurors like adults by telling them that a hung jury is a valid option, but will not be accepted unless a certain number of hours have passed and the foreman verifies that the minority is immovable.

11. Guidelines for Deliberations

Criticism: Deliberations often descend into counter-productive anarchy. As one juror reported to Radio National in 1993, 'The jury spent days arguing about the procedure before even considering the evidence.'
Response: To impose guidelines would interfere with jury independence.
Suggestion: Most jurors would appreciate a simple written guide on the difference between poll-driven and evidence-driven deliberations, on the value of secret and open ballots, and on basic conflict-resolution techniques.

12. Secrecy

Criticism: Jurors are stripped of their freedom of speech during and after a trial.
Response: This is necessary to protect the safety of verdicts.
Suggestion: Maintain the ban on speech during a trial, but ease the restrictions afterwards so that jurors are allowed to disclose and publish what went on in the jury room as long as what they say doesn't interfere with the administration of justice or violate

other laws. That is, allow them to talk after the appeal period has expired (if they convicted) or legislate a standard six-month silence period (if they acquitted).

CHAPTER SIXTEEN

GOING HOME

There's a poignant closing scene to *12 Angry Men*. Dwarfed by the size of the court, the jurors disperse into the night like cockroaches. Henry Fonda is walking down the steps when his first supporter, the old man, Joseph Sweeney, comes up and asks his name. Fonda tells him: 'My name's McArdle.' It's the first time any of the characters has been given a name. There's an awkward silence between the pair, and that's it – 'So long.' The juror returns to the anonymity from whence he came.

If only it were that simple.

For many jurors, the stress only begins when the trial ends. Graham Burnett recalls that the real agony for him started the moment after the jurors had agreed on their verdict. They hug and cry. The juror Adelle then asks: 'If we're doing the right thing, why are we all crying?'

We all want to think we've done the right thing, but putting a person in prison – or setting free someone who may be a criminal – is an immense weight on a juror's conscience.

After the judge gives them some backhanded thanks – congratulating them for doing their service, but reminding them that many of his generation had died giving service to protect democracy – Burnett has another decision to face.

Leaving court, he must decide whether to go out the back door or to go out the front, past the family and representatives of the murdered man. He chooses to go out the front.

> *My instinct was to avert my gaze, out of a sense of decorum, not wishing them to see me looking on at their defeat. But at the same time I realised that my wandering eyes might be interpreted as an unwillingness to look them in the face, as a sign of some uneasiness with the thing we had just done. This would not do. So I made full eye contact, and I held it.*

We didn't have that problem with Steve Rusher. He had no friends in court. He had no friends anywhere. This was, I found, the most striking thing about his case. He'd trusted Les McAtee, a man he'd only known for a few weeks, to arrange two murders. I can imagine a person wanting to kill someone; but it's hard for me to conceive of someone being so utterly friendless in the world that he is reduced to placing such a matter in the hands of a virtual stranger.

As I walked away from the court and went home, a truck pulled up beside me for no apparent reason. For a second I flinched, wondering if Rusher had sent someone to 'serve papers' on me. I couldn't help this feeling, irrational as it was.

But the shakes last. After his trial, American juror Johnathan Carter was at work when he noticed a red laser dot following him around. A workmate, who was pointing the laser as a joke, said: 'You'd better get used to that. He'll be after your ass now.'

Carter thinks:

> *I am sure there are other people [the convicted man] would rather get that are ahead of jurors on the hit parade. Besides, if he does start killing people, that would be just like admitting he was guilty, which he will never do.*

Once the fear has ebbed, depression often sets in. Reading Graham Burnett's account of how he felt after his trial, I knew that I was not alone:

> *Life had been weirdly sapped of its vitality and importance; my work seemed bizarre and insignificant. Conversation with colleagues . . . pained me immensely. In the mornings, perched on the edge of consciousness, I found the trial continuing . . . as if somehow I could continue to discharge a task that seemed impossible to close.*

Jurors will often seek to close the matter for themselves by investigating the person they have convicted (or acquitted). Burnett goes to the crime scene, but it does him no good:

> *I was wasting my time. But my time felt like a waste. Conversation was toothless, books had no life, days were without focus. This disturbing sense largely passed. But it took quite a while . . . Life hands one few such episodes, and they are, in a way, gifts that go on costing.*

Later still, Burnett finds out that Cuffee had previously assaulted victims after luring them as a woman into his apartment. But this, like the visit to the murder scene, fails to satisfy Burnett:

> *Had the messenger descended in the final act, wing-footed, wand in hand, dispelling doubt, bearing the Truth? I could not really see it this way: welcome as the news was, it ransomed our verdict only by bankrupting its logic, which I held so dear.*

It's common for those jurors who resist looking up an accused's history during the trial to do so afterwards. Later I was to research newspaper files on Steve Rusher, and found out that he had been through a previous mistrial. None of this had any bearing on my feelings about convicting Rusher. That wasn't the point in my researches. The point was to express my freedom again, after weeks of confinement, and find some outlet for my lingering anxiety and curiosity.

The 2001 NSW study found post-trial stress to be widespread:

> *A number of jurors expressed surprise that, even though they felt fine during and immediately after the trial, they had experienced sleeplessness, nightmares, depression and phobias in subsequent months . . . A juror who served in a 'very stressful' non-metropolitan trial commented that she kept having 'flashbacks' long after the trial was finished. She added that because she lived in a small town it was difficult to find anyone 'removed from the personalities involved' to whom she could 'unload'.*

Jurors asked for counselling over unresolved concerns such as doubts over the verdict, regrets at caving in or coming to a compromise. Some found consolation in hearing of the convict's prior record, but if this information contradicted their verdict other jurors subsequently felt 'guilty' about their verdict, especially if they had been instrumental in swaying minority jurors to their view or been so swayed by others.

The New Zealand study discovered something similar:

> *Both during and after the trial, jurors used their own methods of alleviating stress. These included 'retail therapy', talking it through with their partner, laughter and having a cry. But . . . some jurors were having considerable difficulty in coping with the impact of their experiences.*

Of the jurors who have contacted me, post-trial stress has been a common denominator:

> *When we were discharged we were read a statement that said we would probably feel strongly about the case for a short while but that it would subside in a few days. More like a few months . . .*

> *We convicted the accused on most of the charges but had to declare 'Not Guilty' on three charges, not because we didn't believe the witness/victim but because there was insufficient evidence to convict. I felt so badly about this, and about how that particular victim would be feeling, that I rang the policewoman in charge of the case the next week and asked her to explain this to the witness/victim. She agreed to do so, but she was obviously rather taken aback. I don't think it's very common for jury members to contact the police.*

I'm unsurprised by this common desire to see someone connected with the case again. Many jurors support each other by getting together for barbecues. My colleague David's jury did. And the NSW study found:

> *Several juries bonded so well that they met regularly to socialise long after jury service had finished. Some jurors who served with complete strangers found that they resided in the same neighbourhood, and they formed ongoing friendships.*

But, it goes on:

> *For other jurors, the experience was less positive. Several jurors said that they hoped never to see their fellow jurors again. A juror who was annoyed by the lack of common*

> *sense displayed by some of his fellow jurors said: 'We were excused from jury service for eight years and I hope that Alzheimer's has set in by then so I don't have to serve again.' . . . For others, tension affected their home lives or their emotional well-being; jurors spoke of not sleeping, 'having a good cry', and domestic tension.*

In British Columbia, judges regularly meet jurors in chambers after trials to help them 'come down' off the trauma of giving their verdict. In most cases, this is because the jurors want reassurance from the judge that they 'got it right'. And it would certainly help judges – not to mention lawyers – to have a structured channel for post-trial feedback. It would be the only chance the lawyers get to find out where they went wrong, or right.

I had no strong feelings about seeing my fellow jurors or the legal officers again. As I've mentioned, I ran into Storeman Foreman a couple of weeks after the trial. He was indifferent to the whole business.

But I couldn't let the matter rest. I was angry at how much the court had left unexplained, at the structural weaknesses in the system. We had a good judge, I kept reminding myself, and a clear-cut verdict, but still it seemed the court had done everything it could to make the jurors uncomfortable and ill-equipped. Or no, that's an exaggeration – the system's failures were in omission, not commission. It had *failed* to equip us with a working knowledge of the criminal trial process. It had *failed* to give us a basic idea of the rules of evidence. It had *failed* those jurors who'd been challenged, by allowing the lawyers to discriminate against their race and appearance. It had *failed* everyone by letting certain professions excuse themselves automatically, by letting some clever dicks excuse themselves with fancy reasons, and by letting two million adults get off by not having registered to vote. It *failed* to encourage us to ask questions of the witnesses. It *failed* to inform us of our highest duty – to justice. It *failed* to set out clearly the fundamental principles of law in the case, and it *failed* to give us proper guidance on how to deliberate. It *failed* us, generally and paradoxically, by insulting our intelligence and over-estimating our level of prior knowledge. It *failed* us by not trusting us as adults. The system *failed* to provide us with adequate physical comforts. Yet it never failed to carry on the lip service about how important we were.

And the funny thing is, whenever a jury appears to get something wrong, whose fault is it? It's the jury's.

My concern about these failures went beyond the Rusher case. We at least found a way to harmonise. My main concern was with all the jurors who hadn't got the lucky breaks our group had.

And I still felt an empathetic wretchedness for Rusher himself. I couldn't stop thinking about how high he'd been, and how far he'd fallen. How grand his life had been as the Hollywood hotshot – even though he was hardly Spielberg, he'd been a player – and how friendless he was as an inmate, now, of Long Bay.

I decided to visit him.

I went with two journalists, one from *The Sydney Morning Herald* and a stringer for several American papers who'd been covering the Rusher trial. On arrival at the jail, we had to give our full names and addresses. I wasn't so happy about this. I had, after all, convicted a man who'd tried to have people killed while he was incarcerated. Could I trust the prison officers not to leak my details to Rusher?

I decided I couldn't, and tried to give my work address. But the guard said I had to give the same address as on my driver's licence, assuring me that there was no way Rusher could get his hands on it.

We had to deposit all our possessions – keys, wallets, pens, handkerchiefs – in a locker. We passed into the prisoners' area through metal detectors sensitive enough to pick up our belt buckles. We'd been scheduled to meet Rusher in the cafeteria, face to face around a table. But some problems with the *Herald* journalist's ID meant that we'd only be able to meet the prisoner at a desk divided by a perspex window.

We were led into the visitors' side of a long gallery of divided desks. My hands were cold and clammy, my heartbeat rapid. The previous night, I'd slept poorly.

We were arranging three plastic chairs at a desk of our choice when the American journalist noticed that Rusher was already waiting for us at another. He smiled generally in greeting. He wore a white jumpsuit torn around the neck. Through the scratched perspex, it gave him the aspect of a wild-eyed mental patient.

He ignored me, pointedly I thought, while he answered the reporters' questions. He complained how hard it was to hear; and complained about the *Herald* stories on his case, which he said 'told only one side'.

The stringer asked him about the progress of his appeal. Rusher said his grounds for appeal were that he'd been entrapped, and that his counsel, Mr Nisbett, had erred by not finding out about the web trace before the jury heard the tapes.

'If my legal support had been better, we'd have been able to plant the doubt about the authenticity of these tapes in the jury's head before they heard them,' Rusher said.

He was down to his last $2,000, he said, having brought $60,000 to Australia. He'd received legal aid for his trial – his assets in the US had been frozen pending the result of the Family Court proceedings, to stop him selling up and hiding the money from Fiona to dodge child support. But Rusher blamed his underfunded lawyers for not having represented him properly.

He said Nisbett wouldn't be appearing for him at his appeal.

Interested in making the story more palatable for his American audience, the stringer asked Rusher about his family.

'My folks are good people, y'know, like, like, they don't associate with convicted bad guys,' Rusher said. 'So they've more or less disowned me.' (I remembered the tapes, when he'd told Les he didn't particularly care whether his mother knew about his circumstances or not.)

The stringer asked him how he felt about 'having fallen so far'.

'Ten years ago,' Rusher said, 'I had my house in Benedict Canyon. Man, I owned Hollywood. I had all my posse. I was like, things can't possibly get better. Well, now I'm here, for protecting SJ – and you know how much more it means to me? Like, infinitely more. I haven't fallen anywhere.'

During the hour or so of the interview, Rusher never once looked my way. He fixed his persuasive staring eyes on the journalists. Now, as I pulled my seat forward to the window, he fixed them on me. They had a madman's penetration. I could see how he could influence people.

'I was a juror in your trial,' I said. 'I just wanted to know if you had any questions for me.'

Rusher smiled warmly, and made a face as if to indicate the penny dropping. 'Oh yeah, dude, you look familiar. Nice to meetcha! Sorry for putting you through all that. I've done jury service myself, and I know what it's like. You always believe the prosecutor first, the judge second, and the accused way down the bottom. That's, like, the way it is. You guys were good honest people, and you acted honourably. But you made the wrong decision – not your own fault, but you could have looked at some of the evidence different. That's what I'd have done if I was a juror. But it should have been presented to you different. Before you heard the tapes, I thought you should have been told there were serious doubts about their, like, validity. You shoulda been told that before you heard 'em.'

He was beginning to rant again, repeating what he'd told the journalists, so I said again: 'Do you have any questions for me?'

'Nah,' he said, 'not at all.'

His charm unnerved me. I'd seen this style before, in the police interview when he'd said he wished nothing but happiness for Fiona and Terri.

As we left the prison, one of the journalists said: 'You can see how he could manipulate people into thinking he's a good man.'

I saw Rusher again about a month later, when I returned to the Downing Centre for the first time since the verdict. This was his sentencing hearing. I wasn't prepared to go to the lengths of the Maidstone jury who, after convicting a man, turned up en masse to see him tried on a second, related, offence. But I was curious. He was listed on the court notice as 'R'. The judge – our old wigless friend – told the court that there had been a suppression order on the names of Fiona, Terri and SJ. He addressed his warning to the handful of journalists who'd come to report on the sentence, drawn by the interest in Rusher since the *Herald* stories.

Steve himself was in his familiar dark-blue suit. He'd had a haircut, his dark blond mane trimmed back around his neck. He carried a large pile of documents.

He was applying for an adjournment. A psychiatrist's report had been delayed because the shrink hadn't listened to all of the tapes, on which he was expected to base his judgment of Rusher's mental state at the time of the crimes. Also, his solicitor had gone to see him in jail the previous day, but Steve hadn't been there. He'd been in court somewhere else attending to other matters. So, on the basis of these two arguments, the judge adjourned the hearing.

I thought that would be all I'd hear or see of Steve Rusher. My wife's pregnancy was nearing its conclusion, and I had started working on this book. Then I received a letter from Rusher. The address was handwritten, and he'd marked it 'Personal'. My first reaction was annoyance that he'd found out my name and address – I still don't know how he got them, but a process of elimination suggests that the most likely source was the prison staff.

He thanked me for my visit to the jail, and said he was aware that I had spoken with his solicitor. He filled another page reiterating, in nakedly and somehow touchingly illiterate prose, his innocence. He wrote of his sadness at being separated from his 'vunerable' son SJ, who, he stressed, was in great danger. Then came the clanger. He wrote that I had 'told' him on my visit that I disagreed with the jury's verdict and 'agreed' with him that Les McAtee and Spike were 'liers' trying to frame him and steal his money. He asked me to write to the court and tell the judge I had been bullied into giving a guilty verdict against my will, so as to help Rusher with his appeal and possibly secure his immediate release. He concluded:

> *I have no idea if this would help my cause but I would of thought they would take notice of what you say.*

Immediately after reading the letter, I rang Rusher's solicitor. He said he did not want to have any discussions about the verdict with me. I said I didn't want to discuss the verdict with him, either. I said there'd been no doubt about the verdict from me or anyone else, and that Rusher was lying, or his memory had failed him, if he thought I'd said anything else at our meeting. I was also very annoyed that Rusher had found my address and written to me – though I have to admit, I can't help a grudging admiration for the man. If there's any loophole, he'll go for it.

I typed a reply to Rusher, telling him he was barking up the wrong tree. I was about to sign it, but something flitted across my mind – an American judge in an earlier trial had said Steve was a 'forger', among other things. Maybe he was after my signature. I left the reply unsigned and posted it to him.

I saw him again in court for what I thought would be his final sentencing. He wangled another adjournment – the psychiatric report still wasn't ready. Annoyed, the judge rescheduled the sentencing and said Rusher was the one who was suffering, as 'he must want to know what's going to happen to him.'

Then, a surprise. Mr Crown got up and said Rusher had sent letters about a juror visiting him in jail to the judge and various other people. Mr Crown asked about an order to stop Rusher harassing the juror.

'It seems to me to be the other way around,' the judge said, before calling my conduct 'extraordinary'.

I smiled. Good old Steve. He copied the judge in on his letter to me, stating that I'd told him I disagreed with the verdict. I looked at him, grinning wryly. He looked away. He was up to every trick in the book. If he'd had some ethics, Steve would have been a first-rate lawyer.

His sentencing took place, finally, almost two years to the day since his arrest. He was no longer represented by his old solicitor and barrister, who had advised him that he had no convincing grounds for appeal. His newest solicitor tried to have the sentencing put off yet again because he'd only had nine days to look at Rusher's brief and Rusher was going to apply for a mistrial due to 'corruption involving a juror'.

While I was falling off my chair laughing, the judge said sternly: 'That has nothing to do with sentencing, and I'll be passing sentence today.'

Still, Rusher had a last desperate card to play. He stood up and asked the judge if he could make an address 'under section 648 of the Criminal Code 1899'.

'We don't have a Criminal Code 1899 in NSW, Mr Rusher,' the judge said.

Generously, the judge gave Rusher ten minutes, during which Steve speechified about various well-trodden matters in his case. It turned out that he had written to Joanne Lees, the Englishwoman whose boyfriend, Peter Falconio, had disappeared, presumably murdered, in the outback in 2001. Lees had been targeted by a nasty whispering campaign, and an ever-hopeful Rusher tried to associate his case with hers – the innocent visitor victimised by those wicked Aussies. The judge was to say that this letter 'does not advance these matters one iota and does not entitle the prisoner to any discount [on his sentence] whatsoever'.

After Rusher had finished, the judge said that contrary to

Rusher's assertions, the vital tapes 'bore no other interpretation' than guilt. 'Not surprisingly,' he went on, 'the jury rejected that there was even a reasonable possibility of Mr Rusher's account being true.'

The Crown case, he said, 'was so strong as to be overwhelming'. As a juror, this felt like being given a pass mark by the teacher.

The judge went on to comment about other issues in the trial.

Rusher had a 'genuine but in my view entirely misplaced concern for his son . . . There was no real evidence whatsoever that Ms Maxfield would do SJ any harm at all.'

Most tellingly, the judge rejected Rusher's story that he acted entirely out of concern for SJ. Instead, Rusher acted 'through feelings of either jealousy and/or resentment . . . and/or to obtain custody of SJ for himself'.

The judge accepted the Crown's submission that Rusher could not be so concerned for SJ's welfare if, as the tapes showed, he would have had Fiona murdered, and, what's more, had her murdered in front of the little boy's eyes.

Rusher had submitted psychiatric reports in which he said he'd been suicidal over his fears for SJ, but the judge referred to contemporaneous assessments of Rusher which showed him to be 'happy', 'alert', 'positive' and 'communicative'. Rusher 'may have been depressed to a degree', said the judge, 'but at the lower end of the scale'.

In conclusion, the judge said Steve Rusher had committed 'a very serious offence indeed, marked by an indifference to the lives [of others and] . . . callous in the extreme'. He had shown 'no remorse whatsoever', and the judge had 'no idea of what his prospects of rehabilitation are'.

Hearing such a wholesale condemnation and rejection of Rusher, the Crown expected a heavy sentence. But the judge said that Rusher's motives were 'not as heinous as' other solicit-to-murder convictions where the motive was money. Therefore, Rusher was sentenced to six-and-a-half years prison, with a five-year non-parole period.

As a juror, I have no comment on this sentence. I don't want to jump onto the misinformed bandwagon of criticising lenient sentences. The judge, no doubt, followed the guidelines and principles in front of him. (Later, on appeal by the Crown, the sentence was increased to eight years with six-and-a-half non-parole.)

But I was told that Fiona and Terri were dismayed, as no doubt was Les. I can only gauge their fears by multiplying the anxiety I myself have felt. That fear has taken time to wear off, since the trial.

Rationally, I don't fear Steve Rusher. One thing that gives me confidence is that when he did want to have someone killed, it took him three failed attempts and eventually he was caught. He trusted people he shouldn't have. He didn't have friends he could rely on.

Anyway, it's stupid, this fear. Steve Rusher is not some crazed psychopath. To me, he seems to be a man who was accustomed to fooling around with the grey areas of the law, and then got carried away by jealousy. He wasn't a threat to the community, just to Terri and Fiona. There's no reason for him to go after me, none at all.

But it says something about the strange, rarefied air of the jury room that most of us, at some stage, were a little bit scared.

'The message here is obvious,' says Johnathan Carter at the end of his account of being a juryman.

> *Do not ever call me for jury duty again. I am ruined for it forever. I could never sit in that box and be open minded again, not after all of the things that I have seen and heard . . . Before they wrap me up in my nice straitjacket and take me away to a padded cell, take this last bit of advice: get out of jury duty, do not be too stupid to get out of jury duty. When the trial was over, I heard that during the jury selection process a woman had screamed that she 'could not take it' and ran screaming from the*

> *room. God bless her, that is one smart woman, and that is exactly what I intend to do the next time I receive a summons. I don't care if it is a one-day trial or not. 'I can't take it! I can't take it!'*

At the end of *Joh's Jury*, the narrator, played by Simon Bossell, says:

> *I saw it as my civic duty. I don't know how I feel about it now, or if I'd go through it again . . . I was angry, and wanted to hold on to it. If I was going to take anything away, it was a feeling of being used.*

But if I'm ever called up for jury duty again, I'll do it with enthusiasm and pride – like my colleague David, who says that 'after trying so hard to get out of it, I found this to be the best thing I'd done all year.'

It's pleasing to see that we're in the majority. The comprehensive New Zealand jury study found that 82 per cent of jurors commented positively on their experience. In all 48 trials surveyed, at least one juror said it was positive. In 18 of the 48, every juror said it was a worthwhile experience.

> *As well as seeing positive personal gains, jurors noted a greater understanding of the criminal trial and reported feeling that a 'civic duty' had been done . . . Some 'found the experience "harrowing"', imposing a heavy responsibility and causing them to feel 'sick to their stomachs', but still found it worthwhile. In particular, they felt that they had made a big contribution, had learned more about the process, had a heightened interest in court cases, and had become more self-confident about putting their view across.*

I'm also greatly encouraged by letters from former jurors who agree that every failing of the jury system could be addressed by better preparation from the courts – not by reducing the use of juries:

> *It seems that the 'failings' of the Court system are currently leading to moves to remove juries, rather than to instruct juries. This will then leave 'justice' to that well-respected group of politicians (frequently being lawyers), judges, barristers and solicitors. Hardly comforting, let alone representative.*
>
> *When I was empanelled we were told nothing other than to listen carefully and decide on the evidence. Was I allowed to raise my hand and ask for something to be clarified? How about ask if I'd not heard something clearly? Was I allowed to take notes? Could I (immediately?) tell my fellow jurors when I picked up a deliberately misleading 'lie' by the prosecutor, designed to make the defendant look stupid or untruthful? Could I ask for an immediate look at the various photos being tendered as exhibits? Despite several days on that jury, and several years since then, I still don't know the answers to any of these questions . . . Our sheriff's officer would not answer any questions except to say that the judge would instruct us fully AT THE END OF THE EVIDENCE (not much use by then! And in our case it never came because something happened, a deal was done, we were thanked and discharged . . .). And of course that is just some of the questions I can remember thinking of at the time. What about the myriad questions we didn't even think about or know were relevant? Maybe a person going into an important job like juror could be prepared by being given (say) a 2-page fact sheet to read while waiting, plus the opportunity to ask questions (of say the sheriff's officer) immediately after*

> *being empanelled. Surely, with all the time and expense of trials, much more attention needs to be paid to the jurors. Otherwise 'the law' and 'justice' will continue to diverge and lawyers' reputations will move below their current parity with used-car salesmen's reputations.*

It's heartening to see how much jurors can contribute to the improvement of our criminal justice system. Now it's up to those other law-makers, the ones who sit in parliaments, to let us help.

Notes

Author's Note

p. xiv 'From the 1500s...' For most of the background information here I have relied on Leonard W. Levy, *The Palladium of Justice: Origins of Trial by Jury*, Ivan R. Dee, Chicago, 1999; and Michael Chesterman, 'Criminal Trial Juries in Australia: From Penal Colonies to a Federal Democracy', 62 *Law & Contemporary Problems* 69, Spring 1999.

p. xiv 'the blackbox of the judicial system' US Justice Patrick Higginbotham, 'Juries and the Death Penalty', *Case Western Reserve Law Review* 41, 1991.

p. xiv 'The quality of finality is lost...' Australian Law Reform Commission, 'Contempt', ALRC 35, 1987.

p. xiv 'What happened in there is your business...' Justice Carter in 1985, quoted in John Fairbanks Kerr, *A Presumption of Wisdom: An Exposé of the Jury System of Injustice*, Angus & Robertson, Sydney, 1987:11.

p. xv 'The others started moving down...' Juror 'Tom', quoted in ibid 28.

p. xv 'we're not allowed to know...' Bret Walker, speaking to the ABC's *Lateline*.

p. xvi 'broadcast more widely among associates...' Mark Findlay et al, 'Jury Management in New South Wales', Australian Institute of Judicial Administration Incorporated, Melbourne, 1994: 7.
p. xvi 'an informed assessment...' ibid ix.
p. xvii 'the whole thing would collapse' Sir Louis Blom-Cooper QC, quoted in Trevor Grove, *The Juryman's Tale*, Bloomsbury, London, 1998: 209.
p. xvii 'there are things to be learned...' D. Graham Burnett, *A Trial By Jury*, Alfred A. Knopf, New York, 2001: 13.

INTRODUCTION: A TICKING IN THE BOX

p. 4 'Jury service is the school...' Thomas Jefferson, quoted in Jeffrey Abramson, *We, The Jury: The Jury System and the Ideal of Democracy*, Harvard University Press, Cambridge, Massachusetts, 2000: 31.
p. 4 'The jury system puts a ban...' Mark Twain, quoted in Kerr 26.
p. 4 'By making men pay attention...' Alexis de Tocqueville, *Democracy in America* (1833), quoted in Abramson 177.
p. 4 'Juries is ineddicated...' Charles Dickens, *Oliver Twist*, quoted in Grove 10.
p. 5 'The jury states a simple verdict...' Thomas Plucknett, quoted in Evan Whitton, *The Cartel: Lawyers and their Nine Magic Tricks*, Herwick, Sydney, 1998: 48.
p. 5 'In "The Emperor's New Clothes"...' Professor Tony Blackshield, La Trobe University, quoted in Kerr 1.
p. 5 'We have a criminal system which is superior...' Mark Twain, quoted in Grove 216.
p. 6 'reflected a deep-seated conviction...' Justice Sir William Deane in *Kingswell v R*.
p. 6 'ahead of formal law reform...' Findlay 8.
p. 7 'We commonly strive to assemble twelve persons...' B.S. Oppenheimer, quoted in Grove 10.

p. 7 'We know, as a nation . . .' Auberon Waugh, quoted in Grove 10.

p. 7 'a group of 12 diverse people . . .' Findlay 6.

p. 8 'asking the ignorant . . .' Hiller Zobel, quoted in Grove 205.

p. 8 'fate of the accused . . .' Warren Young, Neil Cameron and Yvette Tinsley, 'Juries in Criminal Trials: Part Two', Law Commission of New Zealand Preliminary Paper 37, Wellington, New Zealand, 1999: Vol 1, par 30.

p. 9 'A barrister appearing for the Crown . . .' Rule 20 of the NSW Bar Association, quoted in Whitton 40.

p. 9 'something of an anarchist' Nicholas Hasluck from his 1994 novel *A Grain of Truth*, quoted in Whitton 40.

p. 9 'expressly and implicitly silenced . . .' Findlay 137.

p. 11 'As I sat there watching . . .' Judge Alex Kozinski, from his 'Foreword' in Paul Bergman and Michael Asimow, *Reel Justice: The Courtroom Goes to the Movies*, Andrews McMeel, Kansas City, 1996: xii.

p. 11 'Two-thirds of juries end up . . .' This is the conclusion of Young et al in New Zealand and the Chicago Jury Project, though Findlay in NSW suggests (89) that as many as 47 per cent of jurors make up their minds during deliberations.

p. 13 'irresponsible in the extreme . . .' Michael Quinn, quoted in Whitton 158.

p. 13 'Accepting that community confidence . . .' Findlay 28.

p. 16 'When a US President blunders . . .' Alexander Cockburn in *Liberal Opinion Week*, 8 January 1996, quoted in Mara Taub, *Juries: Conscience of the Community*, Chardon Press, Berkeley, 1998: 97.

CHAPTER TWO: PANEL BEATING OR HOW JURORS AND LAWYERS CULL THE POOL

p. 35 'The jury system is actually bizarre . . .' Sonya Hamlin,

What Makes Juries Listen? A Communications Expert Looks at the Trial, Prentice Hall Law & Business, Englewood Cliffs, New Jersey, 1985: 2–3.

p. 39 'At the start, I decided . . .' Burnett 17.
p. 39 'In the twice-exhaled air . . .' ibid 18.
p. 39 'secreted an unexpected libidinous energy' ibid 21.
p. 40 'he studied "philosophy"' Burnett 18.
p. 43 'Then, as now . . .' Abramson 249.
p. 44 'by a blindfolded child' See Levy 77.
p. 46 'in NSW the average time spent selecting . . .' See Philip R. Weems, 'A Comparison of Jury Selection Procedures for Criminal Trials in New South Wales and California', 10 Sydney L. Rev. 330: 340–47.
p. 46 'What are those idiots . . .' Kate Auty and Sandy Toussaint (eds), *A Jury of Whose Peers?*, University of Western Australia Press, Perth, 2004: 27.
p. 46 'In 1982 there were 25 . . .' See Abramson 149.
p. 47 'Favourable to defendants . . .' Clarence Darrow, paraphrased at ibid 146.
p. 47 'If a party's case was primarily emotional . . .' I. Goldstein, *Trial Technique*, 1935, paraphrased at ibid 147.
p. 47 'In medical malpractice cases . . .' ibid 147, including quoted material from Murray Sams Jr.
p. 47 'farmers favoured the state' Melvin Belli, *Modern Trials*, 1963, paraphrased in ibid 147.
p. 47 'cabdrivers, union members . . .' Russ Herman, 'Juror Selection in Civil Litigation', *Trial* 25, January 1989: 71, 75; quoted at ibid 147.
p. 47 'heavy, round-faced, jovial looking persons' F. Lee Bailey, *Fundamentals of Criminal Advocacy*, quoted at ibid 146.
p. 50 '12 people selected from anywhere . . .' Lorana Bartels, 'And So Say Most of Us: The case for the introduction of majority jury verdicts in New South Wales', Master's thesis, University of New South Wales Faculty of Law, 2001: 70.

p. 52 'The jury will be a group . . .' Hamlin 46.
p. 53 'Called up in the 1670 trial . . .' See Levy 62.

Chapter Three: Challenging the Challenge

p. 55 For the following historical account, I owe most to Levy and Kerr. For the etymological note about 'juror' and 'jury', I thank Lorana Bartels.

p. 57 These speculations about the connotations of the number '12' are drawn in part from Kerr and Grove.

p. 57 'a fluke of history' *Williams v Florida* 399 US 78, quoted in Bartels 9.

p. 57 The University of Glasgow study results are as reported by ABC Online journalist Wilson da Silva on 10 September 2001.

p. 58 'A minister, intelligent, esteemed, . . .' Mark Twain, 'Roughing It', 1903, quoted in Abramson 45.

p. 59 For the North and Mapplethorpe stories, see Abramson 21.

p. 59 'We couldn't very well pot him . . .' quoted in A.S. Gillespie-Jones, *The Lawyer Who Laughed*, Hutchinson, Melbourne, 1978.

p. 60 For the history of the Australian jury system, I have drawn from David Neal, *The Rule of Law in a Penal Colony*, Cambridge University Press, Sydney, 1991, Michael Chesterman, Mark Findlay, and the research conducted by Ian Barker QC in 2002.

p. 60 'Aborigines are represented by 0.5 per cent of jurors . . .' See Findlay 5.

p. 61 'an abomination of God' Chesterman 80.

p. 61 'social workers (likely to favour treatment over incarceration) . . .' Kenneth J. Melilli, 'Batson in Practice', *Notre Dame Law Review* 71 (1996), quoted in Abramson xxiv.

- p. 61 'allows the covert expression . . .' Chief Justice Burger in *Batson v Kentucky*, quoted in Abramson 133.
- p. 62 'By history and design . . .' Abramson 8.
- p. 62 'A German psychologist . . .' See Kerr 59.
- p. 63 'comment that the process is a demeaning one . . .' Warren Young, Speech to the Criminal Trial Reform Conference, Melbourne, 24–25 March 2000.
- p. 63 'It was difficult to see any logic . . .' Findlay 49.
- p. 63 'The UK Royal Commission . . .' See Lord Runciman, 'Report of the Royal Commission on Criminal Justice', HMSO, London, 1993; and M. Zander, 'The Royal Commission on Criminal Justice: Crown Court Study', HMSO, London, 1993.
- p. 64 'I felt cheated . . .' Findlay 77.
- p. 64 '42 per cent of potential jurors get off . . .' See ibid 38.
- p. 64 'the court can allow jurors to nominate their availability period in advance . . .' I owe this suggestion and the following one about politicians to Trevor Grove 224 and 251.
- p. 64 '93 per cent of people support the jury system . . .' See Findlay 22.
- p. 65 'The 1994 NSW jury study found that four per cent . . .' See ibid 91.
- p. 66 'In the most recent survey in NSW of 40 trials . . .' See Michael Chesterman, Janet Chan and Shelley Hampton, 'Managing Prejudicial Publicity: An Empirical Study of Criminal Jury Trials in New South Wales', Justice Research Centre, Law and Justice Foundation of NSW, Sydney, February 2001.
- p. 66 'In the 1950s, the biggest-ever survey . . .' Detailed in Hans Kalven and Hans Zeisel, *The American Jury*, Little Brown & Co, Boston, 1966.
- p. 66 'In a case in Geelong in the 1950s . . .' From A.S. Gillespie-Jones.
- p. 67 'There is no guarantee . . .' Grove 128.

p. 67 'Jurors in Athens . . .' Abramson 1.

CHAPTER FOUR: THE FOREMAN WAS A STOREMAN

p. 70 'when relatives of the accused harassed jurors . . .' See Findlay 72.

p. 73 'at that early moment, when relief . . .' Burnett 84.

p. 74 'Few actually discussed it . . .' Young et al Finding 2.51.

p. 74 'In the 1985 study . . .' See Findlay 92.

p. 74 'even though selecting a foreperson . . .' Valerie Hans and Neil Vidmar, *Judging the Jury*, Plenum Press, New York, 1986, quoted in Taub 108.

p. 75 'I have had certain letters . . .' Findlay 132.

p. 75 'an English juror, Anthony Barker . . .' See Grove 179.

p. 76 '[The lawyers] quietly pondered the great question . . .' John Grisham, *The Runaway Jury*, Arrow Books, New York, 1996: 24.

p. 79 'By then, the jurors will have had a chance . . .' Young et al Vol 1 par 28.

p. 79 'the general tenor . . .' Shelley Saltzman (nee Hampton), who interviewed the jurors in the 2001 NSW study (Chesterman et al).

p. 79 'in a significant number of trials . . .' Young et al Vol 1 par 28.

p. 80 'Some of these forepersons . . .' Young et al Vol 2 Findings 6.33–6.34.

p. 81 'as foreman he maintained impartiality . . .' See Burnett 156.

p. 81 'No one wanted to sit down . . .' Mary Timothy, *Jury Woman*, 1974, quoted in Taub 108.

p. 82 'relieved that his jury was able to reach this routine selection . . .' Grisham 59.

CHAPTER FIVE: THE DEFENCE OPENS

p. 89   'The advent of the defence barrister . . .' For some of this background I have drawn from Whitton 76ff.

p. 91   'like a job interview' The comparison is made at Hamlin 110.

p. 91   'sought an exemption . . .' Shelley Saltzman, email to Michael Chesterman, 3 March 2002.

p. 92   'Although the [opening] address . . .' Young et al Vol 2 Findings 2.34–2.37.

p. 92   'Jurors sometimes find it difficult . . .' ibid.

p. 93   'In the 1994 NSW survey . . .' See Findlay 80.

p. 93   'If a formal invitation is made by the trial judge . . .' Justice Ken Mackenzie, 'Conduct of the Trial and Powers of the Trial Judge', Criminal Trial Reform Conference, Melbourne, 24–25 March 2000.

CHAPTER SIX: MEET YOUR NEW FAMILY

p. 94   'We had been frog-marched . . .' Grove 4.

p. 95   'It made us feel like children . . .' Grove 54.

p. 97   'concentration shifts' Hamlin 198.

p. 97   'bystanders rather than participants' Young et al Vol 2 Findings 4.1–4.3.

p. 101 'some jurors thought the instructing solicitors were secretaries . . .' See Findlay 65.

p. 103 'In a Canadian survey . . .' Chesterman et al 30.

p. 103 'prosecutors believed 47 per cent . . .' See Bartels 56.

p. 104 'generic publicity' Chesterman et al 154.

p. 104 'If it were a drug case . . .' ibid 155.

p. 105 'I believe that juries in [country town X] . . .' ibid 154.

p. 106 'When the lawyer finished . . .' Abramson 6.

p. 106 'The 1955 Chicago Jury Project surveyed judges . . .' See Kerr 30.

p. 107 'If jurors like the defendant . . .' Young et al Vol 1 par 233.

p. 107 'anticipate which of the jurors' basic beliefs . . .' Donald Vinson, quoted in Abramson 153.
p. 108 'In an antitrust suit . . .' The IBM and MCI stories are drawn from ibid 151ff.
p. 109 '[Jurors said the accused] was very, very charming . . .' Shelley Saltzman, email to Michael Chesterman, 3 March 2002.
p. 111 'of average ignorance' Glanville Williams, quoted in Whitton 50.
p. 111 'The 2001 NSW jury survey found . . .' See Chesterman et al 48–9.
p. 111 'One respondent to that study . . .' This is drawn from Shelley Saltzman, email to Michael Chesterman, 3 March, 2002.
p. 111 'The 1994 study . . .' See Findlay 60.

CHAPTER SEVEN: LET THEM EAT FRUIT: HOW JURIES SUBSIST

p. 114 'What really makes me mad . . .' Grisham 87.
p. 114 'The hungry judges . . .' Alexander Pope, *The Rape of the Lock*, quoted in Grove 89.
p. 115 'Until 1870, English juries were starved . . .' See ibid 89.
p. 116 'eat the leather of their boots . . .' A. Castles, 'Now and Then – "Boot-eaters" and Majority Verdicts in Criminal Trials', (1992) 66 ALJ 290. I thank Lorana Bartels for pointing out this article.
p. 116 'complained that the jury room was cramped . . .' Young et al Vol 2 Findings 10.31–10.33.
p. 120 'These "problems" varied in seriousness . . .' Young et al Vol 2 Findings 10.42–10.45.
p. 120 'As I wondered why, I realised that I was a single man . . .' Johnathan M. Carter, *Johnny Nine: Capano Juror*, Xlibris Books, Wilmington, Delaware, 2000: 247.

p. 121 'That is a strange situation for adults to be in . . .' ibid 66.
p. 121 'they had forgotten about us . . .' ibid 79.
p. 121 'Out in the narrow, yellow corridor I heard Dan . . .' ibid 75.
p. 121 'But when it comes to food and drink, I envy . . .' ibid 100.
p. 122 'From time to time we were told . . .' Taub 30.
p. 122 'I am of the view . . .' Findlay 117.
p. 122 'I am not suggesting . . .' ibid 133.
p. 123 'Several respondents complained that the air-conditioning . . .' Findlay 59.
p. 125 'thought it obvious that women . . .' Sir William Blackstone, quoted in Abramson 112.
p. 125 'The first American jury with men and women . . .' See ibid 113.
p. 126 'American author Susan Glaspell's 1917 short story . . .' See Abramson 120.
p. 127 'It is not enough to say that women . . .' *Ballard v United States*, quoted in Abramson 119–120.
p. 128 'I believe that the Court . . .' ibid 120.
p. 128 'There is no evidence that women and men . . .' ibid 173.

CHAPTER EIGHT: UNDERCOVER: 'SPIKE' IN SILVERWATER

p. 130 'Many of these men share a manly density . . .' Burnett 49.
p. 146 'I regard the manipulation of the criminal court process . . .' James Wood, quoted in Whitton 95.
p. 146 'with some justification' Adrian Roden QC, quoted in ibid 39.
p. 147 'The rights of accused persons. . . ' Adrian Roden QC in 1989, quoted in ibid 39.
p. 148 *R v Khoo* (2000) NSWCCA 500.

p. 148 'An American survey in 1992 found that only 41 per cent . . .' See National Law Journal/Lexus poll, quoted in Findlay 152.

p. 148 'almost any factual hearing or trial . . .' From James McCloskey, 'Convicting the Innocent', in *Criminal Justice Ethics* Winter/Spring 1989.

p. 148 'There was a trial in Shepparton, Victoria, in 1980 . . .' See R. McGarvie et al, *Order In The Court*, Lothian, Melbourne, 1988.

p. 149 'large force waiting in the wings' Burnett 23.

CHAPTER NINE: CHILDREN OVERBOARD ON THE LOWER GROUND FLOOR OR THE WORLD AS SEEN FROM A ROOM WITHOUT WINDOWS

p. 153 'Eye contact simply says to another human being . . .' Hamlin 159.

p. 155 'jurors disliked Shand's use of words like "otiose" and "moronic" . . .' See Kerr 8.

p. 155 'At some point during the cross-examination . . .' Carter 229.

p. 155 'In two . . . cases, jurors felt intimidated . . .' Young et al Vol 2 Finding 10.17.

p. 156 'Jurors pick up jury folklore very quickly . . .' Grove 55.

p. 159 'Antennae we didn't even know we possessed . . .' ibid 42.

p. 160 'The NSW survey found that in 38 trials . . .' See Chesterman et al xv–xvii.

p. 160 'There was not very much discussion . . .' ibid 82–94.

p. 161 'I was assigned by CBS . . .' Fred Graham, quoted in Abramson 54.

p. 161 'the growth both in intensity and range . . .' Wilson J in *Victoria v Australian Building Construction Employees' and Builders Labourers' Federation*, High Court 1982, 152 CLR 25 at 136.

p. 161 'It is wrong to assume that jurors . . .' *R v Duff* (1979) 39 FLR 315 at 333 (Brenna, McGregor and Lockhart JJ).

p. 162 'It was suggested . . . that jurors . . .' *Attorney General (NSW) v John Fairfax & Sons Ltd & Bacon* (1985) 6 NSWLR 695 at 699 (Samuels JA).

p. 162 'for the system to function we have to assume . . .' Grove 185, 128.

p. 163 'Impartiality is not a characteristic of who or what a person is . . .' *United States v Wade* (1936), quoted in Penny Darbyshire et al, 'What Can the English Legal System Learn From Jury Research Published up to 2001?', *Criminal Courts Review*, December 2001.

p. 163 'a little parliament' Lord Devlin, quoted in Grove 77.

CHAPTER TEN: THE STAR WITNESS: LES IS MORE

pp. 164ff Some of this account has been supplemented by interviews conducted by *Sydney Morning Herald* journalist Sarah Crichton.

p. 173 'indicate their unwillingness to consider the evidence' Bartels 65.

p. 190 'The unschooled public largely and erroneously believes . . .' McCloskey, quoted in Taub 47.

p. 191 'Now, as I look back, some of the hypotheticals . . .' Burnett 61.

p. 192 'understand that a trial is like a play . . .' Abramson 150.

p. 192 'Why don't you sit down and be quiet? . . .' See Hamlin 214.

p. 193 'At a trial in Mildura in 1982 . . .' McGarvie.

p. 194 'I don't know that any juror . . .' Shelley Saltzman, email to Michael Chesterman, 3 March 2002.

p. 194 'Did I look okay? . . .' Auty and Toussaint: 30.

Chapter Eleven: Survivor XII: The Jury Room

p. 195 'Although comradeships were established . . .' Grove 50.
p. 197 'Compared with truth-tellers . . .' Stephen Adler, *The Jury: Disorder in the Court*, Doubleday, 1995, quoted in Grove 118.
p. 197 'frank, forthright and genuine' Young et al Vol 2 Finding 3.21.
p. 197 'The fact that witnesses contradicted themselves . . .' ibid Finding 3.22.
p. 198 'credibility did not pose a problem for most jurors' ibid Finding 3.25.
p. 198 'he only took sketchy notes during the trial . . .' Chesterman et al 184.
p. 199 'The New Zealand jury project proposed . . .' See Young et al Vol 1 pars 84, 85. See also Young's keynote speech to the Criminal Trial Reform Conference, Melbourne, 24–25 March 2000.
p. 202 'one could feel something growing between jurors . . .' Grove 96.
p. 202 'Even before an actual jury retires . . .' Valerie Hans and Neil Vidmar, quoted in Taub 108.
p. 203 'In the 1974 trial of John Mitchell and Maurice Stans . . .' This account comes from Abramson 160.
p. 210 'Should any of them try it on the [train] . . .' Grove 34.
p. 210 'Watch jurors as they wait . . .' See Hamlin 68ff.
p. 212 'The law has always been thought of as a chancy business . . .' McGarvie.

Chapter Twelve: 'Ladies and Gentlemen . . . I Call Steven Rusher'

p. 216 'Jurors in four cases spoke of feeling intimidated and scared . . .' Young et al Vol 2 Finding 10.18.

- p. 216 'thought that perhaps the reason so many of us were suffering various kinds of stress symptoms . . .' Taub 105.
- p. 216 *R v Richards and Bijkerk* (1999) 107 A Crim R 318.
- p. 218 'Again and again I found myself . . .' Burnett 70.
- p. 218 'This was good news . . .' Carter 223.
- p. 219 'shows that jurors find it far easier to convict . . .' Abramson 150.
- p. 221 'You may be misled by the arrangement of the court . . .' McGarvie.
- p. 222 'was not the right to remain silent . . .' For this quote and historical account I have drawn from Levy, Whitton and Justice Geoff Davies, 'The Limits of the Right to Silence', Criminal Trial Reform Conference, Melbourne, 24–25 March 2000.
- p. 222 'Two jurors admitted that they thought it odd . . .' Chesterman et al 181.
- p. 222 'the reality mocks the rule . . .' Davies.
- p. 224 'The witness should look at the lawyer . . .' Hamlin 194.
- p. 228 'whose male members are generally . . .' Grove 143.

CHAPTER THIRTEEN: SUMMING UP OR HOW JURORS ARE SOLD A BILL OF GOODS BY MEN IN GOWNS

- p. 235 'If you say he is guilty . . .' Grove 238.
- p. 235 'When he was a Supreme Court judge . . .' This account is drawn from Gillespie-Jones.
- p. 238 'in other words he thinks . . .' Alan Jones, *Jury Service: A Practical Guide*, Hale, 1983, quoted in Grove 268.
- p. 241 'complex sentence structures . . .' Young et al Vol 1 par 239.
- p. 242 'The New Zealand jury study found that 30 per cent of 312 jurors . . .' ibid Vol 2 Finding 7.27.
- p. 243 'If she is guilty, so be it . . .' See McGarvie.

p. 243 'Once, in the Kimberley Court of Petty Sessions ...' See ibid.

p. 243 'A celebrated recent case of flawed directions ...' See Whitton 157.

p. 243 'a clear pointer regarding the legal issues ...' Chesterman et al 182.

p. 244 'there is a defect in the evidence ...' *Doney v R* (1990) 171 CLR 207 at 214.

p. 244 *Yager v R* (1977) 139 CLR 28.

p. 244 'In the 1697 case *Ash v Ash* ...' See Whitton 48 quoting Langbein.

p. 245 'like the host at some awkward office social event ...' Taub 30.

p. 245 'We wanted a definition of reasonable doubt ...' Chesterman et al 180.

p. 246 'Our study elicited responses ...' Young et al Vol 2 Finding 7.16.

p. 246 'doubt motivated by "reasons"' Burnett 108.

p. 247 'telling jurors to watch a baseball game ...' See Grove 257.

p. 247 'commented that they found the judicial directions confusing ...' Findlay, quoted at Chesterman et al 177.

p. 247 'as the 1994 NSW jury study found ...' See Findlay 64.

p. 247 'legalistic language, insufficient explanation of the rationale ...' Young et al Vol 1 par 55.

p. 249 'over 50 per cent of the jurors surveyed ...' Findlay, quoted at Young et al Vol 1 par 238.

p. 249 'The judge should provide the jury ...' Young speech to Criminal Trial Reform Conference.

p. 252 'in a Victorian Supreme Court case ...' See McGarvie.

CHAPTER FOURTEEN: ONE ANGRY MAN: HOW JURIES DELIBERATE

p. 255 'One cannot flinch . . .' Grisham 471.
p. 260 'a website called CrimeNet . . .' Justice Virginia Bell, 'How to Preserve the Integrity of Jury Trials in a Mass Media Age', Supreme and Federal Courts Judges' Conference, January 2005.
p. 262 'the jurors put one of their number into an esky . . .' Carter 305.
p. 262 'In another . . .' Chesterman et al 85–6.
p. 264 'In a Los Angeles theft trial in 1996 . . .' See Taub 131–132.
p. 266 'the law requires that there be present at this dismal spectacle . . .' Charles Dickens, quoted in ibid 88.
p. 268 'The Chicago Jury Project discovered . . .' See Abramson 197.
p. 268 'In the New Zealand study . . .' See Young et al Vol 1 par 234.
p. 268 'time and again that the best predictor . . .' Hans and Vidmar, quoted in Taub 113.
p. 269 'If jurors are persuaded . . .' Young et al Vol 1 par 118.
p. 269 'Our jury was fantastic . . .' Chesterman et al 158ff.
p. 272 'Accounts of nasty deliberations . . .' See Findlay 114.
p. 273 'There is quite possibly no more demoralising experience . . .' Hans and Vidmar, quoted in Taub 114.
p. 274 'being sent back to the jury room . . .' Shelley Saltzman, email to Michael Chesterman, 3 March 2002.
p. 277 'Despite the jury's deep roots in the Constitution . . .' Hans Zeisel, quoted in Taub 102.
p. 278 'may have reflected an argument . . .' Abramson 182.
p. 279 *R v Cheatle* (1993) 177 CLR 541.
p. 279 'It is illuminating that the jury did not develop . . .' Abramson 182.
p. 280 'Proof beyond reasonable doubt . . .' ibid 191.

p. 280 'The unanimous verdict rule . . .' ibid 204.
p. 280 'It is sometimes argued that attrition . . .' Young et al Vol 1 par 180.
p. 281 '[J]urors returning non-unanimous verdicts . . .' Reid Hastie (ed), *Inside the Juror: The Psychology of Juror Decision-Making*, Cambridge University Press, New York, 1993. See also Abramson 200.
p. 281 'A juror who conscientiously holds out . . .' *R v Black* (1993) 179 CLR 44 at 56.
p. 282 'A mistrial from a hung jury is a safeguard to liberty . . .' *Huffman v Huffman*, quoted in Taub 103.
p. 282 'treasured, paradoxical phenomenon' Hans Zeisel, quoted in ibid 114.
p. 282 'In a New York murder trial in 1994 . . .' See Abramson 177.
p. 283 'punch another jury member . . .' Quoted in Auty and Toussaint: 45.
p. 283 'I distinctly remember thinking . . .' Burnett 91.
p. 283 'We ran the gamut of group dynamics . . .' ibid 12.
p. 284 'He gave us almost no direction at all . . .' ibid 81.
p. 285 'evidence-driven juries spend more time . . .' Young et al Vol 1 par 122.
p. 285 'A jury decision . . . is more than an average . . .' Phoebe Ellsworth, 'Are Twelve Heads Better Than One?' (1989) 52 (4) *Law and Contemporary Problems*: 205–6.
p. 285 'the foreperson should be provided . . .' Young speech to Criminal Trial Reform Conference.
p. 286 'The problem with a compromise . . .' Burnett 116.
p. 286 'What sort of justice is this where verdicts are negotiated between jurors so they can escape from the jury room? . . .' *Age*, 1 November 1985.
p. 287 'The jury was very unusual in its makeup . . .' Chesterman et al 163ff.
p. 288 'What is my real responsibility? . . .' Burnett 129.
p. 289 'It is not only his right, but his Duty . . .' John Adams,

from *Diary and Autobiography of John Adams*, Harvard UP, 1961, quoted in Abramson 30.
p. 289 'You have . . . a right to take upon yourselves . . .' See Abramson 63.
p. 290 'I would hope that in 1850 . . .' ibid xxiii.
p. 290 'regardless of a judge's instructions on the law of a case' Levy 55.
p. 290 'at modest war . . . too severe' Abramson 65.
p. 290 'A Canadian study found that 93 per cent of jurors . . .' See Hans and Vidmar, quoted in Taub 143.
p. 291 'The FIJA membership cuts across political lines . . .' Abramson 59.
p. 291 'juries do it anyway . . .' See ibid 65.
p. 292 'The remarkable aspect of this story . . .' ibid 95.

CHAPTER FIFTEEN: TWELVE ANGRY SUGGESTIONS

p. 294 'Those of us who appear in criminal trials . . .' John Mortimer QC, quoted in Grove 12.
p. 297 'From our unique perspective . . .' Mary Timothy, *Jury Woman*, quoted in Taub 155.
p. 298 'The money paid to jurors is quite inadequate . . .' Findlay 133.
p. 299 'the jury spent days arguing . . .' Radio National, quoted in Findlay 145.

CHAPTER SIXTEEN: GOING HOME

p. 301 'If we're doing the right thing, why are we all crying?' Burnett 167.
p. 302 'My instinct was to avert my gaze . . .' ibid 172.
p. 302 'You'd better get used to that . . .' Carter 368.
p. 303 'Life had been weirdly sapped . . .' Burnett 179.
p. 303 'I was wasting my time . . .' ibid 180.

p. 303 'Had the messenger descended in the final act . . .' ibid 180.

p. 304 'A number of jurors expressed surprise . . .' Chesterman et al 193.

p. 304 'Both during and after the trial . . .' Young et al Vol 2 Finding 10.24.

p. 305 'Several juries bonded so well . . .' Chesterman et al 191.

p. 306 'In British Columbia, judges regularly meet jurors . . .' See Young et al Vol 2 Finding 10.26.

p. 310 'the Maidstone jury . . .' See Grove 217.

p. 314 'The message here is obvious . . .' Carter 376.

p. 315 'As well as seeing positive personal gains . . .' Young et al Vol 2 Finding 10.2.

BIBLIOGRAPHY

BOOKS

Jeffrey Abramson, *We, The Jury: The Jury System and the Ideal of Democracy*, Harvard University Press, Cambridge, Massachusetts, 2000.

Kate Auty and Sandy Toussaint (eds), *A Jury of Whose Peers?*, University of Western Australia Press, Perth, 2004.

Paul Bergman and Michael Asimow, *Reel Justice: The Courtroom goes to the Movies*, Andrews McMeel, Kansas City, 1996.

D. Graham Burnett, *A Trial By Jury*, Alfred A. Knopf, New York, 2001.

Johnathan M. Carter, *Johnny Nine: Capano Juror*, Xlibris Books, Wilmington, Delaware, 2000.

Mark Findlay and Peter Duff (eds), *The Jury Under Attack*, Butterworths, Sydney, 1988.

Philip Friedman, *Grand Jury*, Ivy Books, New York, 1996.

A.S. Gillespie-Jones, *The Lawyer Who Laughed*, Hutchinson, Melbourne, 1978.

John Grisham, *The Runaway Jury*, Arrow Books, New York, 1996.

Trevor Grove, *The Juryman's Tale*, Bloomsbury, London, 1998.

Sonya Hamlin, *What Makes Juries Listen? A Communications*

Expert Looks at the Trial, Prentice-Hall Law & Business, Englewood Cliffs, New Jersey, 1985.

Valerie Hans and Neil Vidmar, *Judging the Jury*, Plenum Press, New York, 1986.

Reid Hastie (ed), *Inside the Juror: The Psychology of Juror Decision-Making*, Cambridge University Press, New York, 1993.

Hans Kalven and Hans Zeisel, *The American Jury*, Little Brown & Co, Boston, 1966.

John Fairbanks Kerr, *A Presumption of Wisdom: An Exposé of the Jury System of Injustice*, Angus & Robertson, Sydney, 1987.

Leonard W. Levy, *The Palladium of Justice: Origins of Trial by Jury*, Ivan R. Dee, Chicago, 1999.

R. McGarvie et al, *Order in the Court*, Lothian, Melbourne, 1988.

David Neal, *The Rule of Law in a Penal Colony*, Cambridge University Press, Sydney, 1991.

Paul H. Robinson, *Would You Convict? Seventeen Cases that Challenged the Law*, New York University Press, New York, 1999.

Mara Taub, *Juries: Conscience of the Community*, Chardon Press, Berkeley, 1998.

Neil Vidmar, *World Jury Systems*, Oxford University Press, Oxford, 2000.

Evan Whitton, *The Cartel: Lawyers and their Nine Magic Tricks*, Herwick, Sydney, 1998.

Reports, Articles, Speeches, etc.

Lord Justice Auld, 'A Review of the Criminal Courts of England and Wales', *Criminal Courts Review*, September 2001.

Australian Law Reform Commission, 'Contempt', ALRC 35, 1987.

Lorana Bartels, 'And So Say Most of Us: The case for the introduction of majority jury verdicts in New South Wales', Master's thesis, University of New South Wales Faculty of Law, 2001.

Justice Virginia Bell, 'How to Preserve the Integrity of Jury Trials in a Mass Media Age', Supreme and Federal Court Judges' Conference, January 2005.

Michael Chesterman, 'Criminal Trial Juries in Australia: From Penal Colonies to a Federal Democracy', 62 *Law & Contemporary Problems*, Spring 1999.

Michael Chesterman, Janet Chan and Shelley Hampton, 'Managing Prejudicial Publicity: An empirical study of criminal jury trials in New South Wales', Justice Research Centre, Law and Justice Foundation of NSW, Sydney, February 2001.

Penny Darbyshire et al, 'What can the English Legal System Learn from Jury Research Published up to 2001?', *Criminal Courts Review*, December 2001.

Justice Geoff Davies, 'The Limits of the Right to Silence', Criminal Trial Reform Conference, Melbourne, 24–25 March 2000.

Phoebe Ellsworth, 'Are Twelve Heads Better than One?', 52 (4) *Law and Contemporary Problems*, 1989.

Mark Findlay et al, 'Jury Management in New South Wales', Australian Institute of Judicial Administration Incorporated, Melbourne, 1994.

Mark Findlay, 'Policies of Secrecy and Denial: Barriers to Jury Reform', *Current Issues in Criminal Justice* Vol. 7 No. 3 pp. 368–381, 1996.

Reid Hastie (ed), *Inside the Juror: The Psychology of Juror Decision-Making*, Cambridge University Press, New York, 1993.

Justice David Ipp, 'Adversarial Justice in Transition', Criminal Trial Reform Conference, Melbourne, 24–25 March 2000.

Bernard Lagan, 'When One Juror Won't Budge', *The Sydney Morning Herald*, 13 May 2000.
Justice Ken Mackenzie, 'Conduct of the Trial and Powers of the Trial Judge', Criminal Trial Reform Conference, Melbourne, 24–25 March 2000.
New South Wales Law Reform Commission, 'The Jury in a Criminal Trial', Criminal Procedure Research Report, NSW Government Printer, Sydney, 1986.
Runciman, Lord, 'Report of the Royal Commission on Criminal Justice', HMSO, London, 1993.
Warren Young, Neil Cameron and Yvette Tinsley, 'Juries in Criminal Trials: Part Two', Law Commission of New Zealand Preliminary Paper 37, Wellington, New Zealand, 1999.
Warren Young, Speech to the Criminal Trial Reform Conference, Melbourne, 24–25 March 2000.
M. Zander, 'The Royal Commission on Criminal Justice: Crown Court Study', HMSO, London, 1993.

FILMS

A Civil Action, (dir: Steven Zaillian), Paramount, 1999.
Joh's Jury, (dir: Ken Cameron), ABC/Southern Star Sullivan, 1993.
Jury Duty, (dir: John Fortenberry), Columbia Tristar, 1995.
Suspect, (dir: Peter Yates), Tri-Star, 1987.
The Juror, (dir: Brian Gibson), Columbia, 1996.
Trial By Jury, (dir: Heywood Gould), Morgan Creek International, 1994.
12 Angry Men, (dir: Sidney Lumet), United Artists, 1957.
We The Jury, (dir: Sturla Gunnarsson), Atlantis Films, 1996.

Text Acknowledgments

Acknowledgments are due to the following authors, publishers and companies for permission to include extracts of copyright material.

Lorana Bartels, reprinted by permission of the author.
D. Graham Burnett, reprinted by permission of Bloomsbury.
Johnathan M. Carter, *Johnny Nine: Capano Juror* ('from one of Delaware's most infamous trials involving one of the most important "behind the scenes" figures in Delaware history'), reprinted by permission of the author.
Michael Chesterman, reprinted with permission of the author.
Mark Findlay et al, reprinted by permission of the Australian Institute of Judicial Administration (AIJA).
John Grisham, published by Hutchinson, used by permission of the Random House Group Ltd.
Trevor Grove, reprinted by permission of Bloomsbury.
Sonya Hamlin, reprinted by permission of the author, a noted jury communications expert, from *What Makes Juries Listen?*, now available in a revised and expanded edition as *What Makes Juries Listen Today?* (Glasser LegalWorks, 150 Clove Rd, Little Falls, NJ 07424, USA).
Joh's Jury © 1993 Southern Star Entertainment. Courtesy of Southern Star Entertainment and Ian David.
Jury Duty © 1995 Triumph Releasing Corp. All rights reserved. Courtesy of Triumph Releasing Corp.
John Fairbanks Kerr, reprinted by permission of HarperCollins Australia.
Leonard W. Levy, copyright © 1999, reprinted by permission of Ivan R. Dee, Publisher.
Suspect © 1987 TriStar Pictures, Inc. All rights reserved. Courtesy of TriStar Pictures.
Mara Taub, reprinted by permission of the author. Distributed by CPR Books, PO Box 1911, Santa Fe, NM, USA.
The Juror © 1996 Columbia Pictures Industries, Inc. All rights reserved. Courtesy of Columbia Pictures.
We the Jury, Jeffrey Abramson © 1994 Basic Books. Reprinted by permission of Harvard University Press.
Warren Young et al, reprinted by permission of the Law Commission of New Zealand.
Hiller Zobel, reprinted by permission of the author.

Every effort has been made to identify copyright holders of extracts in this book. The publishers would be pleased to hear from any copyright holders who have not been acknowledged.

INDEX

A
Aborigines
  Aboriginal jurors, 60
  arrest rate, 60
  bias against, judicial, 243
  imprisonment rate, 60–1
Abramson, Professor Jeffrey, 47, 62, 67, 105–6, 127–8, 192, 219, 278–9, 280, 290, 291–2
accused
  adverse inferences from silence, 222–3, 232
  eye contact, 215–17
  intimidation by, 217
  jury and, 215
  right to remain silent, 221–2
  silence by, 220–3
  testimony by, 219–20
acquittal
  direction by judges, 244
  'leniency bias', 268
  not proven, 288
  Scottish system, 288
Adams, John, 289
Adler, Stephen, 197

advocacy
  eye contact, 153–5
  persuasion, 153
affirmation, 52
Afghanistan, US bombing of, 158
allowances paid to jurors, 70, 119, 298
alternative verdicts, 288
appeal
  criminal convictions, against, 242
  Rusher case, 308
Armitage, Graham, 261
Arnott, David, 51
Ash v Ash, 244
Askin, Robert, 147
asylum seekers, 157
'Atillio', 28, 167–8

B
Bacon, Wendy, 162
Bailey, F. Lee, 47
Balfe, QC, 252
Ballard v United States, 127
Baraka, Sergeant, 165–6
Barker, Anthony, 75

Barker, Ian, QC, 9, 64, 153, 219, 283
barristers
 amount earned by, 100
 eye contact, 153–5
 judges and, 250–2
 legalistic language, 241
 personalities, 193–4
 tools of, 241
 wasting time, 251–2
 wigs, 85
Barry, Marion, 291, 292
Barry, Sir John, 235
Bartels, Lorana, 9, 103, 173, 276–7
Bell, Justice Virginia, 260, 298
Belli, Melvin, 47
bench book, 247
bias, judicial, 243–4
Bjelke-Petersen trial, 12–13, 50, 58, 116, 257, 270
 foreman selection, 76, 77, 79, 80
 Joh's Jury, 12–13, 76, 77–9, 116, 199, 241, 242–3, 246, 257, 270–83, 284, 315
Black direction, 274–6
Blackshield, Professor Tony, 5
Blackstone, Sir William, 125
Blake, George, 291
Blanch, Reg, QC, 90
boat people, 100, 157
 children overboard, 158–9
Bollen, Justice Derek, 243
'Borderline', 100, 110, 140, 173, 188, 227, 228, 230–1, 237, 255
'bottom of the harbour' tax-evasion trial, 286
Boulten, Phillip, 49, 52, 65, 103, 203, 210
Brennan, Robert, 26

Briese, Clarrie, 147
burden of proof, 237
Burnett, Graham, 10, 39, 72–3, 81, 130–1, 149, 191, 246, 257,
264, 301–2, 303
 Trial by Jury, 12, 257, 283–88
 trial of Monte Milcray, 218, 283–88
Bushell, Edward, 53

C
Campbell, Don, 235
capital punishment, 266
Carter, Johnathan M., 10, 120–1, 155, 218, 262, 302, 314–15
censorship, xiv
challenge
 Australia, in, 48
 criticisms, 295
 engineering favourable jury, 45–51
 peremptory, 51, 61–7, 108, 295–6
 period, 45, 55
 suggestions for improvement, 296
Chamberlain, Lindy, 7, 219
Chesterman, Professor Michael, 14, 68, 192
Chicago Jury Project, 1955, 106–7, 268, 277, 290
Choa, Andrew, 203
'Christian Mother', 84, 98, 109, 118, 124–5, 128, 152, 184, 199
Christie discretion, 33
A Civil Action, 105, 241
closing address, 235–6
 Crown, by, 236–7
 defence, by, 237–9
Cockburn, Alexander, 16

compromise verdicts, 286–7
Constitutions of Clarendon
  (1164), 56
conviction
  consequences of, 264
  unsafe or unsatisfactory, 8,
    244
corruption, 146–7
court
  daily routine, 117–19
  delays, 119, 121
  jokes in, 86
  theatre, like, 192
Cowdery, Nicholas, QC, 9, 57,
  61, 90, 147, 265, 295–6
  majority verdicts, 276, 280
credibility of witnesses, 190,
  195–8
CrimeNet, 260
criminal trials, funding of, 101
cross-examination
  Fraser, of, 206
  nature of evidence, 196
  Rusher, of, 228–34
  'Spike', 149–51
Crown
  case, facts of, 69
  closing address, 236–7
  'Mr Crown', 68, 84, 86, 180,
    184, 192–3, 209, 226,
    229–34, 311–12
  onus of proof, 237
  opening address, 69
  role, 9
Cuffee, Randolph, 283, 286, 287,
  303

D
damages, excessive award of, 244
Dao, Tu Quang, 275
Darrow, Clarence, 47
Davis, Angela, 81

de Tocqueville, Alexis, 4
Deane, Sir William, 6
  rights of individual jurors,
    supporting, 281
Death in Bondi, 146
Debus, Bob, 265
defence barrister
  advent of, 89
  closing address, 237–9
  Nisbett, Mr, 68, 84, 86, 88, 93,
    96–7, 100, 101–2, 149–51,
    152–3, 184–6, 189–93, 194,
    223–4, 226, 229, 231, 255,
    308
defence case
  facts of, 31–33
  opening, 83–93
defendant *see* accused
deliberations by juries, xiii,
  253–93
  change of mind during, 268
  guidelines for, 296–7, 299
  hung juries, 254
  length of, 254
  'leniency bias', 268
  minds of jurors made up before,
    268
  secrecy of, 299–300
Dershowitz, Alan, 239–40
Devlin, Lord, 163
di Suvero, Henry, 9, 90
Diamondopoulos, Yanni, 29–30,
  33, 168–9, 207–9
Dickens, Charles, 4, 266
directions to jury, 247, 284
  written directions on law,
    248–50, 285, 296–7
'Doctor Death', 291, 292
Dodd, Judge Ian, 86
Douglas, Justice William, 280
Dowd, John, 10
Downing, R.R., 37

Downing Centre, 37
  juror satisfaction rating, 123
  travel to, 118
Dunford, Justice John, 275–6

E
Ellsworth, Phoebe, 285
Emancipists, 60
Emery, Lorna Fiona, 18–36, 86, 110, 128, 167, 190, 204–5, 225, 250, 255, 314
  arranged murder of, 29–30, 69, 88, 93, 131–45, 168–79, 181, 236, 245, 253, 313
  first witness, 95–7
  Maxfield, correspondence with, 23–4, 101
  opinions of jurors regarding, 99, 102, 109
  payment for murder of, 137
  physical appearance, 22, 101
  pregnancy, 23
  Rusher, first meeting, 21–2
  story of, 17–31
  suppression order on name, 310
Eureka stockade rebels, trial of, 289, 292
evidence
  exclusion of, 33, 146, 259
  jury, withheld from, 94–5
  oral, videotaping, 200
  police, 147–8
  testing by jury, 262–3
  transcripts of, 198–200, 321
exclusionary rules of evidence, 33, 146, 259
jury speculation, 259
Exclusives, 60
eye contact
  barristers with jurors, 153–5

F
Falconio, Peter, 312
Farquhar, Murray, 147
Farragher, Christine, 30, 168–9, 207–9
Fayka, Attilla, 261
federal election 2001, 158
female jurors, 49
Findlay, Mark, 6, 7–8, 9, 13–14, 272
food and drink, 114–29, 297
foreman
  criticisms, 296
  duty, 73
  election of, 71–82
  studies about, 73–5
  successful, 80–1
  suggestions for improvement, 296
  unsuccessful, 80
Fortescue, John, Chief Justice, 57
Fraser, Inspector Jim, 204–7, 209
'Friday Night', 99, 110, 112, 118, 140, 158, 226, 227–8, 255
Fully Informed Jury Association (FIJA), 291

G
Gallagher, Norm, trial of, 286
Gamblee, Joanne Duke, 97
gang rape, 2001, 157
Gaynor, Liz, 46, 194
General Belgrano sinking, 291, 292
Gibbs, Justice Harry, 244
Glaspell, Susan, 126
Goodsir, Darren, 146
Graham, Fred, 161
grand jury, 56–7
Greiner, Nick, 147

Grove, Trevor, 66–7, 94, 95,
    156–7, 159, 162–3, 195,
    201–2,
228, 235

H
Hamlin, Sonya, 35, 52–3,
    210–11, 153, 224
Hans, Valerie, 202, 268
Harrisburg Seven trial, 46
Hasluck, Nicholas, 9
Henry II (1154-89), 56
High Court of Australia
holdout jurors, 277–8, 282
Holt, Lord Chief Justice, 85,
    244–5
Hosking, Bill, QC, 251
Howard, Prime Minister John
    boat people, 158–9
    2001 election, 158
Huffman v Huffman, 281–2
Hughes, Justice Charles Evans,
    163
hung juries, 273–4
    Black direction, 274–6
    John Newman murder trial,
        275
    length of deliberations, 254
    possibility of, 201
    sexual assault cases, 103
    vote, 277

I
IBM antitrust suit, 108
    mock jurors, 108
indigenous jurors, 60
inquest, 56
internet, research by jurors using,
    260–3
intimidation of jurors
    family members of accused, by,
        216–17

Ivan Milat's trial, 216
R v Richards and Bijkerk, 216

J
Jay, John, 289–90
Jefferson, Thomas, 4
Job's Jury, 12–13, 76, 77–9, 116,
    199, 241, 242–3, 246, 257,
    270–83, 284, 315
John Fairfax Ltd, 162
Johnny Nine, 120
Johnson v Louisiana, 280
jokes
    court, in, 86
    jury room, in, 98
Jones, Alan, 157
'JP', 84, 99, 216, 226, 227, 228
judge
    bench book, 247
    bias, 243–4
    counsel and, 250–2
    direction for acquittal, 244
    directions on law, 242
    hints to juries, 242
    role of, 242
    summing up, 245–50
    wigs, 84–5, 200
The Juror, 12
jurors
    Aboriginal, 60
    allowances, 70, 119, 298
    counselling for, 304
    curiosity, 262
    eye contact by counsel, 153–5
    female, 49, 59
    food and drink, 114–29, 297
    freedom of speech, 256,
        299–300
    going home, 301–2
    holdout jurors, 277–8, 282
    identification, xiii
    ignorance of rights, 78–9, 112

indigenous, 60
note taking by, 198–200
origin of word, 55
own research, doing, 259–64
post-trial feedback, xvii, 306
post-trial feelings, 307-7
post-trial stress, 301–5
questioning regarding trial, xiii
records, 14
sense of fear, 216–17
settling-in-period, 296
statutory declarations, 70
stress symptoms, 186, 216
video for, 42–3
wildcard juror, 50–1
women, 59, 125–9
jury
bonding, 202–3
criticisms and suggestions, 294–300
daily routine, 117–19
deliberations by *see* deliberations by juries
demographics, 110–11
dominant characters, 203
drowsiness, 97
dysfunctional, 272
equity, 104
evidence-driven, 284–5
failure, 272
grand, 56–7
guessing juries, 209–14
'leniency bias', 268
petit, 56–7
poll-driven, 284–5
psychological anchors, 103–7
second, 56–7
size, 57
testing what was said in court, 262–3
types of people on, 110–11
unaccountability, 5

Jury Assembly Room, 37, 38–44
jury consultants, 46
consultancy businesses, 107
jury duty
avoiding, 38, 40–1, 43
country jurors, 41–2
electoral rolls, 41
employers and, 119–20
fine, 41
statistics, 41
statutory exemptions, 41
Jury Duty, 42, 73, 95
jury equity *see* jury nullification
jury forecasting, 106
jury nullification, 104
America, in, 289
Eureka stockade rebels, trial of, 289, 292
history, 53, 289
legitimate, 292
meaning of, 288
jury room
conditions in, 115–16, 120–3
suggestions to improve, 297
windows, 116, 297
jury selection
America, in, 46
average time, 46
criticisms, 64, 295
disguise, 50
numbered juror cards, 44
panel selection, 35–54
race, effect, 45, 47
suggestions for improvement, 295
wildcard juror, 50–1
jury studies
Chesterman study, 14, 187, 274–5
Chicago Jury Project, 1955, 106–7, 268, 277, 290

NSW Law Reform Commission, 1985, 14, 74, 75
NSW 1994, 64, 74–5, 93, 101, 111, 122–3, 247, 249
NSW 2001, 79, 91, 104, 108, 111, 194, 198, 222, 243–4, 245–6,
262, 269, 286–7, 304
NZ, 2000, 14, 63, 73–4, 79–80, 91–2, 97, 107, 116–17, 120, 155, 197, 198, 199–200, 216, 241, 242, 246, 247–8, 249–50,
268–9, 280, 285, 304, 315
UK Royal Commission, 1993, 14, 63
jury system
changes in NSW, 14
criticisms of, 35, 294–300
failures of, 306–7
history, 55
suggestions to improve, 295–300
Jury Woman, 297

K
kenbet, 57
Kevorkian, Jack (Doctor Death), 291, 292
King, Rodney, 7
Kozinski, SJ, 11

L
Laidlaw, David, 126
law, written directions on, 248–50, 285, 296–7
Laws, John, xv, 157
Lees, Joanne, 312
Levi, Roni, 146
liars, good, 197
Lilburne, John, 222
Lombroso, Cesare, 62

M
McAtee, Les, 18, 25–33, 59, 130, 131, 137–45, 164–94, 230, 302, 311
McGarvie, Justice Richard, 212
Magna Carta 1215, 56
majority verdicts, 275–83
Mapplethorpe, Robert, 59
Mark Foy's, 36–7
Martin, Judge, 60
Maxfield, Terri, 19–36, 69, 86–7, 96, 108, 200, 255, 314
arranged murder of, 26, 28–30, 69, 93, 131–45, 165, 167, 168–79, 183, 225, 232–3, 245, 253
Emery, correspondence with, 23–4, 101
opinions of jurors regarding, 293
payment for murder of, 137, 232
second witness, 101–3, 151
sexual abuse, alleged, 166–7, 236–7
suppression order on name, 310
MC1 antitrust suit, 108
Mead, William, 53, 289
'Mechanic', 99, 109, 112, 118, 188
Mellon, Brian, 27
Milat, Ivan, 216
Milcray, Monte, trial of, 218, 285–7
Mitchell, John, 203
mock jurors, 108, 128
Molomby, Tom, 9, 51, 53–4, 65–6, 85, 90, 93, 153–4, 155–6,
196, 213–14, 260, 297
'Morgo', 133–9, 142, 144, 145, 151, 175, 182

Morison, Adam, 49, 50, 52, 91, 147, 153
Mortimer, John, QC, 294
Murphy, Justice Lionel, 7, 147, 155, 244
  first trial, 288

N
Newman, John, 275
Ngo, Phuong, 275, 280
Nielsen, Juanita, 36–7
Nisbett, Mr *see* defence barrister
North, Oliver, 58–9

O
oaths and affirmations, 52
objections
  frustration with, 192
  O.J. Simpson case, 192
O'Bryan, Justice, 243
'Old Hand', 82, 83–5, 98–9, 100, 109, 118, 128, 152, 156, 184,
189, 200, 202, 226, 227, 228, 255, 256
Operation Wilko, 131, 169
Oppenheimer, B.S., 7
Optus, web trace from, 206–7
Orrell, Jessica, 207

P
Pauline Hanson's One Nation, 157
payment to jurors, 70
Penn, William, 53, 67, 289
peremptory challenge *see* challenge
perjury, corruption by, 146
petit jury, 56–7
physical appearance of defendant, 207–8
Plucknett, Thomas, 5

police
  corruption, 146
  evidence, 147–8
  popular-culture representations, 10–13
post-trial feedback, xvii, 306
post-trial feelings, 301–7
post-trial stress, 301–5
Pottle, Patrick, 291
prosecutor *see* Crown
psychological anchors, 103–7
publicity, xvii–xviii
  effect on jurors, 104, 160

Q
Quinn, Michael, 13

R
R v Cheatle, 279
R v Duff, 161
R v K, 261–2
R v Khoo, 148
R v Richards and Bijkerk, 216
race
  effect on jury selection, 45, 47, 177, 188
  psychological anchor, as, 105
Ramage, Malcolm, QC, 48, 123, 125–6, 154–5, 209, 232
Randle, Michael, 291
rape conviction, 2002, 260
reasonable doubt
  closing address, 237
  meaning of, 245–6
  summing up by judges, 245–50
recorded conversations, 131–45, 170–84
  authenticity of tapes, 194
Refugee Review Tribunal, Rusher at, 225
Reginald, Tony, 209

'Retired Gent', 99, 102, 109, 112, 118, 121, 124, 140, 156, 158, 159, 178, 188, 189, 190, 207, 228, 242, 255, 293
Roden, Adrian, 146–7, 251
Rose, Reginald, 10, 118, 257
Rosenbaum, Yankel, 62
The Runaway Jury, 12, 46, 76–7, 82, 114
Rusher, Steve, 59, 69–70, 86–7, 97, 100, 130, 131–45, 302, 303–4
  appeal by, 308
  arrest, 183
  cross-examination of, 228–34
  evidence by, 224–6
  first wife, 21
  letter from, 310–11
  Long Bay, visit at, 307–310
  police-cell interview, 204–6
  principal defence of, 230–3
  psychiatric reports, 313
  recorded conversations, 131–45, 170–84
  Refugee Review Tribunal, at, 225
  sentencing hearing, 310, 311, 312–14
  story of, 17–34
  witness box, taking, 215–34
Rusher case, 17–34, 69–70, 83, 86–8, 93, 95–7, 130–51, 164–94, 215–34

S
Saltzman, Shelley (nee Hampton), 79, 91, 194
Samuels, Justice Gordon, 162
Saul, John Ralston, 15
Schmidt, H.S., 63
second jury, 56–7

secrecy of deliberations, 299–300
security check, 117
sentencing guidelines, 264
sentencing hearing, 310, 311, 312–14
Sexton, Michael, SC, 261, 276, 298
sexual assault cases
  hung juries, 103
  women jurors, 126
Shand, Alec, 155
Shaw, Luke, 50, 58, 76, 77, 80, 270, 282–3
sheriff's officer
  excuses offered to, 38
  jury room, 70
  no discussion of cases with jurors, 109
'Shut The Gate', 100, 102, 110, 118, 158, 199, 226, 227, 254, 293
silence of accused, 220–3
  adverse inferences from, 222–3, 232
  right to remain silent, 221–2
Simpson, O.J., 7, 47, 292
  acquittal, 291
  defence objections, 192
  defence team, 240
Skaf, Bilal, 260, 261–2
Skaf, Mohammed, 260, 261–2
solicit, xv
  meaning of, xiii, 236, 245
Spencer, Herbert, 58
Spigelman, Chief Justice James, 161–2, 265, 266
'Spike', 30, 130–51, 164, 194, 232, 311
  cross-examination, 149–51
  recorded conversations, 130–45
Stans, Maurice, 203

statutory declarations for jurors, 70
'Stickybeak', 84, 98, 110, 118, 128, 158, 187, 188, 199, 202, 226, 255, 293
Stockholm Syndrome, 202
'Storeman Foreman', 99, 112, 118, 152, 156, 186, 211, 216, 226, 255, 306
stress
 during trial, 216–17
 post-trial, 301–5
 symptoms, 186, 216
summing up, 236–52
 writing, in, 299
Suspect, 11–12

T
Tampa, the, 157
Taub, Mara, 10, 122
Teague, Cliff, 164
Tedeschi, Mark, 275, 280
terrorism
 September 11, 157, 158
 war on, 158
Thangaraj, Murugan, 50–1, 90–1, 126, 251
three strikes law, 264
Timothy, Mary, 10, 81–2, 126, 297
transcripts of evidence, 198–200
 criticisms, 298
 opening submissions, 211–12
 suggestions for improving, 298
Trial by Jury, 12, 257, 283–93
Twain, Mark, 4, 5–6, 58
12 Angry Men, 10–11, 116, 118–19, 152, 200, 246, 253, 257–70, 284, 301

U
UK Royal Commission into juries, 14, 63
unanimous verdicts, 269–70, 277–83

V
verdict
 alternative, 288
 'art form' of receiving, 255
 compromise verdicts, 286–7
 gender and, 126–9
 majority, 275–83
 Rusher case, in, 255
 safety of, 8, 14, 287
 unanimity in, 269–70, 277–83
 unsafe, 8
videotape
 oral evidence, 200
 police-cell interview of Rusher, 204–6
Vidmar, Neil, 202, 268
Vinson, Donald, 107
voir dire, 34, 203

W
Walker, Bret, SC, 14–15
Watergate, 150, 203
Waugh, Auberon, 7
We The Jury, 105
web trace, 206–7
wigs, 84–5, 200
Williams, Professor Glanville, 66–7, 111
Wise, Detective Peter, 169, 209
witnesses
 credibility, 190, 195–8
women on juries, 59, 125–9
 America, in, 125
 sexual assault and domestic violence cases, 126

Wood, Justice James, 146, 261, 275
Wood Royal Commission, 146
Woodward, Louise, 8
Wran, Neville, 147
Wright, Pauline, 261, 265
written directions on law, 248–50, 285, 296–7
Wu, George, 264–5

X
'X-Files', 100, 111, 118, 199, 255

Y
Yager v R, 244
Young, Chief Justice, 252
Young, Professor Warren, 8, 14, 63, 124

Z
Zahra, Peter, 265
Zeisel, Hans, 277–8, 282
Zobel, Hiller, 8

Other books by Malcolm Knox

A Private Man

Fame...
Pornography...
Family Secrets...

It is two days since Dr John Brand's death and his eldest son, Davis, suspects a cover-up. *Survived by two sons*, the death notice said. *Peacefully*. Someone has lied: there are three sons, and the circumstances of their father's death are murky. No-one seems able to tell Davis where and when – and with whom – his father died. The Sydney Test Match is on, and Davis's brother Chris, a famous cricketer, is batting to save his career. Their mother, Margaret, watches Chris on TV, seemingly inert in her armchair. Hammett, the unacknowledged third brother, lurks on the edges, banished but not forgotten. Scattered over Sydney, the Brands' lives – and John Brand's funeral – are put on hold for the duration of the game: fives days of suspense, silences, revelations, recriminations and redemption.

Filtered through two arenas of masculinity – sport and pornography – *A Private Man* is at once a poignant story of a family's grief, an artfully constructed thriller and a provocative dissection of Australian men and their private passions.

'Knox is, quite simply, a fabulous writer.'
Literary Review, UK

'Wonderfully accomplished'
New Statesman

Summerland

'You might want me to tell you how we decorated our houses, what labels and fabrics we allowed next to our skin, where we ate, what we ordered . . . But the material lives of the rich are of little consequence . . . It is the interior lives of the rich that are truly foreign . . .'

They are society's golden ones, endowed with the privileges of youth and wealth, bred to live in a world of limitless possibility.

Richard sits on the shores of Sydney Harbour, a hollowed-out man remembering the loss of his paradise, recounting the years he spent with his best friend, the charismatic heir Hugh Bowman. Gliding through a life of endless celebration, they formed a charmed quartet with their childhood sweethearts, Helen and Pup.

As adults they married and continued their tradition of summer holidays at Palm Beach, giving every appearance of leading immaculate lives. Like those mythical people in magazines, their skin was unblemished, the lighting just so.

But as Richard tries to rebuild the perfection of his memories, he must confront the secrets and subtle cruelties which blew their small world apart.

Summerland is at once an artful dissection of friendship and a searing social exposé. This first novel by Malcolm Knox enters fresh territory in Australian literature.

'A contemporary Australian *The Great Gatsby*.'
US Publishers Weekly

'Stylish . . . This is a wise and savvy novel, with a nice sense of play, good humour, wry and pensive thought.'
The Age